Robert Morley Eric Keown Cyril Ray Kenneth Bird
David Langdon Alan Coren F.M. Evans L. Raven Hill Dilys Powell P.J. O'Rourke
Miles Kington Keith Waterhouse A. G. Agnew L. G. Illingworth Charles Grave Michael Heath
Shirley Brooks
Richard Mallett
James Thurber
H.R.H. Prince Charles
F.H.Townsend
H.R.H.Duchess of York
J.G.S. Linacre
Lord Stevens
Norman Mansbridge
H.R.H. Princess Anne
H.R.H. Princess Margaret
Bud Handelsman
John Tenniel
David Taylor
Alan Coren
Arnold Roth
David Thomas
Bernard Hollowood
F.C. Burnand
Owen Seaman
E.V. Knox
Kenneth Bird
Malcolm Muggeridge
Mark Lemon
William Davis
E.V. Knox
Ewan S. Agnew
Percival Leigh
A.P. Herbert
Barnard Hollowood
Horace Mayhew
Michael Bywater

earle Hunter Davies E.T. Reed H.F. Ellis F.C. Burnand Gilbert á Beckett
Boyd Russell Davies Sheridan Morley J.B. Boothroyd Frank Reynolds Anstey Guthrie
R.G.G. Price Christopher Hollis David Taylor B.A.Young John Betjemsan
Mahood Alan Brien Richard Gordon

The PUNCH TABLE: circa 1986

Arnold Roth

◎

Free Lance

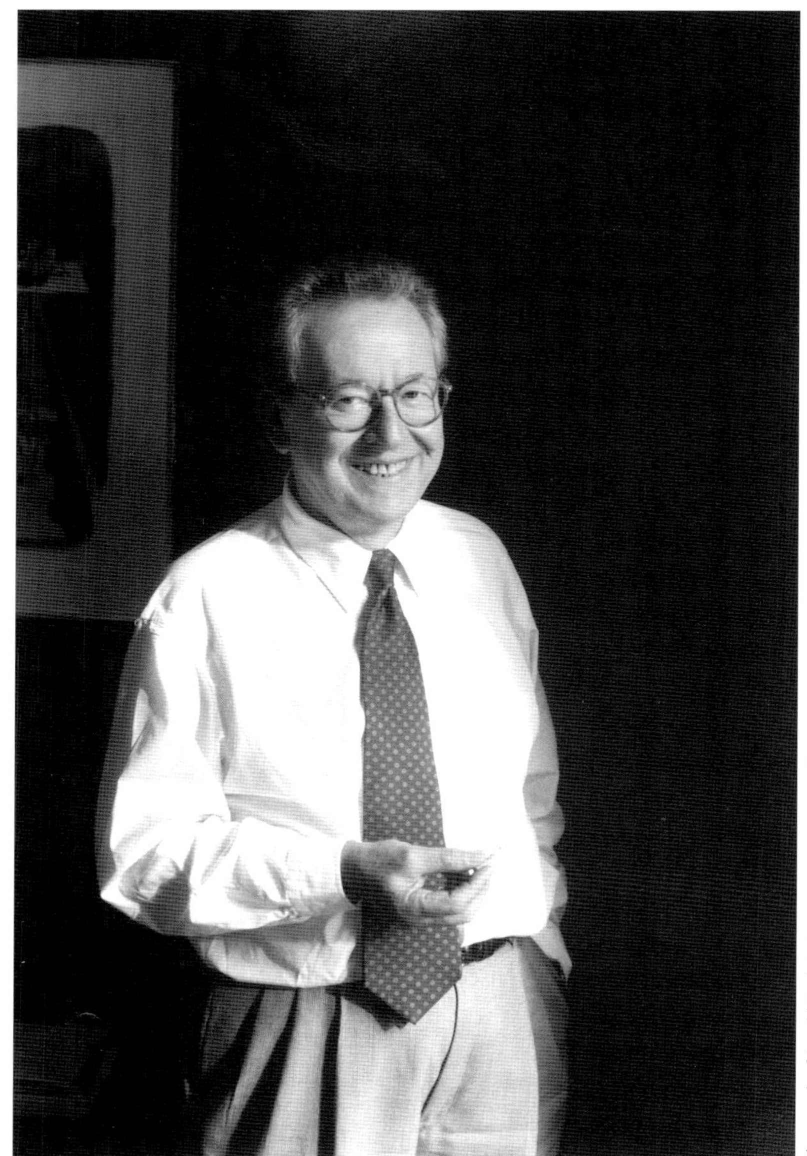

Photograph of Arnold Roth in August 1996 © Anne Hall.

Arnold Roth

Free Lance

A Fifty Year Retrospective

FANTAGRAPHICS BOOKS

Arnold Roth: Free Lance

Editor: Lucy Shelton Caswell
Editorial Liaison: Gary Groth
Designed by Preston White
Promotion by Eric Reynolds
Published by Gary Groth & Kim Thompson

FANTAGRAPHICS BOOKS
7563 Lake City Way NE
Seattle, WA 98115 USA

For a free full-color catalogue of comics and cartooning,
including other work by Arnold Roth, call **1-800-657-1100**.
Our books may be viewed — and purchased — on our website at
www.fantagraphics.com.

Arnold Roth: Free Lance is co-sponsored by The Ohio State University and
University of the Arts. Publication of this book is supported in part by
a grant from the Richard Florsheim Art Fund.

Printed in China.

ISBN: 1-56097-438-9

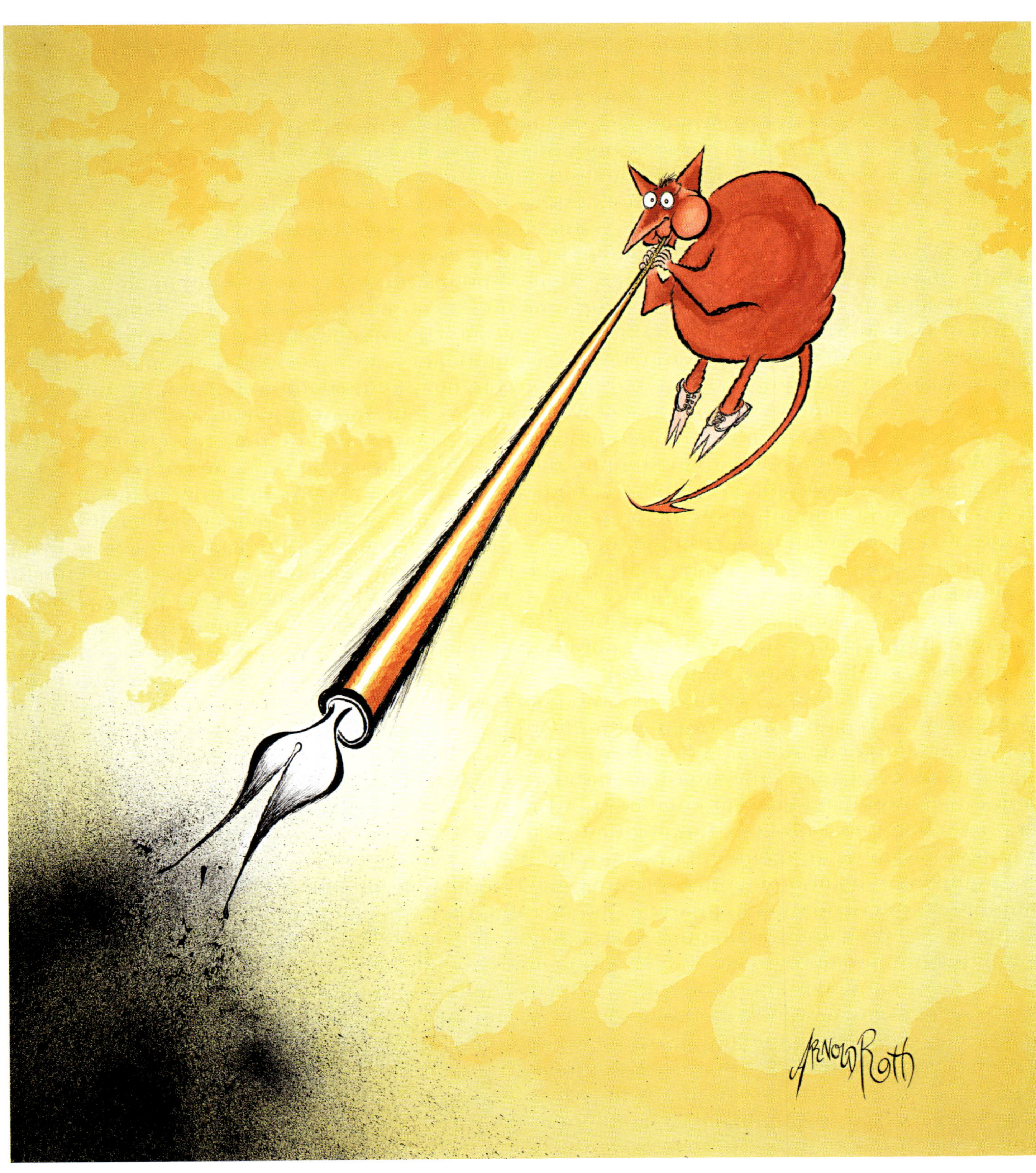

Figure 1
Philadelphia College of Art Poster
Philadelphia College of Art Gallery 1980

Introduction

This exhibition might be advertised as celebration of the all-American success story. Robert C. Harvey's biographical sketch of Arnold Roth in this volume tells about a Jewish boy growing up in a rough Philadelphia neighborhood. He makes good through talent and hard work. He teaches himself the saxophone and plays so well that during hard times he can support himself with band gigs. He contracts tuberculosis, but recovers. He meets a beautiful, talented, intelligent woman and enjoys a half-century of married life with her. They have two fine sons who share their parents' creativity. Even though he is dismissed from art school, his skills are such that he is hired at one time or another by virtually every major magazine published in the United States between 1951 and 2001.

There is no question that Arnold Roth's talent and accomplishments are remarkable. His work is the result of long hours at the drawing board and a fierce determination to make each deadline. What we celebrate with this book and the related exhibition is, however, the fun that Roth has had — and has shared with us — for fifty years. The cover illustration Roth did for the November 1994 issue of *INKS: Cartoon and Comic Art Studies* provides a visual summary of his career: he sits with his bow tie on at his drawing board, laughing as he draws, while a scowling neighboring artist who is searching for an idea looks jealously though the window. Arnold Roth knows what he wants to draw and enjoys doing it. His hand is sure and facile as it moves to create images that capture their viewers' imagination, pictures that seem already to be completed in his mind and flow onto the page. His sense of color is subtle, adding to the drawing but never overwhelming its lines. His bravura control of watercolor, breathtaking.

Unlike many artists of his generation, Arnold Roth was successful in having his original work returned to him by the editors and publishers who commissioned it. To be sure, some important work such as his art for *Trump* and *Humbug* is lost; but hundreds of pieces dating to his student days remain in his possession and were considered as this exhibition took shape. The final selection was guided by an effort to document the breadth and scope of Arnold Roth's freelance career as completely as possible without overwhelming viewers. Roth's work must be read carefully, not simply "looked at." It requires the active participation of the viewer to catch the subtleties that are, in fact, the heart of his work. Keeping this in mind, the decision was made to limit the works in the exhibit to a number that would not cause glazed eyes or exhibit fatigue — since either would betray the playfulness that is Roth's hallmark.

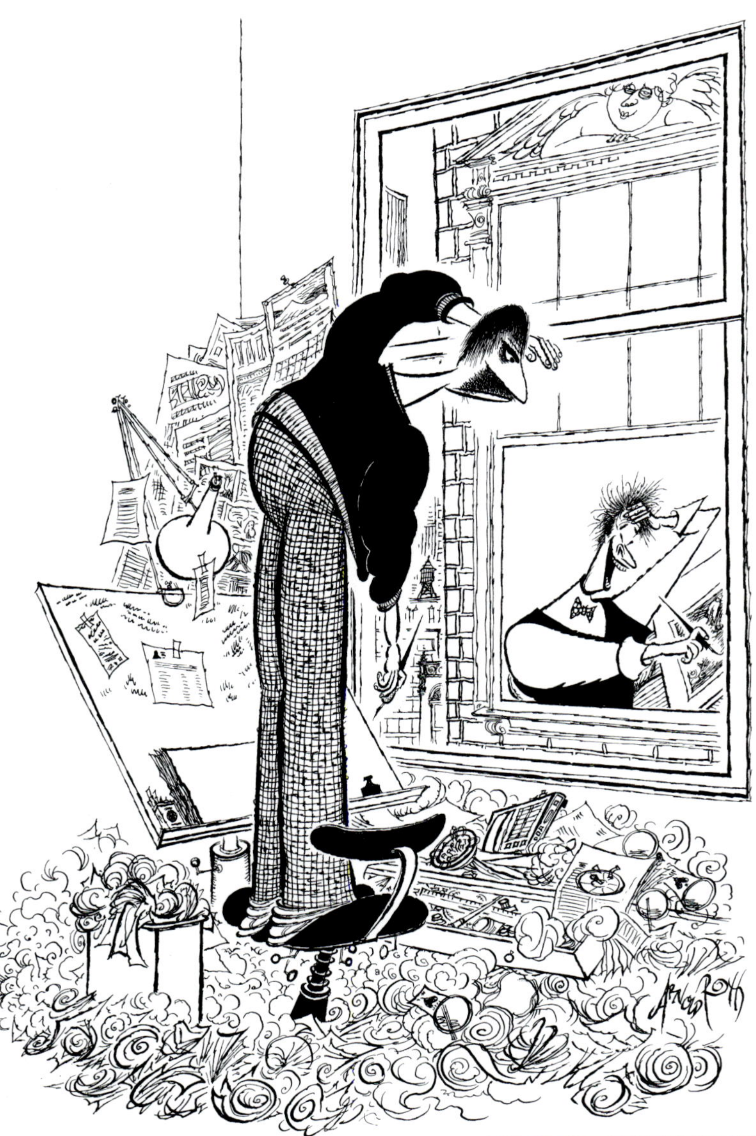

Arnold Roth: Free Lance is a celebration of many things: an outstanding talent, a long and remarkable career, success and many honors; but most of all, it is a celebration of the joy of making art and the pleasure it brings to others.

— Lucy Shelton Caswell
Professor and Curator
The Ohio State University
Cartoon Research Library

PREFACE

In common with countless millions of adolescents on both sides of the Atlantic, and very probably on both sides of many another other serious waterways, too, I began buying *Playboy*, some forty-odd years ago now, because it had Arnold Roth in it.

Few of us, of course, dared admit to this, sheepishly handing over our rattling sockfuls of monthly savings to some inquisitive newsvendor, or being caught by a sharkfaced headmaster on the farthest perimeter of a football field with our *Playboy* concealed inside *The Big Boy's History of Belgium*, or having a caring mother tiptoeing into our rooms late at night to find out why the bed was shaking plaster off the dining-room ceiling, we were quick to explain that we bought *Playboy* only for the interesting photographs of big women, because no other serious publication contained quite as many big women as this one did, and if you needed to study big women properly, maybe some day majoring in them, or indeed going on to a PhD, or even making a career in, say, cosmetics or the slavetrade, you would be well-advised to learn as much as you could while your brain was still young and receptive. All this was something older people immediately accepted.

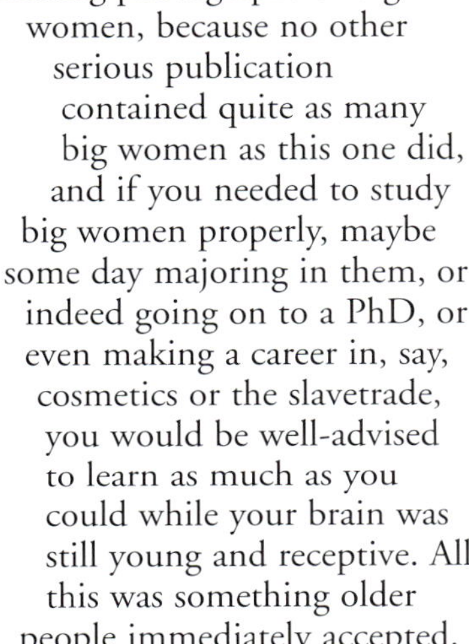

Had we, on the other hand, confessed to buying *Playboy* because it carried the work of the world's greatest living cartoonist, we should almost certainly have received a good hiding. The fifties, remember, were a period when corporal punishment was still a flourishing pastime, and not only would a sharkfaced headmaster or caring mother happily lash out at any young person who threatened what had been established as the status quo, but even an inquisitive newsvendor would be ever on the qui vive to floor any teenage customer who gave him what he considered to be a smart answer. Had I, for example, told my mother that what the bed was shaking with was uncontrollable laughter, my parents would have required only the briefest of discussions concerning my incorrigible want of gravity before hauling me out of school and packing me off to be a chimneysweep or whaler. Whereupon, I have little doubt, they would have begun making strenuous, albeit elderly, attempts to conceive again, praying that this time they would succeed in constructing an offspring reliably humorless enough to become an orthodontist.

Thus, subversion was perforce the keynote of my life, just as (for those who grow impatient for the knitting of disparate strands) it is the keynote of Arnold Roth's. Scour this benighted planet for someone who might succor us against those who daily sucker us — the monarchs and the presidents, the shamans and the bureaucrats, the bishops and the generals, the bankers and the architects, the lawyers and the scientists, in short the movers and the shakers — and you would be hard-pressed to come up with a champion likelier to move and shake these false gods to their feet of clay than the iconoclastic genius we honor here today, feller of the mighty, scourge of the bogus, deflater of the pompous, seamless fusion of brain and soul, word and line, and thus the cartoonist supreme (also a saxophonist, but probably not to another saxophonist).

And also, for ten years, my employee. Forgive me, that isn't literally true, I just like saying it. It makes me feel like a Medici, it helps me to argue dat mah libbin has not been in vain, for the fact is that Arnold cannot be described as anybody's employee, because there was never a freer lance than his; it's simply that, down the long arches of the years, some editors have been fortunate enough to have him walk through their doors, stand his lance in their corners, and lay on their desks artwork of such impeccable quality that they had no option but to reach immediately — or, at least, as soon as they had stopped marvelling, roaring, slapping their thighs, calling to their colleagues to come in here right away, and generally undermining their bargaining position irremediably — for their checkbooks. Those ten years of mine were spent as Editor of *Punch*, then (the 1980s) the finest humorous magazine in the world — even granted that this is an opinion for which the editor of *The New Yorker* would have called me out to Central Park at dawn and offered me the choice of weapon — and thus a fitting showcase for the world's finest cartoonists. Than whom there was none finer than Mr. Roth. Issue after issue, he graced our fortunate pages with his unique comic vision of America in all its joys and lunacies, which, to the million-strong States-smart British readership that *Punch* enjoyed, stood him in line not simply with US cartoon legends like Peter Arno and Saul Steinberg and Charles Addams, but also with the great literary wags, from S. J. Perelman and James Thurber to Joseph Heller and Woody Allen (also a clarinettist, but probably not to another clarinettist).

And if, in all those years of rejoicing over Arnold Roth's work, I had one regret, it was that my readers would see that work only in the miniaturized reproduction of the magazine. None but my staff and I saw the wondrous originals, in their original size, their original line, their original color, their original, in every sense, brilliance. That this splendid exhibition finally allows a wider world to relish what only a fortunate few have hitherto seen not only allows me to rekindle my own rejoicing but also to rejoice that the rejoicing can, at last, be shared.

— Alan Coren

For the Fun of It: The Lively Art of Arnold Roth

By Robert C. Harvey

Seldom do we see a signature that tells us more about the artist, his work and his vision than Arnold Roth's. The last name's initial letter stands on one spikey leg while the other, giving a chorus line kick, swoops down and around and curlicues into the letter "o," pinwheeling in on itself with the fizzing frenzy of a July Fourth firework. An antic letter if ever there was one.

Roth's signature didn't always betray so vividly its owner's attitude toward the world at large. As this retrospective of his work reveals, Roth once signed his name in an entirely normal manner. No curlicues, no maniacal pinwheels. Just "R-o-t-h," fini. It is as if, with maturity, the artist saw the world more clearly, and with clarity of vision came comprehension: he could see that we had all gone a trifle mad in the mid-day sun, and our foolishnesses deserved to be examined. Minutely. And the more Roth looked, the more acrobatic his signature become, dancing crazily to the music of the spheres that was, perforce, not so much harmonic as discordant. Or so it would seem here in this fanciful prelude.

A prelude of extravagant metaphor, no question; but there is something about Arnold Roth's work that brings out the extravagant in us all. And if it seems from what I've said that Roth has changed as the years rolled by — that he became more sheerly perceptive and satirical — that is but the trick of the metaphor. In actual fact, probably the world around him has never seemed entirely sane to Roth. Throughout his work, we have his risible gloss on civilization as we know it — or, more accurately, as we've tried to ignore it, an enterprise Roth seems dedicated to undermine by making us face ourselves. What he makes us see is not so much any congenital ugliness or evil as it is a somewhat bent reality that is oddly inconsistent with our more exalted aspirations. Roth's satiric vision seems more attuned to highlighting the nature of the human condition than to reforming it. He doesn't want to change us so much as he wants us to take some sort of perversely comical delight in our own idiosyncrasies as a species.

On the most straight-forward unabashed level, Roth shows us exactly how a perfect lemon pie affects the consumer in "Seasoned Cook: Lemon Pie" (Fig. 33). Here ordinary physiognomy goes violently agog. Lips are not merely pursed: they are stretched beyond anatomical possibility. And the eyes bulge out of the head altogether to underscore the sensation — to illustrate, to dramatize, the delicious sourness of that first bite. The sharp angularity of the man's arms adds a sense of startled rigidity to the portrait, precisely the kind of attention riveting that the inaugural taste of tart stimulates. Exaggeration of the most extreme sort makes the point, Roth's visual rendition of the taste of a lemon pie — his caricature of lemon pie eating.

In the same manner — in the manner of a fusillade — we have "New Orleans" (Fig. 31) , the portrait of a couple dining on oysters at Antoine's in the Crescent City. We can harbor no doubts whatsoever that oysters and jazz don't mix. The city's traditional jazz is more atomic than atmospheric here: every visual element in the picture is blown away by the very sound of the music. Roth recruits even the chandelier hanging from the ceiling to his purpose. Everything goeth before the blast. Everything is exaggerated. Everything is in caricature.

Perhaps the best bird's-eye view of Roth's sportive sense of anatomy is on display in the whimsical frieze of readers he produced for *The New York Times Book Review* as a "History of Reading" (Fig. 45). Here his selection of visual details and the distortion of the figures and their visages is regulated by the gleeful satiric impulse, not the sober anatomical or photographic or realistic proclivity. Anatomy is determined solely by the role the figure is playing. Under Roth's pen, anatomy *is* the satire in such efforts as "All Jogging Aside" (Fig. 16) for *Punch* or "For Your Two Legs Only" (Fig. 28), a comment on the jeans fad for *Esquire.* ("This was during that time when it was more important what label was

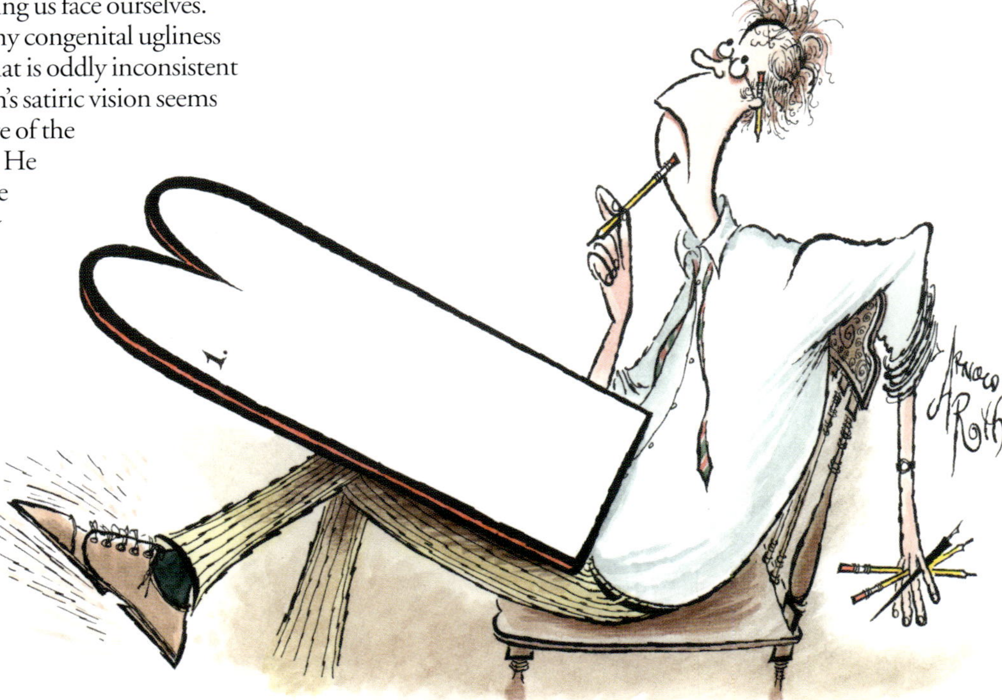

on the jeans than what they actually looked like," Roth explained when we talked in the fall of 2000.)

In "The Original Pushers Return to Washington Square" (Fig. 53), anatomy is again shaped by the personalities Roth is portraying — Greenwich Village types — and vice versa. But the comedy here also derives from the juxtaposition of the picture and its title. In the best traditions of cartooning, the words play as large a role in the final result as do the pictures, neither words nor pictures achieving alone without the other quite the same effect as they do together. And here, in that tradition, "pusher" attains a meaning from the pictures that is not inherent in the term itself — just as the picture gains greater meaning from the words used to describe it. And in the visual pun inherent in "Blind Date" (Fig. 26), we have the ultimate blend of word and picture. Roth's mastery of verbal-visual blending is complete, and when the blend is achieved through the exaggeration of caricatural rendering, the very essence of cartooning emerges, its madcap drollery paramount. In the two-page spread for *Punch* on "Assertive Woman" (Fig. 15), we find both word-play and picture-play running giddily rampant. Pure cartooning. Funny pictures that complete the meaning of the words and vice versa.

As revealed in his work, Roth is clearly what many of us mean when we say "cartoonist." He is a maker of funny pictures — funny pictures often yoked to accompanying words. And vice versa. He has been a cartoonist all his life, and for most of that time, he has freelanced, snatching a living by hustling one assignment after another in a highly competitive market, the wolf kept at bay by ingenuity and energy. And talent. And luck, lots of luck.

"It's great to try to be good at what you do," Roth told me, "but you can't try to be lucky. It sure helps, though. Of course, if you count only on luck, you might be caught short if you have to back it up sometime."

Roth had the luck to be born in 1929 on the cusp of the dawning Great Depression, and so he learned the survival value of scrambling for gainful employment as he grew up. And Philadelphia was a good place for a kid of artistic bent to grow up in. Roth and his older brother (by four years) shared the same interests and frequented the cultural environs of the Philadelphia Art Museum and the Free Library of Philadelphia.

"From age seven or eight, we were allowed to go anywhere in the city," Roth said. "I think because there were no neighborhoods worse than ours so our parents figured if we went someplace else, we were safer."

They went to exhibitions and shows. They borrowed books from the Free Library. They attended events at the University of Pennsylvania. Ever since, whenever Roth has worked for these institutions, he has done so as cheaply as he could by way of paying them back for the free education he'd received. While a teenager, he worked in the Free Library, first as a page and then as a repairer of books and bound volumes. As he repaired torn pages in stacks of *Harper's Weekly* from the Civil War era, he studied the drawings that made the magazine famous. He also saw cartoons in *The New Yorker* and in *Esquire* (thanks to an uncle who subscribed to the latter).

And he went to movies like any other youth of the period. Unlike most, he fell in love with jazz and learned to play the saxophone. "We always listened to music growing up," he told Gary Groth in an interview for *The Comics Journal* (June 1961, No. 142). "With six kids there was a different radio playing different music everywhere in the house." Although he took lessons briefly, most of his learning about the saxophone was by observing other players and talking with them.

Roth also drew pictures and sold a few, and he worked in an "art factory" — a so-called studio that mass-produced hand-painted works of art for sale in dime stores. And he worked in a toy factory one summer: "I painted eyes on ducks," he explained.

Upon graduation from high school in 1946, Roth was awarded a full scholarship to the Philadelphia Museum School of Industrial Arts. But he finished only two years. "I was put on probation after the first year," he explained, "and expelled after the second." But it wasn't for lack of talent; it was for lack of punctuality. He seldom arrived at class on time.

"It was a strict school," Roth said, "and you had to be there at nine o'clock. And when I say I was late, I don't mean five after nine: I mean ten-thirty. That kind of thing."

He was late because he had been up until the wee hours of the morning playing in jazz bands around town.

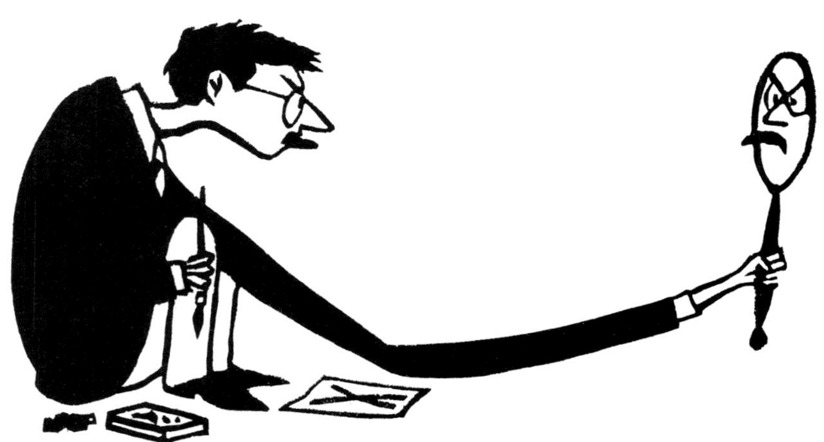

Although Roth started freelancing artwork in the summer of 1948, music remained his most dependable source of income. But by late that fall, he was diagnosed with tuberculosis. In December, he entered a sanitarium, where he spent the next fourteen months. While there, he read voraciously. And he drew a lot, sending postcards to friends by the hundreds. He left the sanitarium in late January 1950 and re-enrolled in art school but left a month or so later to take care of his mother, who was dying of cancer.

Upon her death in March 1951, he and his five siblings inherited $719 each, and he staked himself to a career as a freelance cartoonist. He and ten other creative entrepreneurs set up a studio in a twenty-foot by fifteen-foot room in a historic building near Independence Hall. Many of his studio-mates used the address as a mail-drop and never spent any time on the premises. But Roth did. All week long, he prepared a portfolio of drawings to sell. He hustled them around Philadelphia, and once a week, he took the train to New York, a recognized Mecca for commercial artists, where he peddled his wares.

Looking for any sort of work that would yield an income, Roth did all kinds of menial artistic tasks for a time. He did silk screen designs for Pennsylvania Dutch lampshades for Levittown. He did cocktail napkins that were designed to be sold to habitués of nudist camps. Once he took an assignment whiting-out the specs that blemished velox prints. His only steady work was with Temple University medical school for which he did lettering on medical charts. He did anything thrown his way. None of the jobs paid much, but they *paid.*

Toward the end of 1951, one of the editors at *The New Yorker* manifested great interest in Roth's work. But the magazine ultimately bought no cartoons from Roth at the time. "Although they showed interest in my work," he said, "their system and my temperament were not compatible."

Had Roth been published in the magazine, his career would have taken flight and soared as a result. But he realized very early that if he drew cartoons based upon the "corrections" and suggestions of others, he would sacrifice the very spontaneity and invention that made his work uniquely his own. He learned to set ground rules early in a working relationship.

"I explain if you want my best work, the work you've seen, this is how I do it," he said. "I won't do preliminary sketches for advance approval, and I won't draw what I'm told to draw. They can't give me the idea. I won't make piddling changes. They have to trust me. I'm not going to do a cartoon about a rainstorm if the story is about furniture. If it's a new magazine or I don't know the people very well, I'll ask if there are any taboos, if there's something that is a sin to draw. I just don't work well under any other circumstance. I tighten up. I get to be too careful. I start considering too many ancillaries. It takes the playfulness out of the job."

To do his best work, Roth must be free to follow his maniac muse wherever it might lead him. Pursuing that muse is the fun of the work. That's why Roth is a cartoonist — for the fun of the work.

"I made mistakes in the beginning," Roth admitted. "But I was working for people who weren't paying me much. And I managed to avoid people who wanted to 'do' the drawing. It's like a band leader telling a guy what to play in his jazz chorus. If you have to tell him, he shouldn't be playing a jazz chorus to begin with. If I'm not doing it right, I don't belong in the business. And if I *am* in the business, in all probability, I'll know more about it than they do."

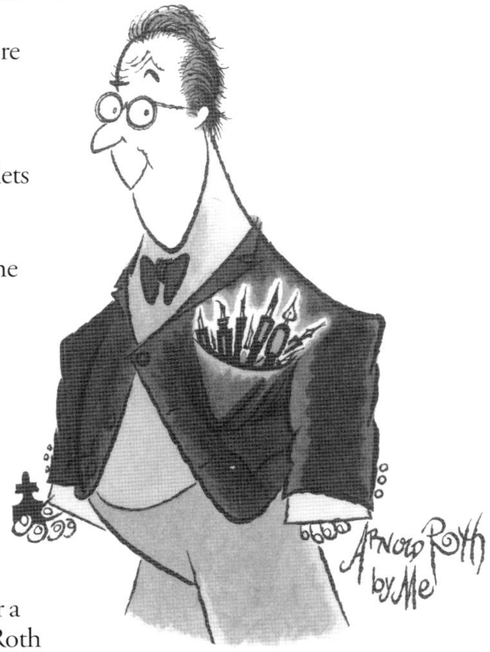

In 1952, Roth started getting lucky. He began finding better outlets for his work. It was a watershed year.

Charm magazine began buying spot drawings at ten dollars apiece, two a month. "It kept me going," Roth said. And by a "pure fluke," he got in on the ground floor with *TV Guide.* A special dummy issue was being prepared as part of *TV Guide's* bid for a national audience, and Roth did a drawing for that issue.

Walking down a street in Philadelphia one day, he ran into an ad agency friend who was working on the dummy issue. "He was desperate because they were in a big hurry," Roth said. "And he said, 'Could you do a pencil drawing — if we give you the information — of where the tv cameras will be for Eisenhower's inauguration?'"

Roth did the pencil drawing and, later, the finished version for publication. His second drawing for the magazine — a picture of a man on a roof sprouting tv antennas — was so well received that he began getting regular assignments with *TV Guide.* It became a steady account, and his relationship with the magazine continued until Walter Anneberg sold it decades later.

With increasingly regular assignments, Roth felt financially confident enough to marry Caroline Wingfield, who he'd met at art school. They were wed in October 1952. About that time, Roth met Paul Desmond and the rest of the Dave Brubeck Quartet.

He and Caroline frequented the jazz clubs in Philadelphia, so Roth knew the Brubeck group was in town for five weeks, but he didn't expect one of them to show up at his studio. One of the photographers sharing the room had advertised a camera for sale, and when Brubeck and his cohorts saw the ad, they chipped in to buy the camera as a birthday gift for Desmond, who had developed a passion for photography. This happenstance led to a life-long friendship with Desmond and Brubeck — and to numerous assignments doing album covers for the Quartet and others.

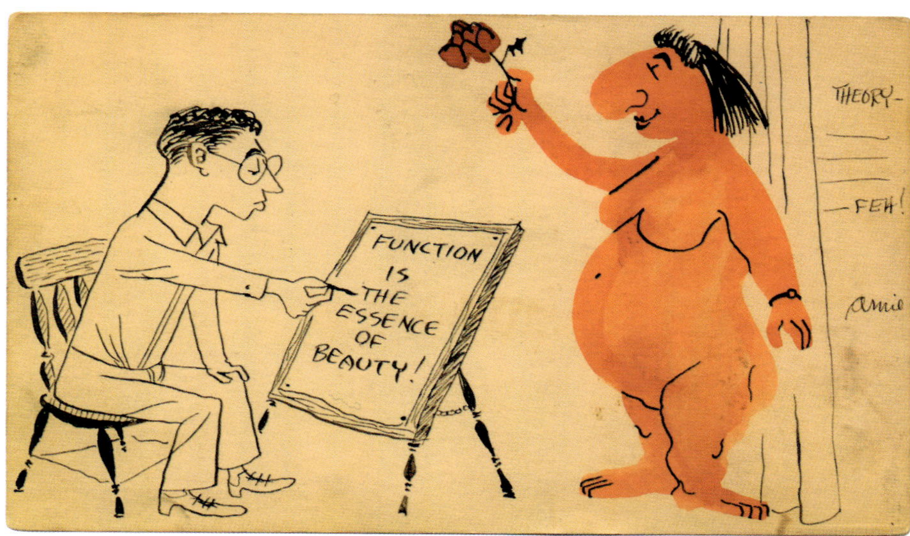

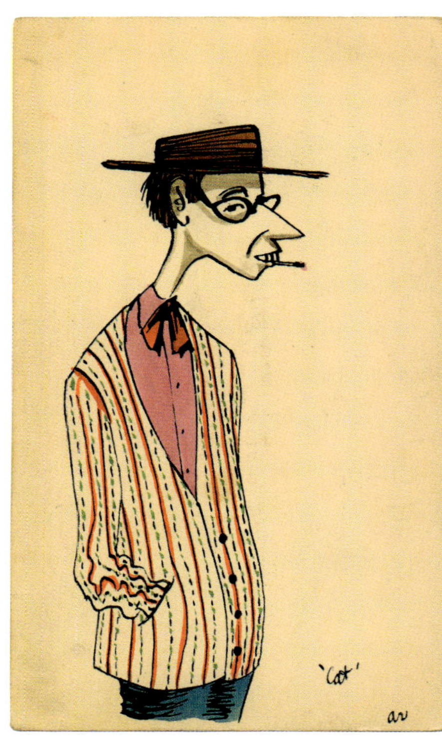

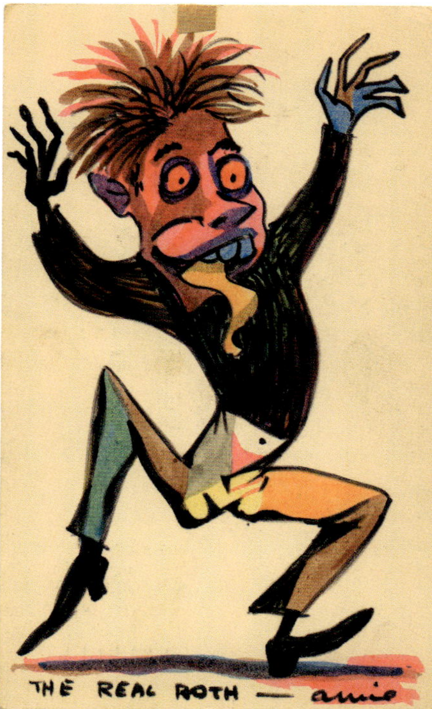

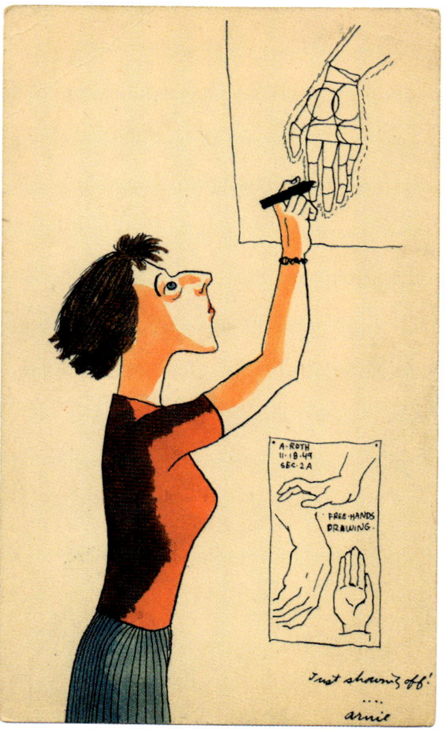

In 1949 it was found that I was qualified for hospitalization for tuberculosis. During the year-plus that I spent in the Deborah Sanatorium, Browns Mills, New Jersey, many of my bed-ridden hours were spent by frequently doing drawings on postcards which I sent to classmates and friends at the University of the Arts.

I've been told that the recipients would leave the cards in the open mail rack after reversing the cards so the drawings could be seen. That produced a permanent exhibition of constantly changing exhibits.

I was forced back into what passes as normal life when my qualification for recuperation lost its validity. Naturally, production of the cards ended. To celebrate that fact, my very kind classmate Charlotte Kaplan and many others returned almost 250 of the cards to me.

Seeing the cards, now, I understand why.

— Arnold Roth

Once Roth had done a few album covers for the Fantasy Records releases of Brubeck music, he got similar assignments at other record companies, including Columbia Records. Then in 1954 came another lucky break.

Roth arrived at the offices of *Glamour* magazine late in the afternoon. At first, the art director told the receptionist he wouldn't see Roth, but then he suddenly came out and wanted to look at Roth's drawings. He browsed through the portfolio and then said:

"Would you sell all of these drawings?"

"Sure," Roth said, " — that's what they're for."

"I just had a double-page spread killed," the man explained, "and we have to go to press tomorrow."

The drawings were all humorous, not gag cartoons, and without any particularly unifying theme. But *Glamour* printed them all and gave them a theme, entitling the double-page spread, "New Talent of 1954" (Fig. 3).

At about the same time, television began to emerge as a vast new outlet for advertising. The new medium had a voracious appetite for material, and animation found an enthusiastic welcome in commercials. Roth was soon into it. In 1955-56, he started contributing ideas and character designs to Storyboard, Inc. Started by John Hubley, one of the founders of the UPA animation enterprise and a creator of Gerald McBoing-Boing and Mister Magoo, Storyboard manufactured material for ad agencies to use in tv commercials. With steady sales there plus *TV Guide, Charm* magazine and a few sales to *Esquire* and elsewhere, Roth was at last making enough money to say that he was making a living as a cartoonist. Feeling fairly secure in his profession, he and Caroline started their family with Charles Perino, born in 1956, and Adam Wingfield, in 1958. About the same time, Roth made his big break-through.

Hubley had two cartoonists on staff as art directors — R. O. "Bob" Blechman and Gene Deitch. Talking with Blechman, Roth heard about *Trump,* which, at the time, didn't have a name. But it had an editor — or founder — and Roth knew the reputation of the editor. Harvey Kurtzman did the kind of cartooning Roth did, and Kurtzman was looking for people to help with his latest project.

Kurtzman was the comedic genius who launched *Mad* comic book in the fall of 1952 for Entertaining Comics (EC). Paul Desmond had introduced Roth to *Mad.* "He picked one up in an airport when he was traveling around to gigs," Roth said, "and he brought one to Philadelphia to show me and said, 'You've got to be reading this! This is great!'"

At the time, though — roughly 1953 — Roth wasn't thinking about comic books; he was aiming for magazines, the "slicks" not four-color pulp. He didn't pursue the matter then. But in 1956, when Blechman mentioned Kurtzman's new project — and when Roth heard about it again from *New Yorker* cartoonist Ed Fisher — it seemed a promising venue.

By then, Kurtzman had moved beyond comic books both physically and intellectually. During the first couple of years with the *Mad* comic book, Kurtzman had honed the device of parody into a weapon of sharply pointed satire. Beginning with takeoffs of comic strips, movies, tv shows, and literary classics, he expanded into the larger realm of popular culture generally. By 1955, Kurtzman had become increasingly impatient with the limitations of the form. He converted the comic book to a magazine format, but he was soon lured away by Hugh Hefner, publisher of *Playboy,* to produce a luxurious new satirical magazine that would deploy all the resources of magazine publishing — color and photographs as well as cartoons and text — to achieve through elaborate parody the ridicule of popular culture that Kurtzman aimed for. Hefner set him up in his *Playboy* branch office, a handsome rowhouse on 37th Street across from the J. P. Morgan Library.

Roth went to see Kurtzman, and Kurtzman immediately put him on retainer.

Kurtzman was sitting at a table in an office, Roth remembered, and on the table was a sheet of paper with the names of about fourteen young cartoonists on it. "And every one of those names — which I could remember for years — belonged to cartoonists who would later have great careers in publishing or animation," Roth said. "Harvey was great at spotting people and giving them a chance."

The first issue of *Trump,* cover-dated January 1957, contained work by *Mad* alumni Wally Wood, Jack Davis, and zany Will Elder as well as a host of others from Kurtzman's list — Al Jaffee, Ed Fisher, Russ Heath, Bob Blechman, and Howard Schneider among others. Roth illustrated a Roger Price article, "Why Christmas Is Nice." The second issue (March) was more lavishly produced with many more pages of color. Roth was now listed on the masthead as "Staff Artist (Asst. Ed.)," and he contributed pieces mocking the Russian tendency to claim epoch-making inventions as their own, the influence of ballet on everyday life, and "Movie Scenes You Must Have Seen," a send-up of celluloid cliches.[1]

Roth had continued freelancing to a growing list of client magazines, but he produced a good deal more material for *Trump,* too — much of it put aside for future issues of the magazine.

Alas, *Trump* was out of business before it hit the stands in late 1956. The March issue was its last. The problem was a nervous bank. Hefner's success with *Playboy* had established him as the boy genius of Chicago, and that was good enough for the bank for awhile. But *Playboy* was making an expensive move into new offices at the time, and a brief recession resulted in a dip in the magazine's advertising and sales revenues. Moreover, it wasn't a good time for magazines, and when the venerable *Collier's* magazine folded in January 1957, the bank refused to renew Hefner's line of credit. To absorb losses, Hefner stopped drawing a salary for awhile. And he canceled *Trump,* which, like all newly minted magazines, had already lost a considerable sum with its inaugural issues.

But Kurtzman and his crew had tasted success. Kurtzman expected *Trump* to be making money by the fourth or fifth issue, and with that expectation, he wanted to continue the crusade — but with another vehicle. He was able, without much effort, to persuade five of his cohorts to join him in a partnership to publish another national satirical magazine. Elder, Jaffee, Davis, Roth, and Kurtzman's lifelong production manager, Harry Chester, signed on. Hefner, feeling contrite, gave them free office space in his new Manhattan headquarters at Madison and 57th Street, and the partners put up cash as well as talent to publish their brainchild, *Humbug.*

Humbug was a much more modest production than *Trump:* it was smaller in size and page count, and it was published on cheap newsprint paper. But it, too, was a doomed effort. Just as it debuted, the biggest magazine distributor in the country folded. American News Service owned newsstands in hundreds of transportation centers and most of the best corner locations in big cities. Kurtzman, Roth recalled, tried to see beyond the immediate tragedy: "Look," he said, "we're not in the worst trouble: *The New Yorker* doesn't have a distributor either!"

Humbug struggled along for eleven issues from August 1957 until August 1958.

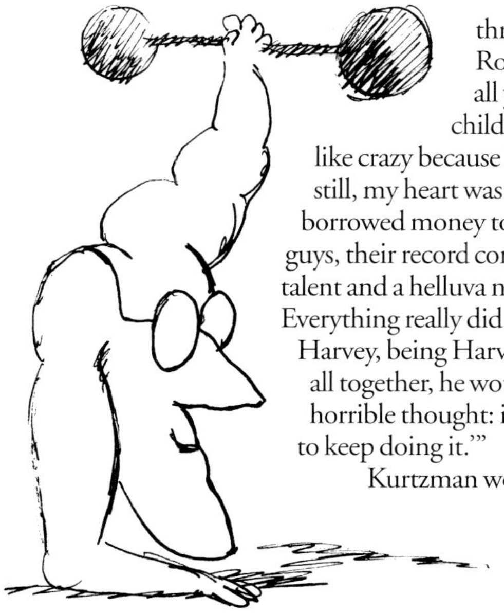

"We really went through hardship to do it," Roth remembered. "We were all young. We had young children. And I was doubled-up like crazy because I had to make a living. But still, my heart was in the magazine. I even borrowed money to help — from the Brubeck guys, their record company. We had a lot of talent and a helluva nerve but we had no brains. Everything really did conspire against us. But Harvey, being Harvey, when we were getting it all together, he would say, 'Gee, I just had a horrible thought: if this makes a hit, we'll have to keep doing it.'"

Kurtzman would pursue his dream in yet another low-budget production, *Help!,* which lasted for twenty-five issues, coming out periodically until August 1965. Roth contributed occasionally, and when Kurtzman and Elder teamed up to produce the world's most lavish comic strip, the painted full-color *Little Annie Fanny*, for *Playboy* (starting in October 1962), Roth, Jack Davis, and Al Jaffee sometimes helped Elder. By this time, Roth was in demand in numerous other publications. Still, he regards his time with Kurtzman on *Trump* and *Humbug* as the biggest break he had.

It was a signal if not salutary experience not just because of the fellowship of the crew but because of their focus. "I was doing purely humor," Roth said. "And it wasn't just piece-work: it was filling up the magazine. Although I've always done funny ideas, this wasn't just one album cover for which you create an idea suitable to the subject and then go on to the next, which would be something completely different. And so that was one of the best things that ever happened."

He enjoyed working with Kurtzman and learned much from him. Kurtzman had a reputation for meticulousness, for a fastidiousness in layout and rendering that carried perfectionism to an wholly impractical extreme. When editing the adventure comic books and *Mad* for EC, he produced detailed layouts for every story, and he demanded that the artists follow his layouts precisely. But he didn't do layouts for Roth; Roth did his own.

"Harvey and I used to argue and fight all the time," Roth said, "although we were in absolute philosophical agreement, our ways of working were very different. I've always thought, Well, if it's not that hot, you do another one. But Harvey wanted to hone and re-do. And I've never worked well in that way. I want to do it and then do another one. So I'd say, 'Harvey, I don't want to have a life where I've done one terrific drawing. I want to do a lot of crummy ones,'" he said with a laugh. "It's just like the two Egyptian kids looking at the pyramids, and one saying, 'Wow — you know how good we are at doing these now? Imagine how good we'll be in 5,000 years.'" He laughed again.

His regard for Kurtzman was at least as enduring as the Egyptian rock piles. And when he published *A Comick Book of Pets* with Scribner's in 1976, he dedicated it to Kurtzman — "the master."

In the wake of *Humbug's* collapse, Roth increased his efforts to find more markets for his work. He sent three cartoons to *Punch* magazine in England. All three were purchased. And he worked up an idea for a newspaper comic strip.

Called *Poor Arnold's Almanac,* it was designed as a Sunday feature, and it proved to be the sort of cartooning Roth would be most adept at — and the kind he liked most to do. Like his later "History of Sex" series for *Playboy,* each installment of the *Almanac* picked out a single subject, and Roth played variations on the theme in the manner of a jazz musician. The opening panel announced the topic for the day, and in subsequent panels — sometimes in narrative sequence as a comic strip, sometimes singly as stand-alone gag cartoons — Roth turned the subject this way and that, inspecting it from every angle and finding inconsistencies in human behavior and naked emperors everywhere he looked. Typically, his hilarities resulted from yoking pictures to words: the pictures revealed the comedy in the verbiage. But his format permitted him simply to play with words alone, punning and making lunatic lists and reciting with sportive abandon whatever drollery he discerned in some aspect of his subject. It was vintage Roth buffoonery. And he would eventually continue in the same mode for *Punch* and for *Playboy.* It was the way Roth liked most to work.

He presented four completed strips to Harry Welker, the comic editor at the New York Herald Tribune Syndicate, the distribution operation of its namesake newspaper, the nation's most literate daily paper. Welker bought it immediately. The syndicate didn't have many comics, but what they had was quality — Johnny Hart's *B.C.,* Mell Lazarus's *Miss Peach*, Al Jaffee's *Tall Tales* (which had just begun). *Poor Arnold's Almanac* started appearing on May 31, 1959. It was a regular gig, as Roth put it — steady income. Living on what he earned with magazine work, Roth used the *Almanac* money to pay off his debt to the Brubeck record company. Within a year, he had discharged the debt.

Roth had always wanted to go to England, and now, with a regular check from his comic strip and assignments from New York magazines, he could afford to risk the venture. In London, he would supplement his income by doing work for *Punch,* which had been buying from him with some regularity. He packed up everything he owned, and he and his wife and two kids moved to London in August 1960.

Punch was the English-speaking world's most revered humor magazine — in legend, at least, if not in fact as well. Allegedly launched from the back room of a tavern in the summer of 1841, it was one of many British attempts of that time at duplicating the satirical and comedic impact of *La Charivari*, a daily paper in Paris, founded in 1832 by Charles Philipon, who had earlier (1830) achieved notoriety with a caricature of King Louis Philippe in his weekly paper *Le Caricature*, the magazine that made caricature famous (due more to its chief contributors, Honoré Daumier and Gustave Doré , than to Philipon). At the time of Roth's initiation into *Punch,* its editor was Bernard Hollowood, a sometime cartoonist himself who had served as the magazine's deputy literary editor and radio and television critic. The soon-to-retire cartoon editor was Russell Brockbank ("a wonderful guy who was a very good cartoonist himself," Roth said), who had brought into the magazine such personages as Ronald Searle, Francis Wilford-Smith ("Smilby"), Michael ffolkes, and Gerald Scarfe among others. A great many cartoonists were connected to the magazine, but *Punch* needed them: a weekly, it published about thirty cartoons in every issue.

Much of the planning for every issue of the magazine occurred on Thursdays at a weekly meeting dubbed "the *Punch* lunch." Like many things in England, it had a long and mellow tradition. The meeting of editors, writers, and cartoonists took place at a large table that could seat about twenty-four persons. The table, sometimes called "the Mahogany tree" (because of a poem William Makepeace Thackeray wrote about it in 1847), is not a particularly ornate piece of furniture; it is, rather, an inexpensive but sturdy piece of Victorian office furniture in ordinary deal (not "mahogany" at all). Its distinction, however, lies in the carved initials that adorn its surface. To symbolize the permanence of the institution, "members of the Table" were invited to make their marks thereon. The invitations were not lightly extended. By 1979 — after over 120 years — only 79 sets of initials appeared, including those of such literary and artistic lights as Thackeray, Searle, A.A. Milne, John Leech, George du Maurier, Phil May, Malcolm Muggeridge, and John Tenniel. The only American by then was James Thurber. Mark Twain had been invited to inscribe his initials but declined, saying he would be quite satisfied to share the last two letters in Thackeray's beautifully executed monogram. ("Everyone assumed that he was simply too drunk to handle a penknife," Roth said with a chuckle.)

The meeting was an evening dinner until 1925, when it became a mid-day meal. It began, without fail, in the editor's office with drinks, starting about noon. "There was about an hour of boozing," Roth said, "and then, you'd go into lunch, which was served by liveried guys with white gloves on, one of whom looked like Mr. Punch. I always thought they got him from central casting. The editor sat at one end of the table, and the publisher at the other."

The walls of the "banquet room" were decorated with framed drawings from *Punch* and photographs of various dignitaries, including a painted portrait of Mark Lemon, the first to edit the magazine single-handedly. (At the beginning, the editorship was shared by Lemon and two others.)

The meal was a traditional five-course Victorian feast, beginning with soup and including a hearty main course like saddle of lamb and ending with desert and cheese, all lubricated by bottles of claret. "You didn't have to eat or drink for a couple of days afterwards," Roth said. "And by the end of the thing, everybody was pretty much in the bag."

In addition to staff members, the company might include a special guest — a politician, entertainer, writer, or other notable. During the meal, the conversation was general around the table — general gossip, rude jokes, bad puns, obscene limericks, and other forms of verbal horseplay. If there was a guest, that person might be queried about an interest or activity. Eventually, the talk would turn to current events, and staff members would comment on aspects of the conversation.

"And so the editor would say, 'Well, good — why don't you get me a hundred words on that for next week's issue,'" Roth said. "And then a cartoonist might mention something, and the editor would say, 'Oh yes — why don't you do something on that?' The meetings lasted most of the

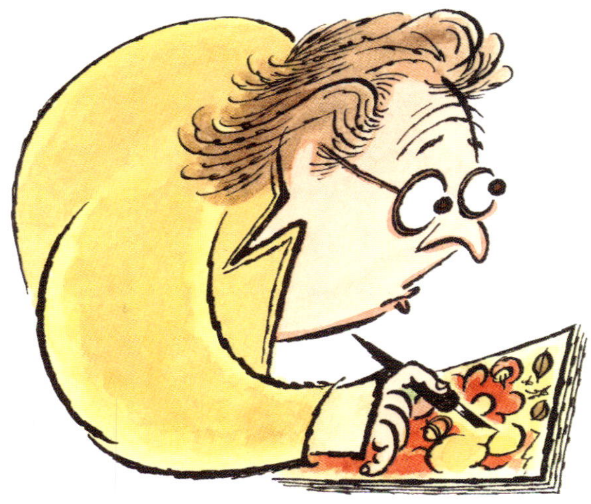

afternoon. The editor told me that the next morning there were always all these phone calls from people who'd been there: 'Ah, I neglected to jot down the subject you assigned to me.'" Roth laughed: "They were lucky they remembered how to get home!"

Roth contributed exclusively to *Punch* for the next year. Although the edgier *Private Eye* magazine invited him to contribute, he didn't. "I always try not to draw for the competition if I'm doing a lot of work for somebody; I don't think it's the right thing. It would just be egregious."

Working for American magazines, however, was not working for competitors. While in London, Roth received a couple of assignments from Kurtzman at *Help!* He went to Moscow and Berlin ("the pleasure domes of Europe") to do cartoon reportage. He also did a lot of color work for *Esquire* — illustrations as well as cartoons. Then in the late spring of 1961, the syndicate rug was pulled from under him.

Shortly after Roth was informally assured that his contract with the Herald Tribune Syndicate would be renewed, he received another letter telling him that his contract was terminated. Later, Roth found out that the newspaper and the syndicate were quarreling, and the newspaper canceled *Poor Arnold's Almanac.* Once the flagship newspaper no longer carried a syndicated feature, it became difficult for the syndicate to sell the feature. About forty newspapers carried the *Almanac,* but salesmen still had no way to counter the scathing comment they met with from many editors they visited: "If this strip is so good, why don't you [the syndicate's home-base paper] carry it?"

Roth immediately wrote to another syndicate to see if it would distribute the strip. But by then, it was too late. "As soon as a syndicate decides to kill you, they tell all the client papers that the strip is ending," Roth said. And all those papers promptly drop the strip and put another in its place. Had he found out earlier about the impending demise of the *Almanac,* he could have negotiated a transfer of the feature to another syndicate that might have been interested in acquiring a strip that came with a ready-made string of subscribing papers. But since he was in England, Roth heard no rumors in advance, inklings that might have prompted a salvage maneuver. The last strip ran on May 14, 1961; it had completed two full years. In August, Roth packed up the family and returned to Philadelphia, where he lived for the next two years, moving then to Princeton, New Jersey.

He continued to do work for *Punch* by mail, occasionally making a quick trip to London. Then in 1965, he inherited the magazine's regular monthly two-page feature, "Report from America," which had been contributed for years by P.G. Wodehouse, by then in his nineties. His report had slowly deteriorated over the years until it consisted of little more than a miscellaneous collection of clippings from U.S. magazines and newspapers. Bernard Hollowood asked Roth to take it over.

"I wrote what I was sure were the funniest two pages ever written in English and mailed them off," Roth recalled. "They came back and in red on top of the page in big letters it said, 'You fool, I meant *draw* two pages!' My wife said, 'Gee, they're really angry at you.' I said, 'No, if they don't call you at least a *swine,* they're not even serious.'"

Roth did a monthly two-page spread of cartoon reportage on American foibles for the next twenty-three years. Deploying again the method he'd perfected in *Poor Arnold's Almanac,* he examined such topics as the cutback in funding of the National Endowment for the Arts, the struggle between smokers and non-smokers, the jogging fad, hypocritical U.S. immigration policies, and so on. As in the *Almanac,* he mustered the entire arsenal of cartoon weaponry — single-panel cartoons, humorous illustration, mini-strips of several sequential panels as well as a healthy dose of verbal high jinks (like the delicious pun in the immigration report on the "Open Dour Policy" [Fig. 19]). He loved doing it. The format was a perfect reflection of his comedic sensibility; he was therefore stimulated to ever more prankish flights of hilarity. And he enjoyed absolute editorial freedom.

"It was the perfect symbiotic arrangement," Roth said. "I knew I had to fill two pages every month, I did two pages, I sent them in, they never said a word, they printed them, and then they underpaid me. And everyone was happy!" He laughed.

In September 1986 came the ultimate accolade. Roth received a letter from Alan Coren, then the editor of *Punch* (and Roth's favorite in that chair), inviting the cartoonist to carve his initials into the Table next time he was in town. Next time? Roth turned to Caroline and said, "Pack our bags — we're going to London. Don't want to miss this opportunity."

"What it meant was that I was considered staff," Roth told me. "And the staff is very small." It was a signal honor, and one that had been conferred upon very few other Americans.

One of the beneficial effects of the *Trump* adventure was that Roth started being published regularly in *Playboy.* Many of his efforts were illustrations for articles executed in his usual maniacal manner — such as "Intermission" [Fig. 23], "Euphemisms: George Carlin" [Fig. 25], and "Camilla Parker-Bowles" [Fig. 27]. But perhaps his most celebrated contribution to the magazine is a series that started in the late 1970s, "The History of Sex," from which we have in this volume Chapter Four, "Olympian Games" [Fig. 22], a perfectly representative example of the sort of verbal-visual jape that distinguished the series.

In setting out on this project, Roth negotiated an arrangement with Hefner. He knew that Hefner had ambitions to be a cartoonist himself when young and that he couldn't refrain from making suggestions for changes in cartoons submitted to *Playboy*. (Jules Feiffer, among others, agrees that Hefner is a very perceptive editor of cartoons. According to Feiffer, Hefner often produced several pages of detailed critique with ideas for "improvements" in a single cartoon with the sole intention of making the cartoon work better. "And often he would bring up things that he was absolutely right about," Feiffer said.) But Roth, as we've seen, doesn't feel comfortable working in that manner.

"I made a deal that if he didn't like something, I wouldn't do it over, but I would replace it," Roth explained. "If you agree to changing things and doing them over, you'll be doing it to everything. I didn't want to collaborate with Hefner. Although I admire and value his editorial judgement, I think he can't leave well enough alone. I only had to replace a few things out of lots of cartoons I submitted. It was filthy and fun — though I think with one or two exceptions, my favorite jokes were clean ones: they had nothing to do with sex."

But when Hefner saw in the "Olympian Games" the picture of King Midas whose magic touch had turned his penis to gold, he couldn't stop himself.

"He sent a three-page single-spaced letter," Roth remembered, "about how he really didn't want me to replace it, he liked it a lot, but the only thing is, he didn't like the way I drew the penis. And Caroline opened it, I was working — and I was in a horrible rush on a job — and she was reading this letter to me, and she's dying laughing, and she says, 'I can't believe this guy is heading a two-hundred million dollar a year business and has time for this.' She showed me the memo — with 'From the desk of Hugh M. Hefner' at the top — and here was a sketch. It was three red lines — two parallel with an inverted V on top. He's showing me how to draw a penis! So I wrote back and said, 'You're right. The way you indicated *is* the way to draw a penis, but unfortunately that's the way I draw *noses,* so for clarity's sake — ,'" he chuckled, the conclusion of the sentence obvious. "And that was the end of that," he said.

He never cleared his ideas in advance. "At the magazine," Roth said, "they had no idea what was coming: every chapter, I would just do it. And they'd ask me: 'How long is this going to go on?' And I'd say, 'As long as I'm paying tuitions for my kids in college.'"[2]

In the mid-1960s, Roth had added *Sports Illustrated* to his list of major outlets. The list would eventually number in the hundreds of publications, including *Time* and *Newsweek, Fortune* and *Forbes, Harper's, Gentleman's Quarterly, Holiday, Horizon, Life, American Health, Audubon, Modern Maturity, Mother Jones, The Nation, Money, National Lampoon, New Woman, Parenting, People, Premier, The Progressive, Psychology Today, Saturday Evening Post, Rolling Stone, Smithsonian, Town and Country,* and the *Wall Street Journal* and other newspapers, particularly in New York. He became one of the most published cartoonists. Then in the late 1970s, Roth had perhaps the most serious financial setback of his career.

He had concocted another cartoon feature for syndication. Called *Downtown,* it was intended to reflect an emerging population shift. People were moving back into city centers from the suburbs — single people. And Roth set his cartoon locale in a downtown bar where all sorts of odd and engaging characters would congregate. "The premise," he said, "was much like the television show, *Cheers*" (which began in September 1982). An agent placed the feature almost immediately with a syndicate, and Roth began to cut back on his magazine work to give himself time to produce the cartoon on a daily basis. He did about three months' worth of cartoons, but the syndicate kept stalling on releasing the feature, telling Roth all the time that it would be launched "any day now." Eventually, however, the enterprise collapsed altogether. But by then, Roth had turned away scores of assignments. "And when you turn away people too often," he remarked, "they start to think you're not in the business anymore."

At age 50, faced with near financial disaster, Roth rented a six-foot by nine-foot "open plan" space in a studio shared by commercial artists in Manhattan. This "office" permitted him to meet with clients, show his portfolio, and do the work those efforts yielded. He commuted daily from Princeton three or four days a week, working at home in New Jersey the rest of the week. A few months later, he was back on reasonably firm financial footing. After a year or so, the illustrator Ed Sorel told Roth about the availability of a small apartment below his own in a rowhouse building.

"We seized it," Roth said. "It replaced the 'open plan' space. Since I could work and sleep there, my commute was reduced to once a week."

The Roths left Princeton in 1984 for an apartment in New York, the cartoonist taking a studio elsewhere in the city. He has lived and worked in separate places since then.

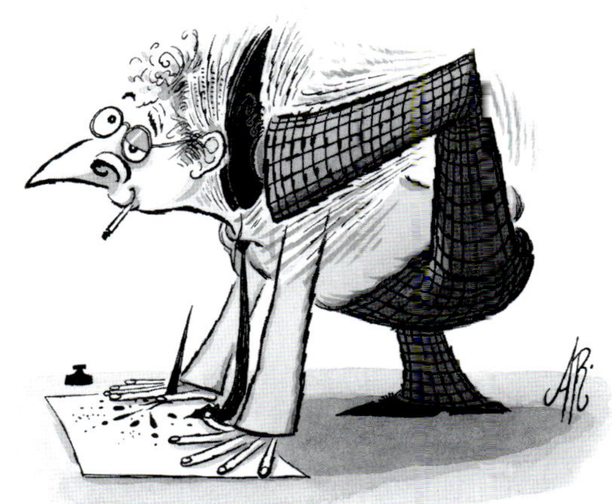

A Portrait of the Artist As A Young Flea Owner

The 1980s was a good decade, Roth said. Not only did he appear regularly in the pages of numerous national magazines, but he was elected president of the National Cartoonists Society in 1983. The next year, the Society named him Cartoonist of the Year and awarded him the Reuben. He had won NCS awards previously for sports cartooning in *Sports Illustrated* (1976 and 1977) and for cartoon illustration (1976 and 1979), and he won the latter annually through the eighties (so regularly that he withdrew himself from consideration after 1989). A member of the Association of American Editorial Cartoonists and the Society of Illustrators, he won many gold and silver awards in the Society's annual shows.

He appeared on the "Tonight Show" with Johnny Carson and David Letterman. He lectured at the Philadelphia College of Art, the School of Visual Arts, Pratt Institute, Cooper Union, Parsons School, Princeton University, and Yale, among others. He filled in for vacationing editorial cartoonists Bay Rigby at the *New York Post* and for his father Paul at the *New York Daily News,* indulging in a little political commentary as well as social satire.

Roth's approach to editorial cartooning is amiable rather than adversarial. He believes cartoons should laugh the pompous off their perches rather than skewer them to the wall. The agenda is to deflate not to destroy. For Roth, "liberal" is middle ground, not "left."

"I've done a lot of political stuff from the very left to — well, not the very right," he told me. "Like today, I'm working on a job for a magazine here which I've worked for steadily, *City Journal*, which is, I'd say, middle conservative. Not a right wing. And they're a pleasure to work for. I worked for *The Progressive* for six or eight years — that's up in Wisconsin, the old Lafollette paper, and they're pretty toward the left. And I've done work for *The Nation*, too, which some say is very left."

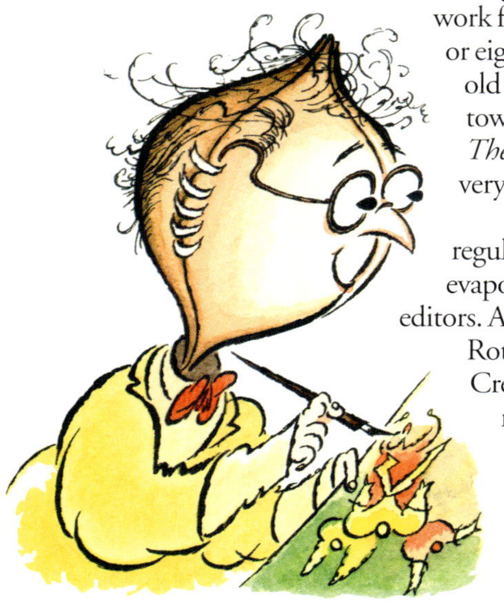

By the end of the decade, his regular assignment at *Punch* had evaporated with the rapid turnover of editors. At the urging of *B.C.*'s Johnny Hart, Roth revived *Poor Arnold's Almanac* with Creators Syndicate. He avoided the mistake he'd made with *Downtown:* he continued to accept magazine assignments while doing the cartoon. But this time, the strip was daily as well as Sunday, and the combined magazine and strip workload was exhausting. The circulation of the cartoon simply wasn't great enough to justify this all-out effort. Still, Roth carried on for almost two years before he discontinued the *Almanac.* But there was good news from other quarters.

In 1992, *The New Yorker* acquired a new editor — Tina Brown, a young English woman whose rise in magazine journalism had been meteoric on both sides of the Atlantic. Brown had done some writing for *Punch* shortly after graduating from Oxford, and she knew Roth's work. Soon after taking the editor's chair at *The New Yorker,* she invited him to submit material. Lee Lorenz, then art editor and cartoon editor for the magazine, phoned Roth and said, "She'd like to see ideas."

As always, Roth was loath to do sketches (but the first one he did became a *New Yorker* cover).

"I'll tell you what, Lee," he said. "I'd like to do double-page spreads for you. Would you be open to them?"

Lee said he would, and Roth continued: "Okay, I'll just do a couple finished, and if you like 'em and want to buy 'em, good. And if not, I'll know this is not for me."

Roth did two spreads in his customary jazzman manner. *The New Yorker* bought one but passed on the one he did about bicycling in the city. Thereafter Roth appeared sporadically in the magazine until David Remnick succeeded Brown a half-dozen years later, and then the cartoonist started getting commissions regularly, frequently for the magazine's Back Page, a single page cartoon feature.

"They call up and say, 'Could you do a Back Page?" Roth said. "And the way I work — I say, 'Okay — do you have an idea of the subject? Is it a theme issue?' 'Oh, no,' they say; 'we'd just like something that goes with the season.' And that's the way I like to work. And I'll do sketches for them because with a commission, I know they'll pay me for my time and effort whether they publish the work or not. As I always say — if they'd paid me to go to art school, I wouldn't have been late," he finished with a laugh. "I've had thousands and thousands of deadlines and never missed one."

Some years later, casting about for a subject for one of the Back Page commissions, Roth remembered the two pages he'd done on bicycling. Owen Phillips edited it down to the customary single page allowance and titled it "As You Bike It." Another Back Page, "Animal City" [Fig. 65], is perhaps a better example of how Roth works because it was designed as a single page, as a unified work.

The literal idea — the joke, the humor — is paramount, but in the execution of the drawing, Roth strives for aesthetic qualities as well as technical, narrative clarity. "I try to make the composition attractive," he explained, "so that the way I stage each panel and where they are in relation to each other make an attractive, balanced appearance. When I say 'balance,' I don't mean axial balance. If there's heaviness or darkness here in one area, there should be something to balance it elsewhere so the whole page will be attractive — so it will be appealing to the eye — and will read easier."

Although there are five separate drawings in "Animal City" [Fig. 65], each of them is related to the others in an overall design. The two smaller panels at the top of the page are balanced by the large panel at the bottom. The huge shaggy dog at the upper right is balanced against the cluster of figures at the lower left, including a big fat horse the anatomy of which echoes that of the observer on the bench at the left. But aesthetic balance is more complex than simply weighing visual elements, one against another. The action of the third panel is diagonal from upper left to lower right; this diagonal is countered by a diagonal in the opposite direction in the next panel (the stairway and the falling flower pot point from upper right to lower left), the visual impulse directing the eye to the left side of the panel below, which continues the same diagonal composition element in the line of observers, leading, ultimately, to the fat man on the bench whose comment sets up the final joke. The action across the bottom of the page at the right duplicates the diagonal of the third panel and acquires a kind of visual impetus as a result.

At the same time, each individual drawing is composed for narrative clarity. The rat in the first panel points with his nose to the girl in the chair, the rat's nose and the girl's arm creating a diagonal that leads to the speech balloon that, coupled to the picture of the rat itself, makes the joke. The picture here, although humorous, is not a joke without the words; and the words make no comedic sense without the picture. The next pictures are all humorous in themselves. The huge dog is contrasted with its owner, a tiny woman; but the size of the dog and the comparatively tiny plastic receptacle that she plans to use in scooping up the dog's deposit creates the comedy at the heart of this picture.

"I try to make everything be funny," Roth said, "but that huge face of that huge dog — I wanted him to look like a digestion machine. And in the last panel, the visual joke is the contrast between the running horse and the plodding one."

And, again, the verbal content taken in conjunction with the visual content creates a joke that neither words nor pictures achieve without the other.

Every drawing represents an artistic challenge as well as a narrative one. The cartoonist must not only make the literal humorous point clearly — the narrative chore — but must make it in a way that is aesthetically pleasing — to the artist as much as to the reader. In meeting this challenge, Roth thinks like a jazz musician.

"I enjoy doing it," he said. "I try to give myself little problems. Dave Brubeck, years ago, was on a symposium and somebody asked him, 'Would you describe what playing jazz is?' And he said, 'It's getting yourself into and out of trouble.' I thought that was a good way to put it. If you're not doing that, you're really hacking it, doing the same thing over and over. I always want to push it a little.

"When you're illustrating," he continued, "usually there are givens. The subject matter. Whether I make up the subject — let's say biking — or it's an article about bikes, you shift into that gear; you start going through that channel. You start to gather pieces of the puzzle. You might know what you want to do at the end — what the joke is going to be. And a lot of times, there's no real joke. It's just exaggeration that is funny — which is what cartooning is. But there are all these pieces that you want to incorporate. And that to me is the fun of it; that's very exciting. And that's where the art comes into it — doing an attractive or interesting or effective drawing that somebody wants to look at — instead of turning away.

"When I illustrate," he went on, "I do a funny drawing about that subject. I won't just illustrate an occurrence in the story. I want the drawing to be comprehensible and entertaining apart from the piece. My experience is that people look at the pictures first and then they read the piece. If you're a straight illustrator, you depict an incident from the story, and the reader thinks, 'Wow — that looks exciting.' But what's the point of me drawing Joe putting his hat on the rack while Mary shoves her lover out the back door? You can do that with a photo now. Straight illustrators used to do those things. I figure my function is to entertain the person and get them into the piece.

"I had a great teacher in high school who was a painter named Frederick Gill," Roth said. "Composition was his main interest and it's always been mine, also — how to put things together to make a picture and, in my case, to tell a story. I think the thing he imparted most was the idea of working 'honest,' and by that, I mean not to go for effect. He taught me not to go for the cheap shot or the obvious and easy solution. He taught me to create a problem for myself and try to solve it. And no tricks. We get into habits about the ways we solve problems. If we're not really concentrating, we solve problems in an almost automatic way. It becomes a part of our iconographic language. It's like saying 'like' a lot. After awhile, you're not thinking: you're just saying 'like' all the time. I'm thinking constantly. I give it absolute concentration when I'm working, but these automatic things can creep in, and you have to be wary of them and try to avoid them. If you rely on them — after awhile, it kills the fun of doing the work. Automatic makes it uninteresting."

A pronounced mannerism in drawing — artistic style itself — can be such a crutch. Style for Roth is like handwriting: he draws, and his style emerges.

"People ask me how I worked out my style," Roth said with a chuckle. "Well, I didn't. It sort of like the way you sign your name. I just do it. When I was very young, I went once to the studio of a couple of guys I knew in art school, and they hoped to be gag cartoonists. And I would say, 'What are you working on?' And they would say, 'I'm working out my style.' And I said, 'You mean you're twenty years old and you're going to work out how you're going to draw everything for the rest of your life?' It was something I never believed — you just drew. If I'm doing a drawing where I want a lot of tension rather than something that looks pleasant, I think it does affect the way I inscribe the line. And I think that's the explanation for it."

Sometimes a raggedy line indicates texture; but sometimes it suggests tension in a scene. Fat, smooth lines suggest repose, placidity. Roth feels such emotions as he works, more-or-less consciously. If he has a rush job, for instance, he

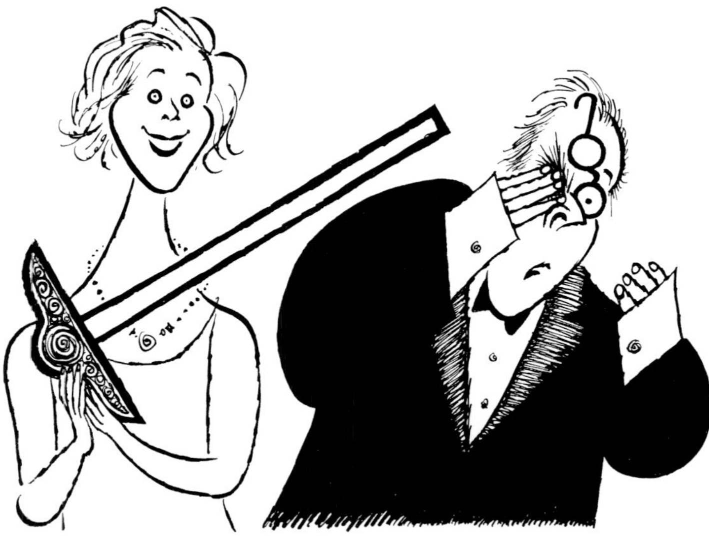

frequently works at a larger scale than usual. But it isn't entirely intentional. The more rapidly he works, the more his hand sweeps back and forth across the paper, a large gesture that results in a large drawing.

Roth typically blocks out a drawing with pencil, sketching lightly and loosely. Most of the detail is added as he inks with a pen. "Sometimes I'll do more pencil if it's a very complicated piece," he explained. "A lot of times I'll just put in the main figures and then fill in the ancillary jokes in the background as I ink."

And sometimes the incidental comedy is added as he works and realizes that he's leaving negative space or other visual awkwardnesses that need to be filled with something so they won't detract from the main purpose of the picture.

"Sometimes you want a huge, fairly empty space," Roth said. "In the biking piece, for example, the guy stealing the bike would be a case like that. I have the tree, the huge chain, and the guard — an ineffective overly armed guard — humorous elements, of course. But then we come to the guy speeding away. And I had to show that he was speeding away on a bike that had no handlebars, no seat, no front wheel because the bike owner had taken those thinking this was now a useless bike because it wouldn't work. The empty space around the picture enables me to show how comically little of the bike the thief has stolen."

Once the linework of the drawing is completed in black ink, Roth begins to lay in color. Since he doesn't work from color sketches, he goes slowly, starting with light tints and building up the color as he goes and sees how the over-all composition is developing. "It takes a little time," he said, "but in watercolor, once you commit too much, you're stuck. I have in mind what I want — and a lot of the color is determined automatically by the thing being colored — but my technique allows me a lot of flexibility as I go."

The more time he has, the more care he can lavish on the painting. "If the clock is ticking and I can't really get into more complicated painting, I use over-all tones of colors, warms and cools, and then just suggest color. Others I can really develop."

In the "Intermission" piece for *Playboy*, for example, much of the background detail was added at the coloring stages without linework. Here (particularly on the left), the color is deeper, stronger than in other drawings. In some works, the color is lighter — pastel almost. "It depends upon the idea and the feeling I want to get into it," Roth said. "When you do it in black and white, you use your line for emphasis — to tell the story and get the mood and character — and color should work to enhance all that. Black and white is color with a very limited palette. Line can be very colorful, especially if the blacks are handled well. Design possibilities are endless. You can achieve depth and form simply by placing densely worked areas against white space."

Although Roth's work is commercial, he feels completely free artistically. "I feel very journalistic about it," he said. "If a drawing is a little weaker than I want it to be, then I'll just make the next one a little better — if time allows. If time doesn't, I make it as good as I can under the circumstances. There's no other choice. If you break your leg and need to run for help, you can't say, 'I'm not going to run; my leg's broken.' You run as best you can.

"In the short run," he continued, "the most important thing — for salability and communication — the most important thing is the joke. But in the long run, the most important thing is the art, the actual graphic work. Nobody cares what Gillray's politics were, or Rowlandson's views; you just look at those pictures. They're funny and they're great. They're beautifully done.'"

Looking at Gillray and Rowlandson and Roth, we have the sense that they were all having fun being funny. We know Roth is having fun. We know he does it for the fun of it. And from the evidence before us, we know that when Roth does it for the fun of it, he creates works of art as well as works of comedy.

---

[1] None of Roth's original art from this period is still in his hands; all of it has disappeared (which is why this exhibition includes no samples from either *Trump* or *Humbug)*. Roth has heard various stories — the artwork was destroyed in a flood; it was appropriated by a collector in Long Island. Otherwise, the work in this volume from various magazines is roughly in proportion to the amount of work Roth did for those publications.

[2] All of Roth's "History of Sex" for *Playboy* has not yet been published. He has completed three or four installments that the magazine has yet to run. The last chapter to be published appeared nearly ten years ago. Since the series began, *Playboy's* attitude about frontal male nudity has changed: Roth has had to change his art in some instances to eliminate phallic offense.

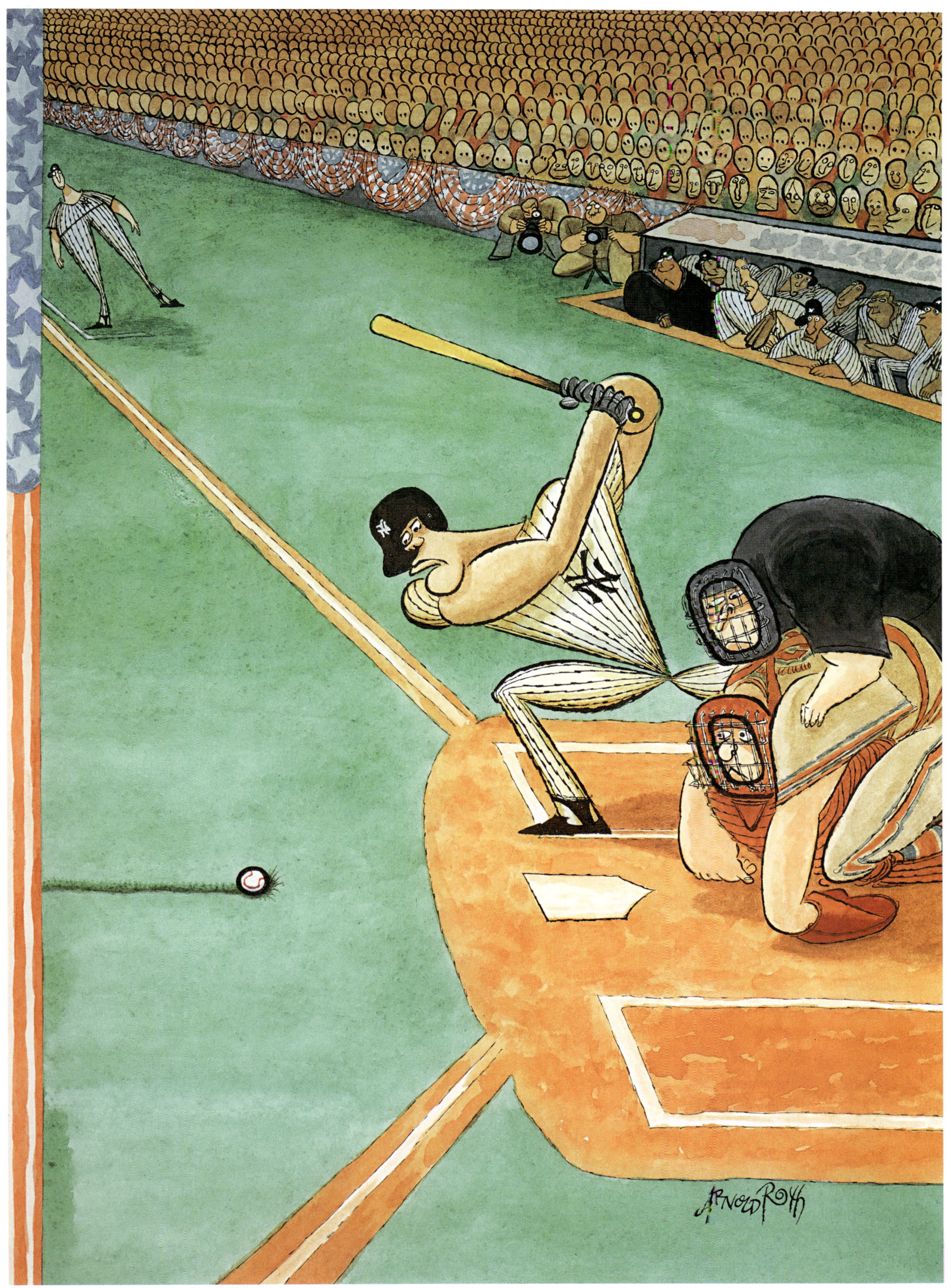
ARNOLD ROTH

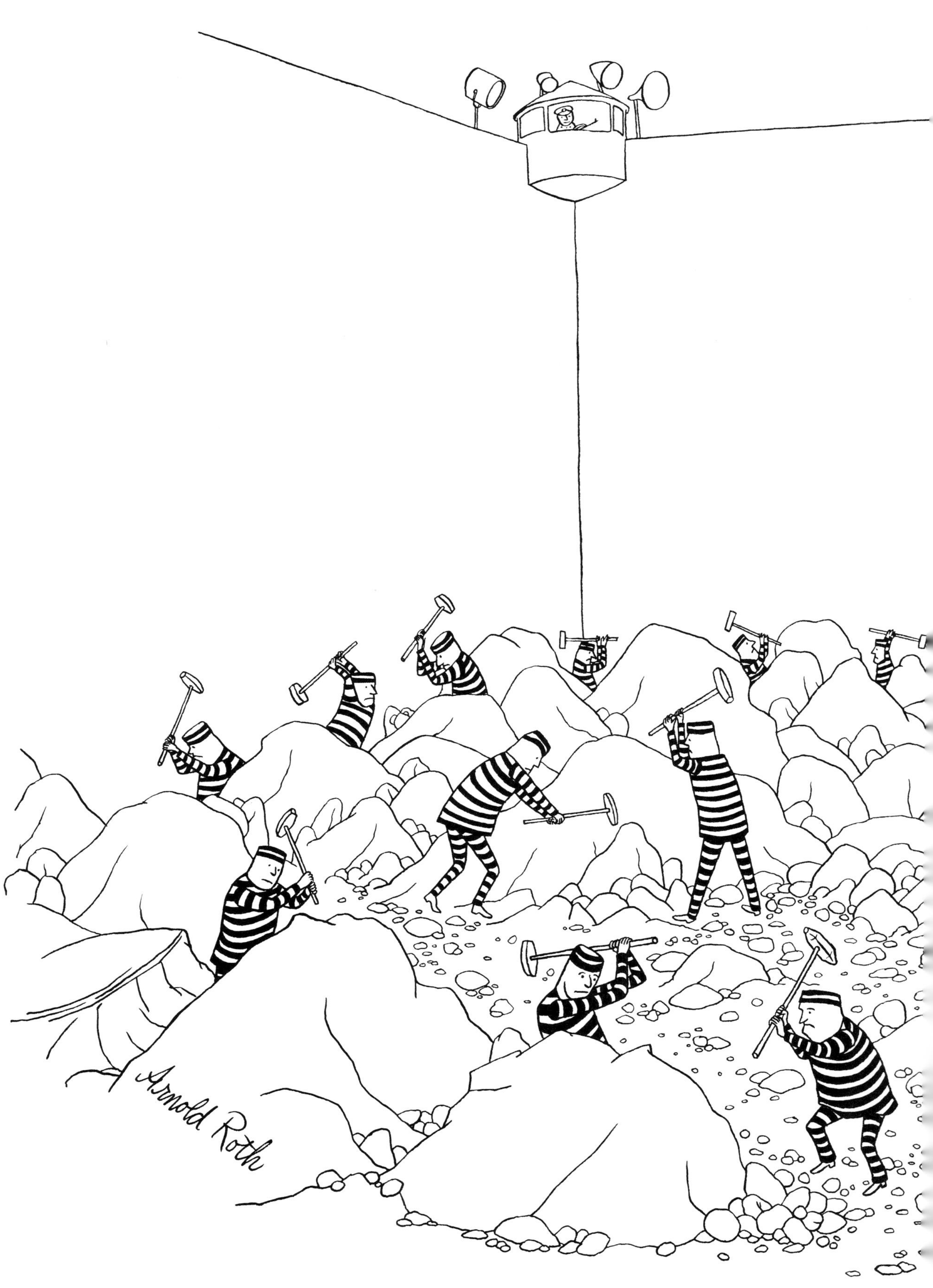

Overleaf:
Figure 2
"The First Pitch"
The New Yorker 2000

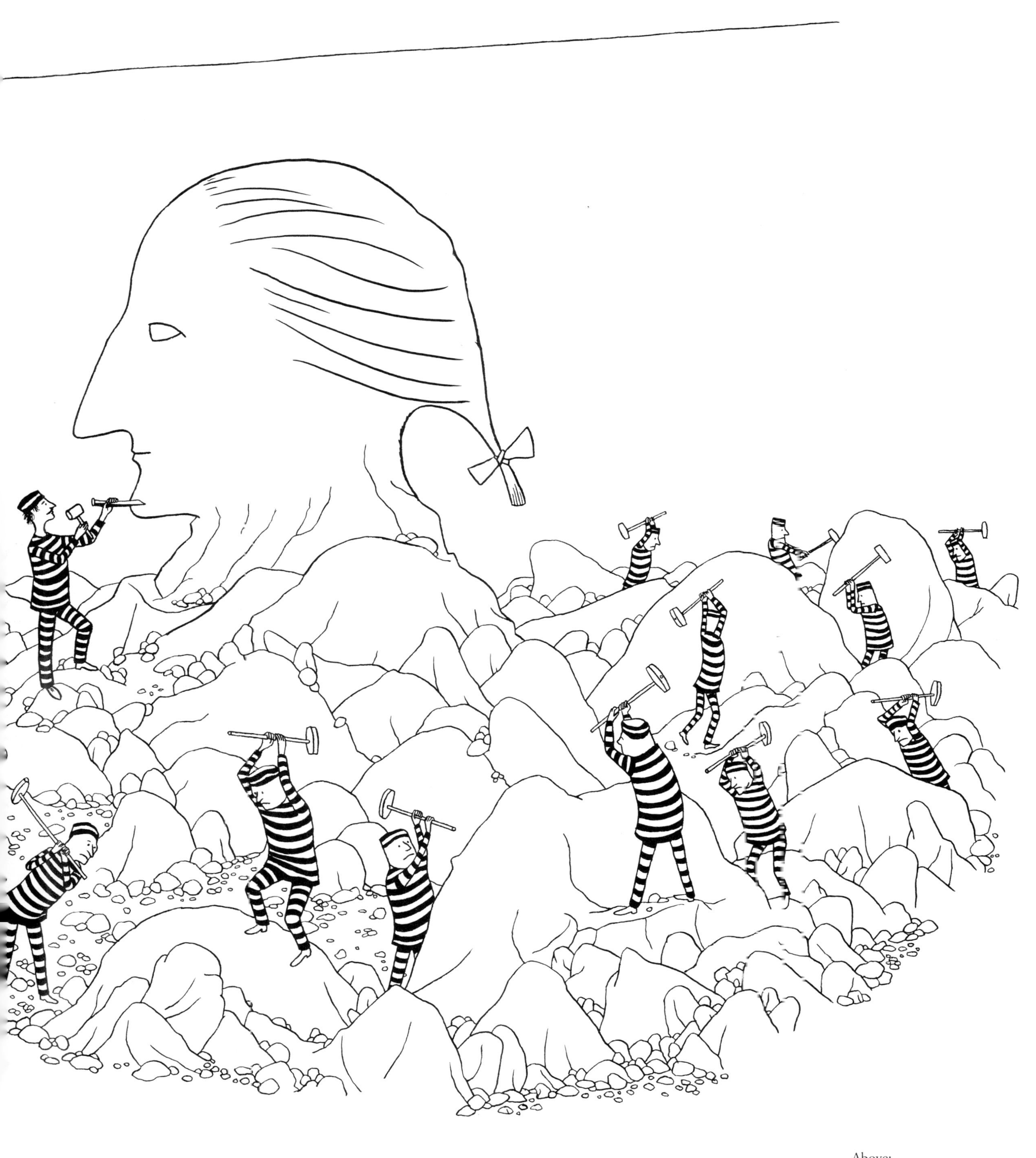

Above:
Figure 3
"New Talent of 1954"
Glamour 1954

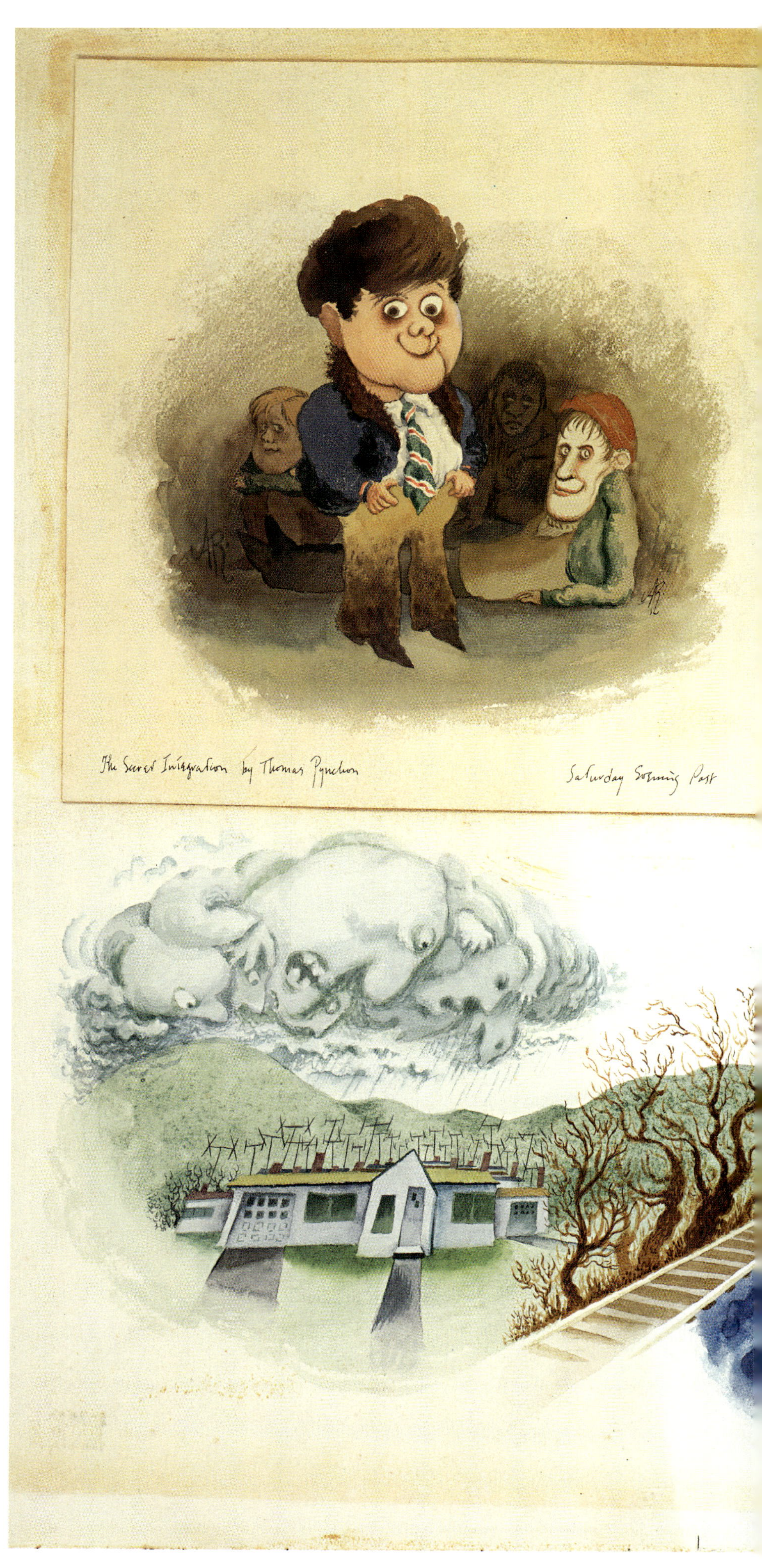

Figure 4
"The Secret Integration"
Saturday Evening Post 1964

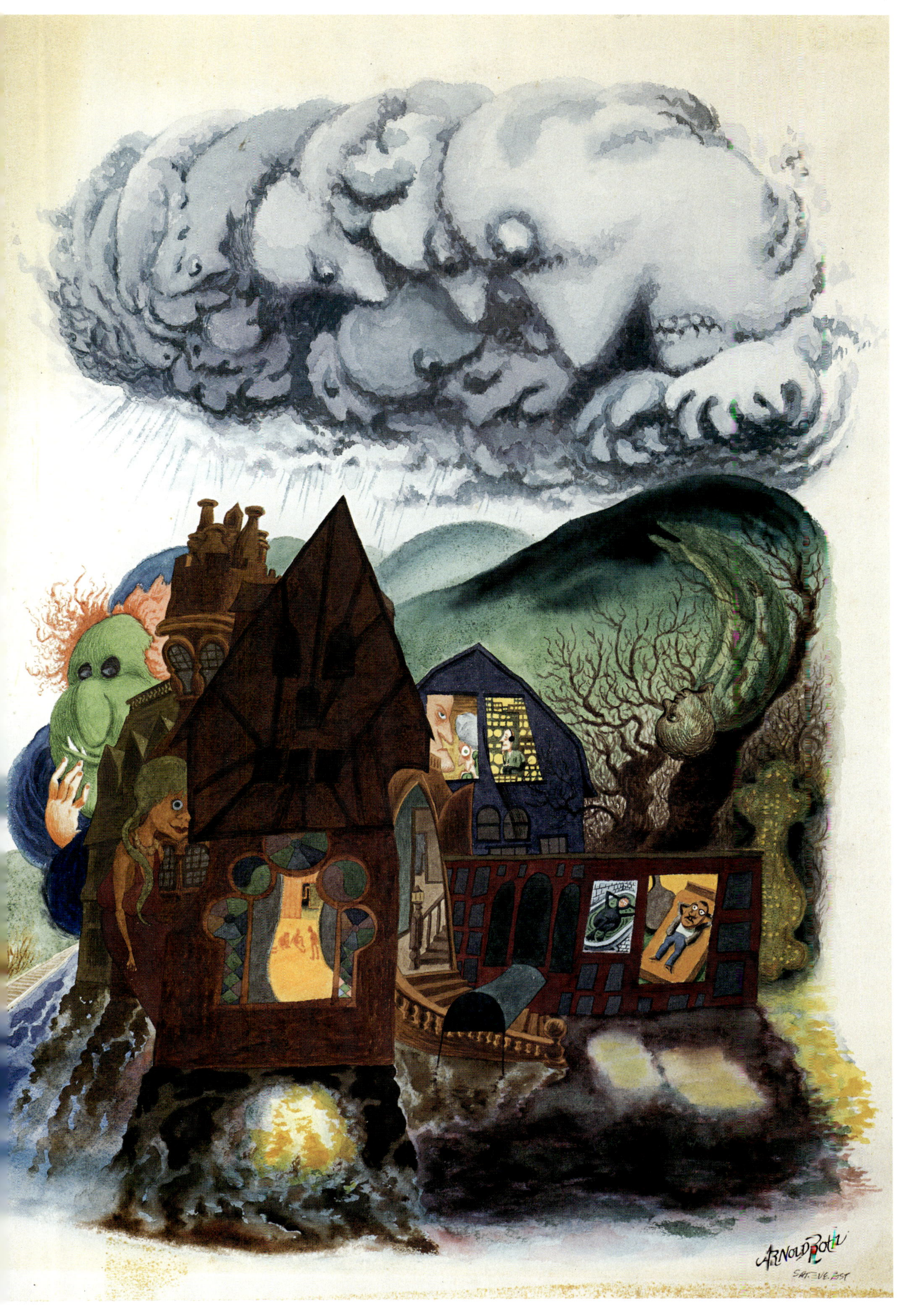

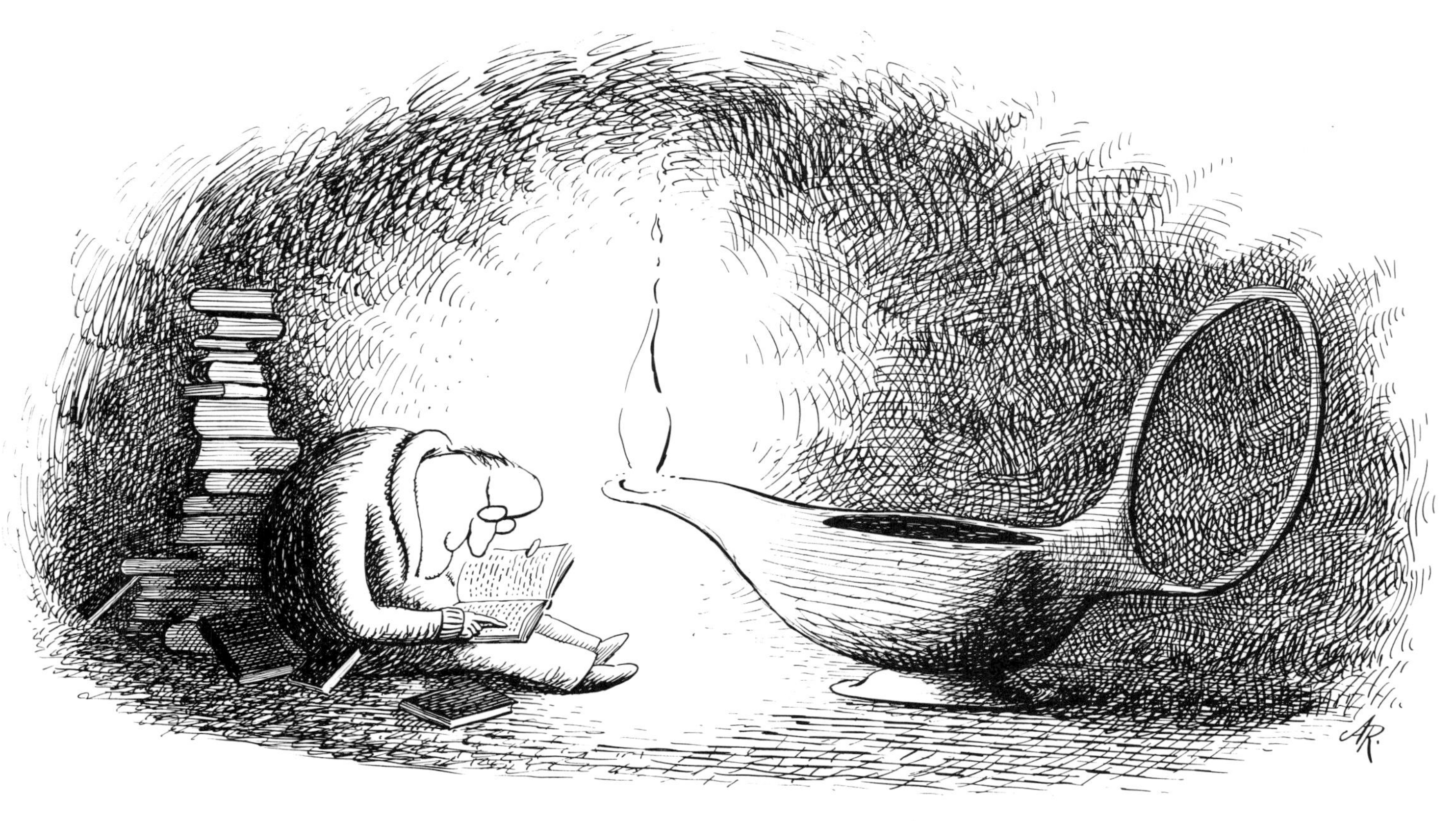

Figure 5
"The Reader"
Holiday circa 1955

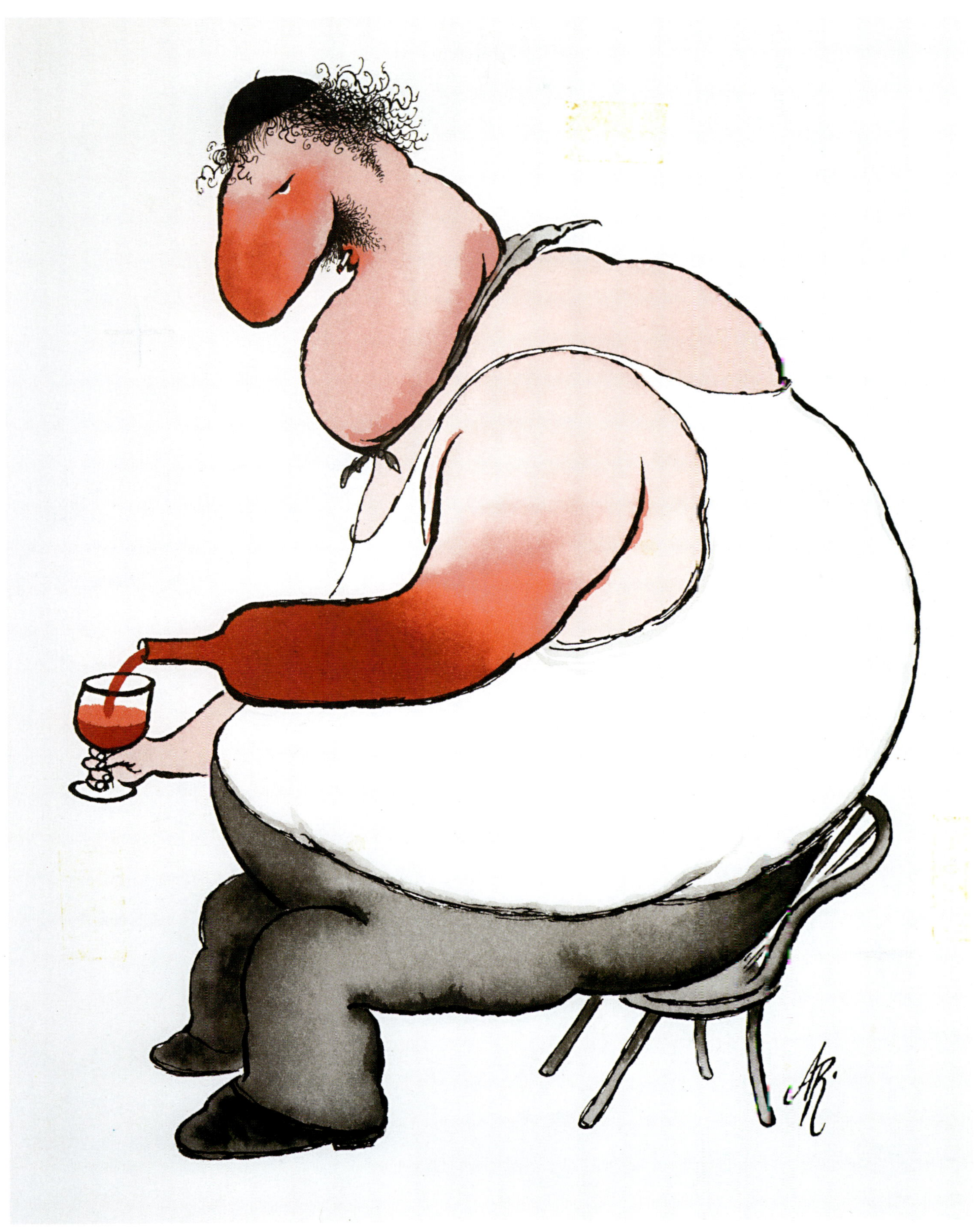

Figure 6
"Red Wine"
Choosing and Enjoying Wines 1965

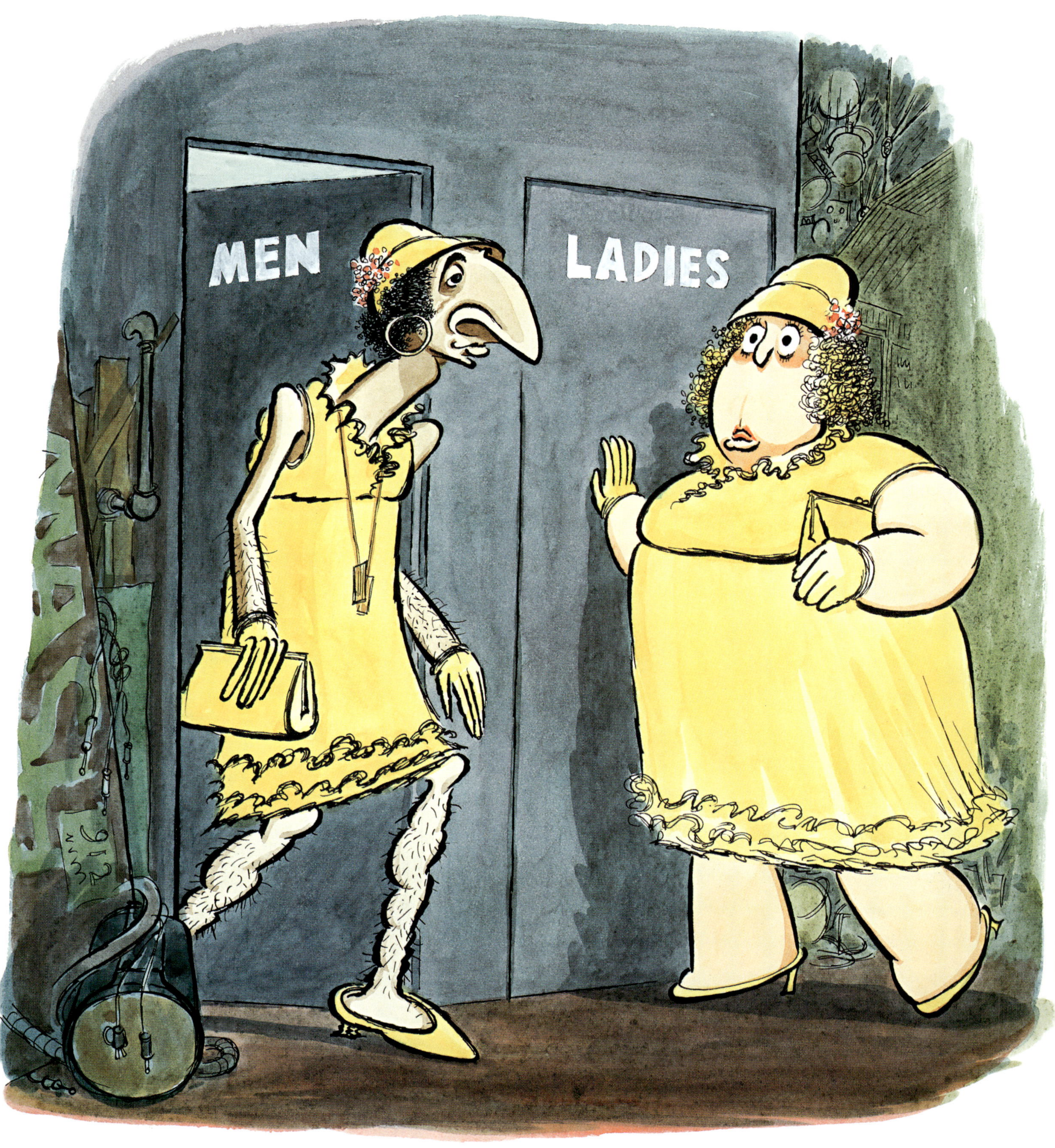

Figure 7
"R & R"
TV Guide 1977

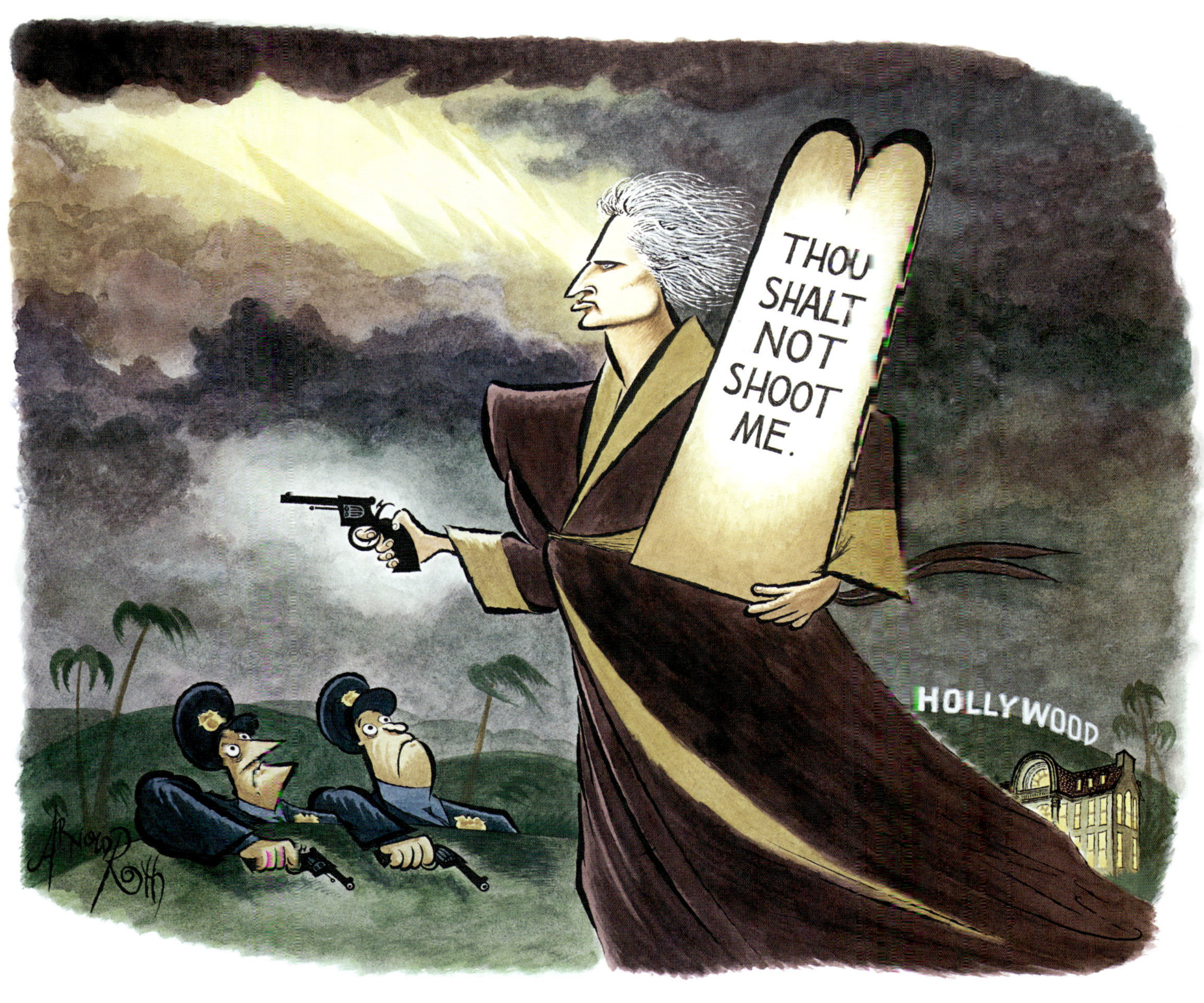

Figure 8
"Charlton Moses Heston"
TV Guide 1987

POOR ARNOLD'S
ALMANAC

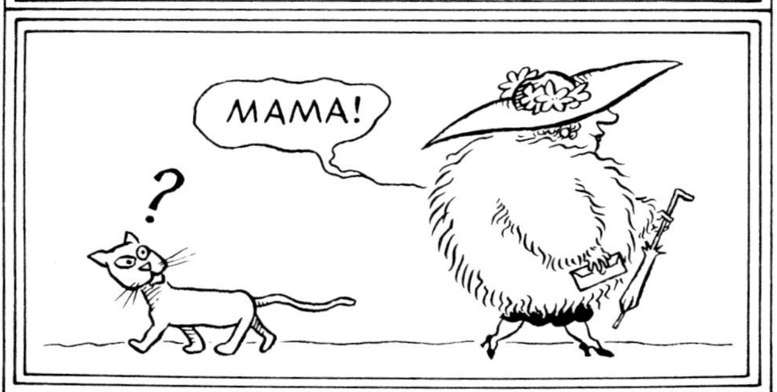

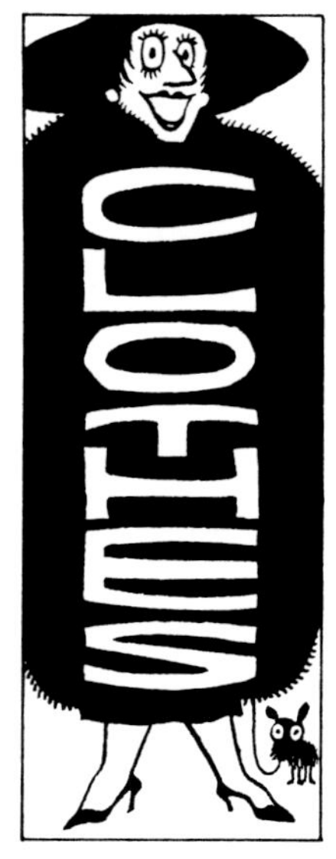

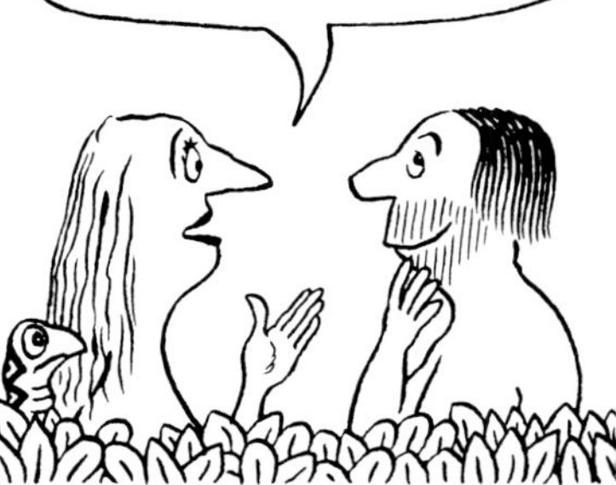

CLOTHES CHANGED; PEOPLE DIDN'T!

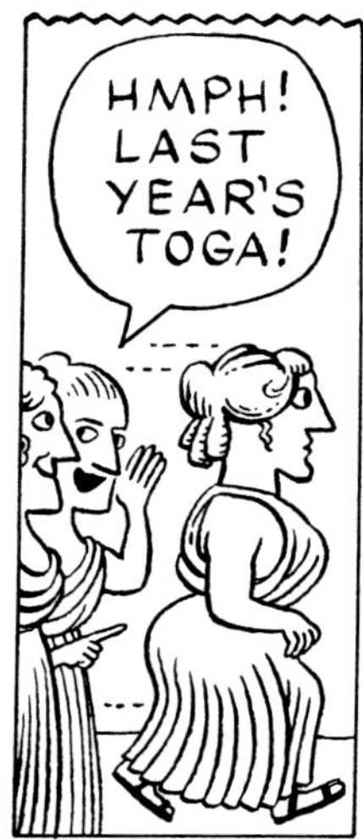

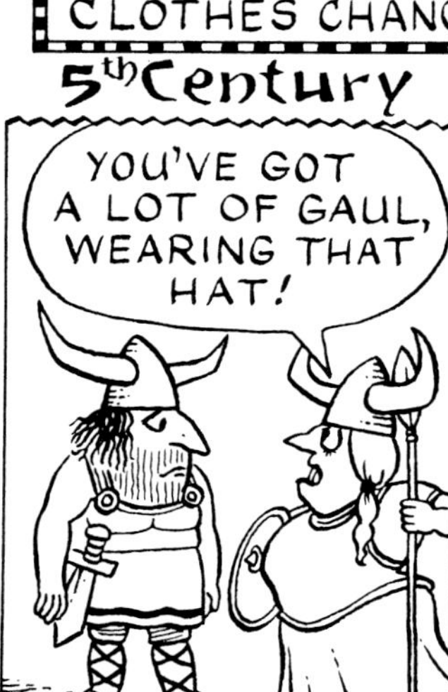

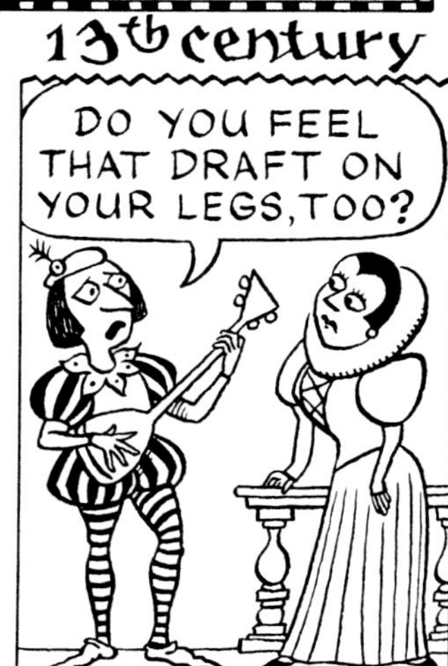

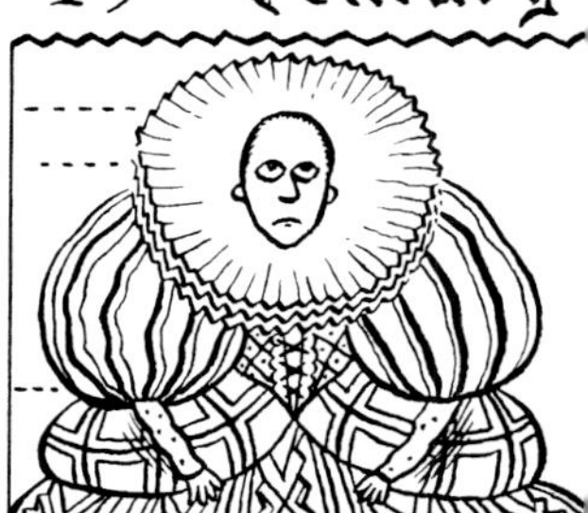

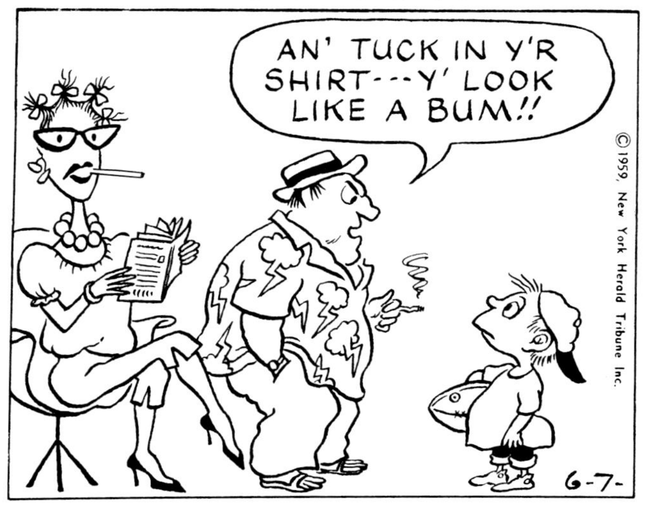

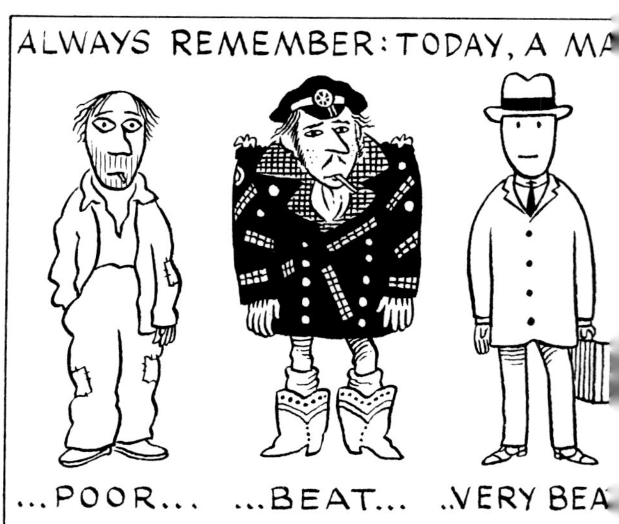

Figure 9
"Poor Arnold's Almanac"
New York Herald Tribune Syndicate 1959

SO, SOMEONE OPENED A STORE...

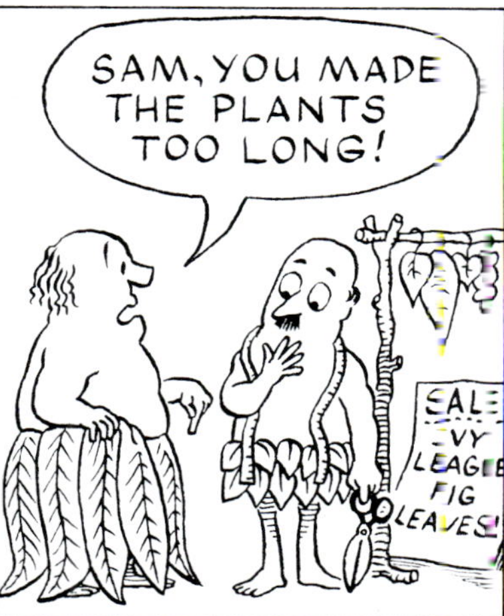

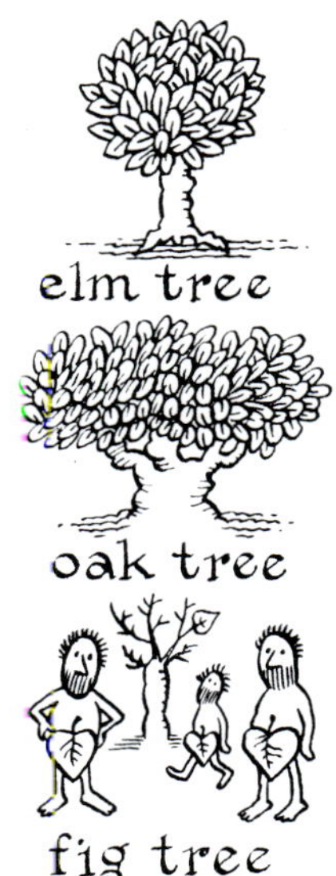

1,000,000 B.C.:
FUR BECOMES FASHIONABLE:

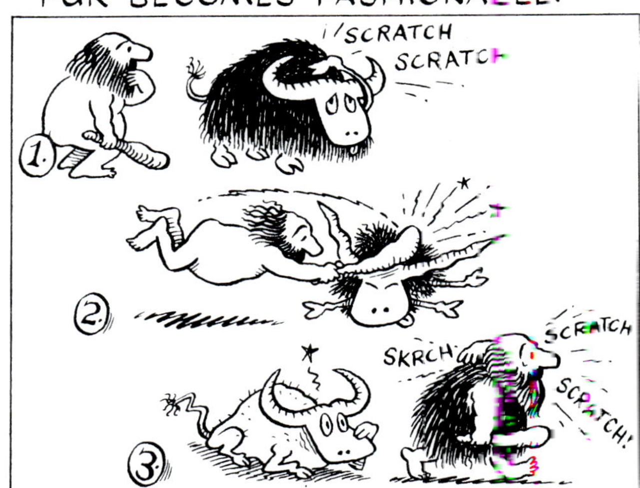

17th Century

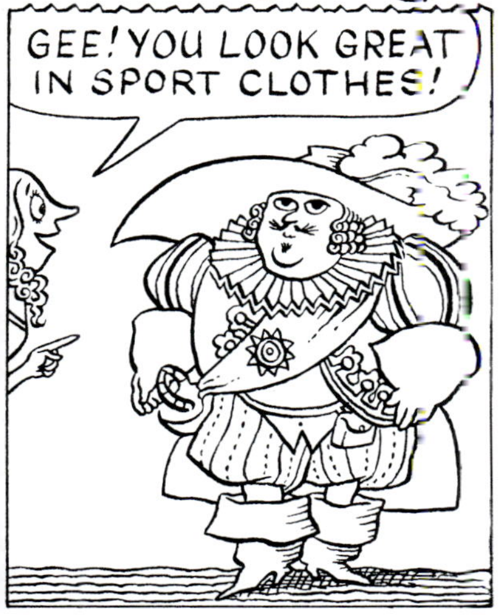

18th CENTURY

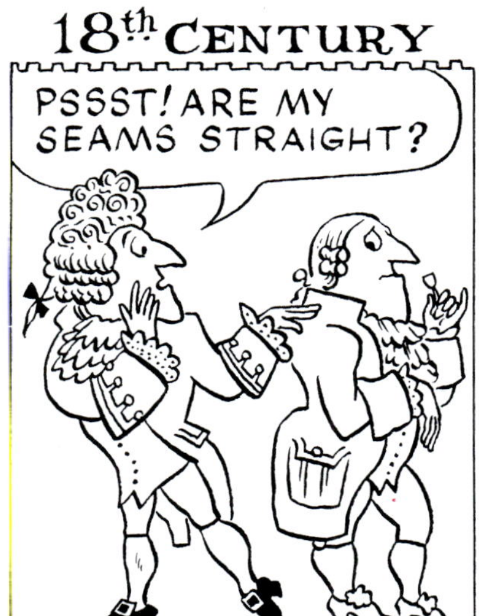

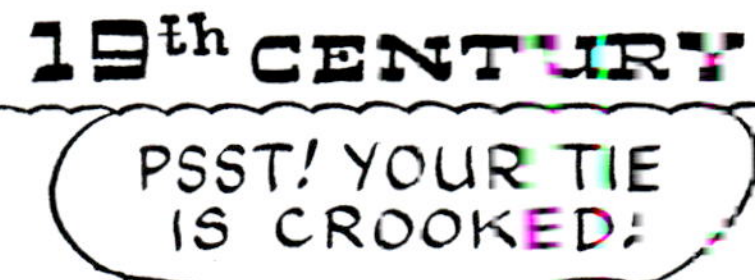

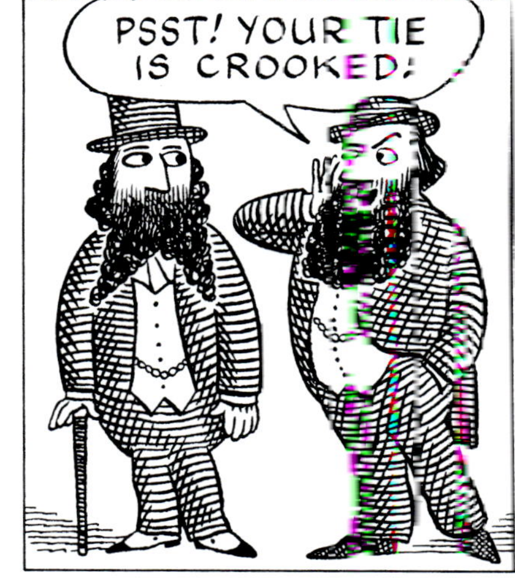

IS JUDGED BY HIS APPEARANCE....

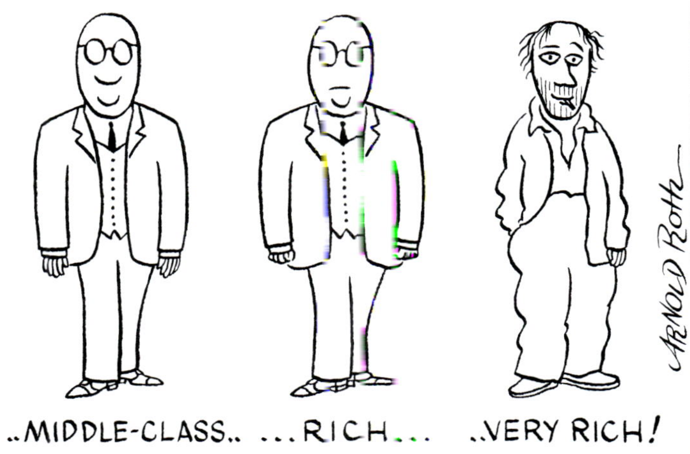

QUESTIONS for STUDENTS:

1. CLOTHES WERE INVENTED BY:
   (a) cavemen ☐
   (b) prudes ☐
   (c) Brooks Brothers ☐

2. MAZZERELLA IS:
   (a) an Italian shirt ☐
   (b) an Italian cheese ☐
   (c) a darned good musician ☐

3. DRESSES HAVE:
   (a) Hems ☐
   (b) Hers ☐

4. CLOTHES MAKE THE:
   (a) man ☐ (b) woman ☐ (c) money ☐

SCORE:
If you answered 'yes' to all the questions—you just didn't understand the quiz!

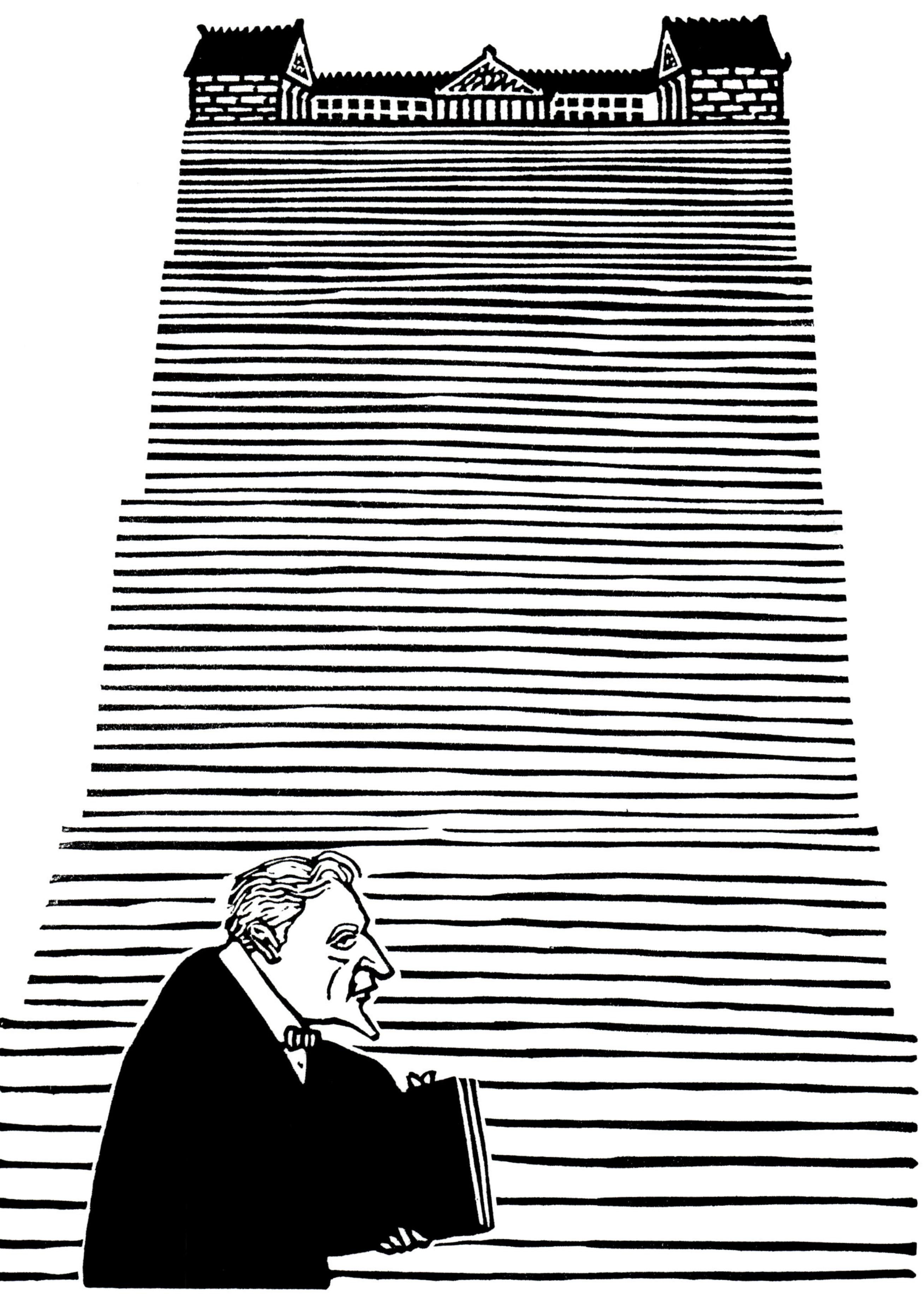

Figure 10
"Carl Zigrosser"
Philadelphia Print Club 1959

Opposite:
Figure 11
"Street Musicians"
Punch 1961

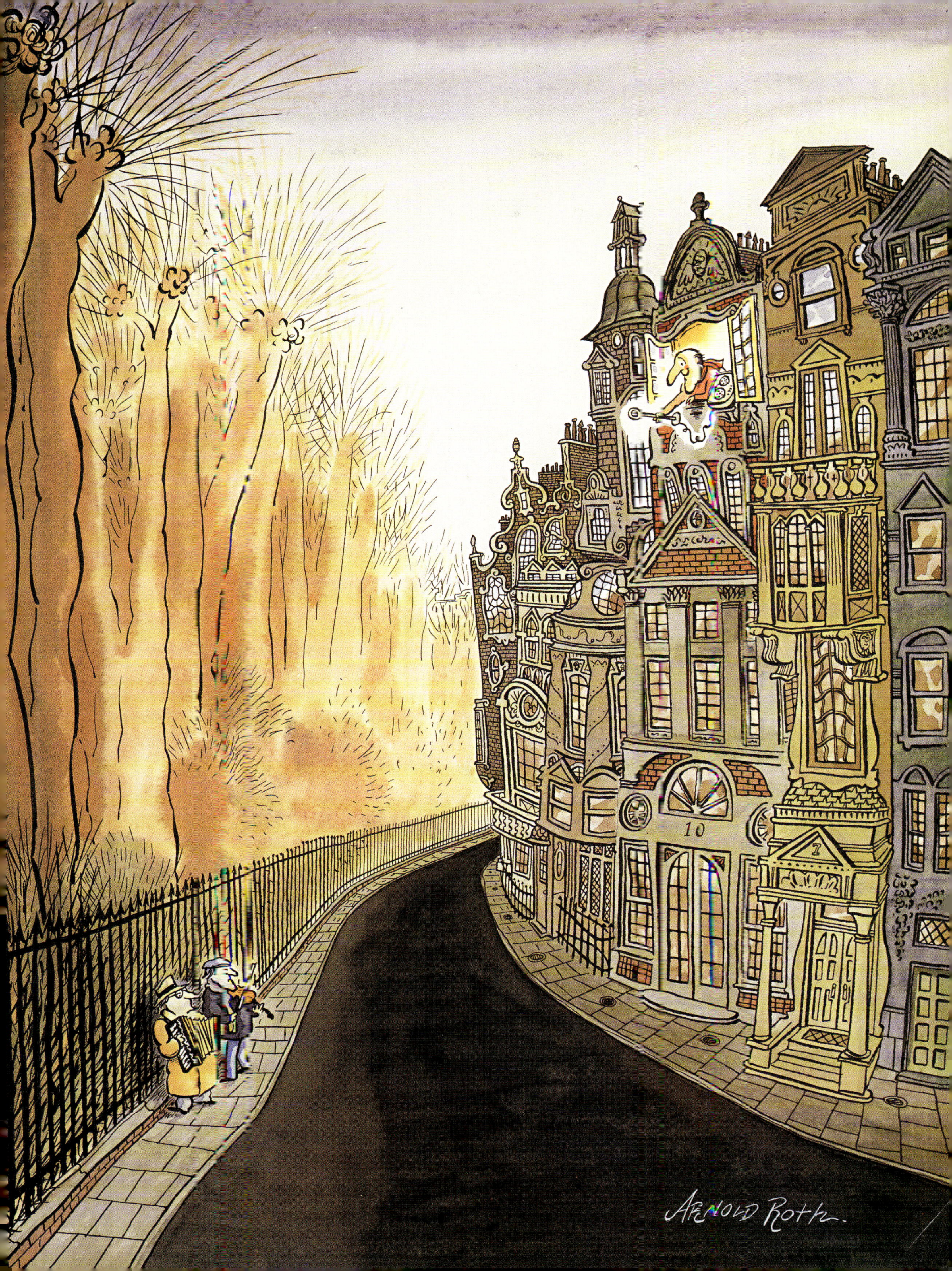
10
7
ARNOLD ROTH

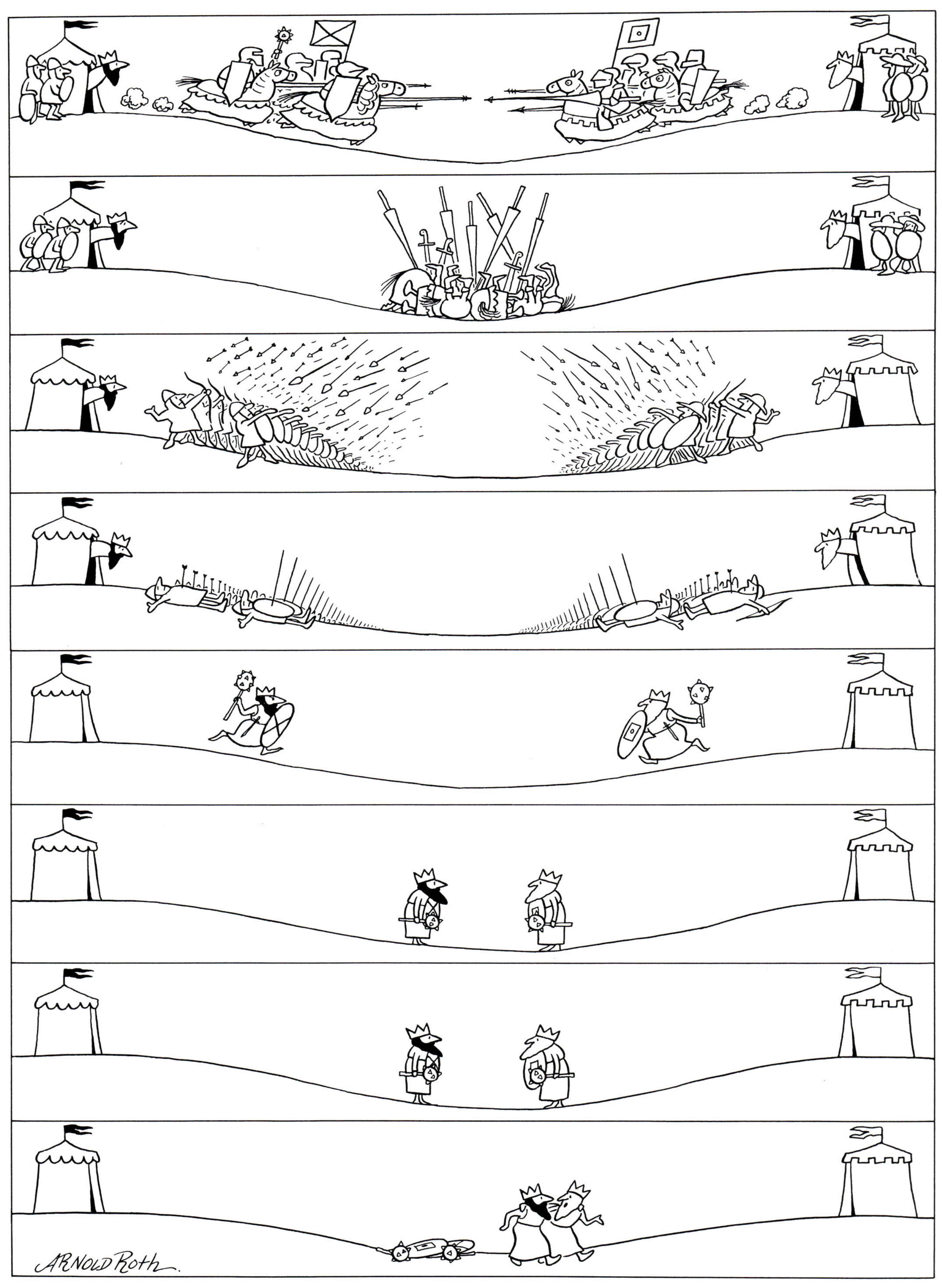

Figure 12
"War Kings"
Punch 1960

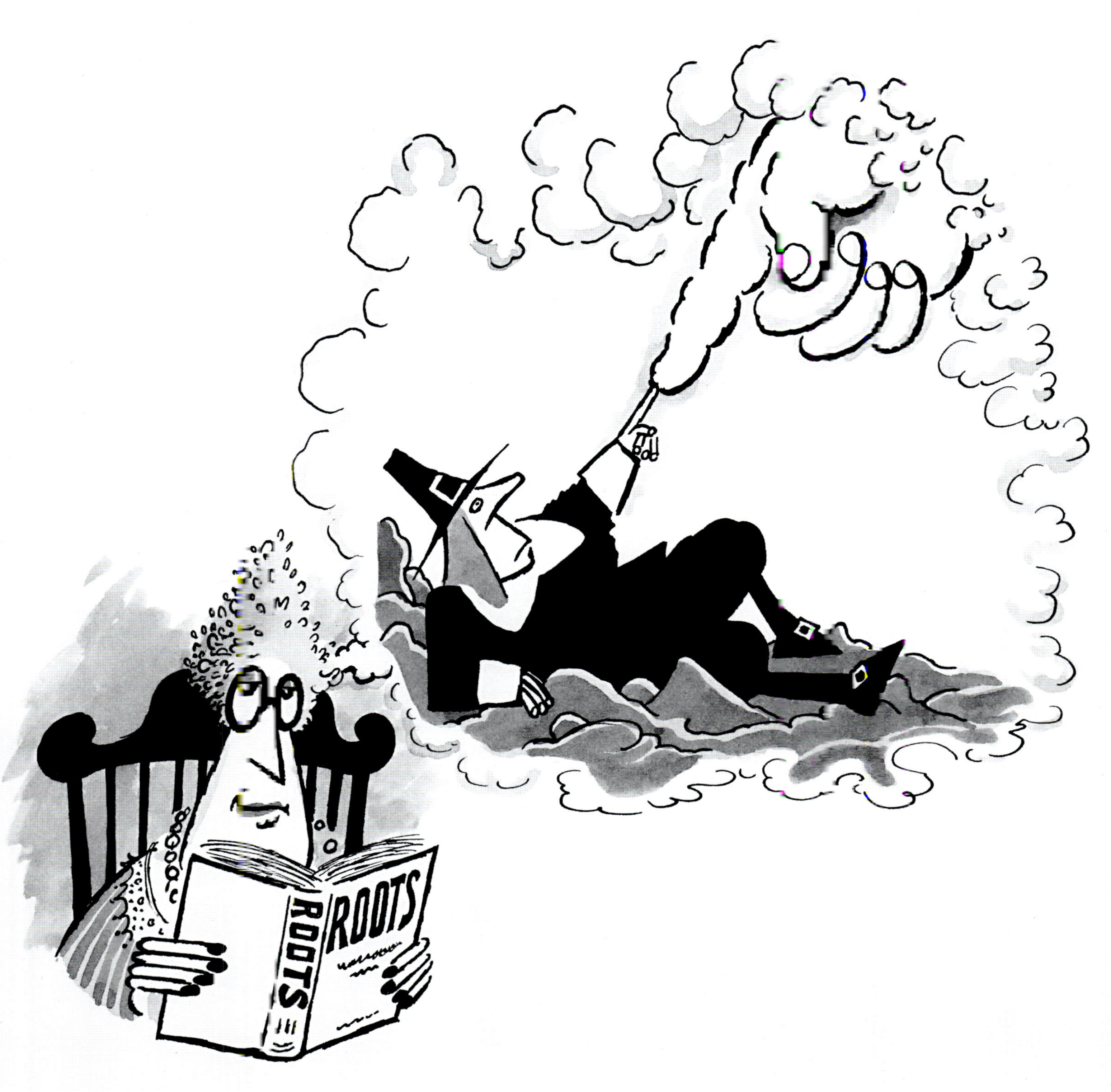

Figure 13
"Roth's Roots and Ruts"
Punch 1977

The WAR Between the NonSMOKERS & the SMOKERS

AS EYE, EAR, NOSE & THROAT WITNESSED
by ARNOLD ROTH

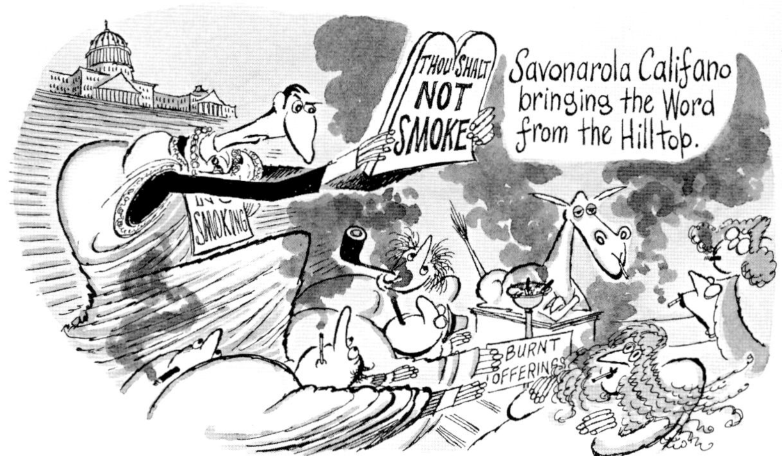

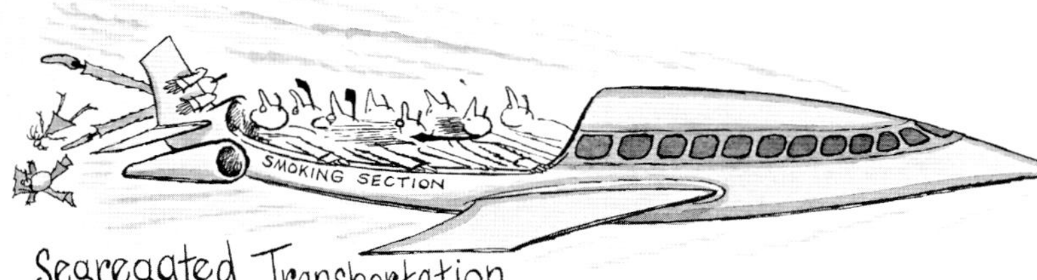

Segregated Transportation

The Purge

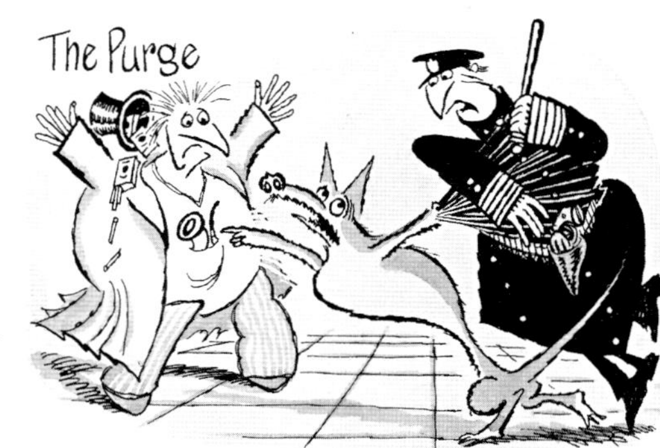

The Trial

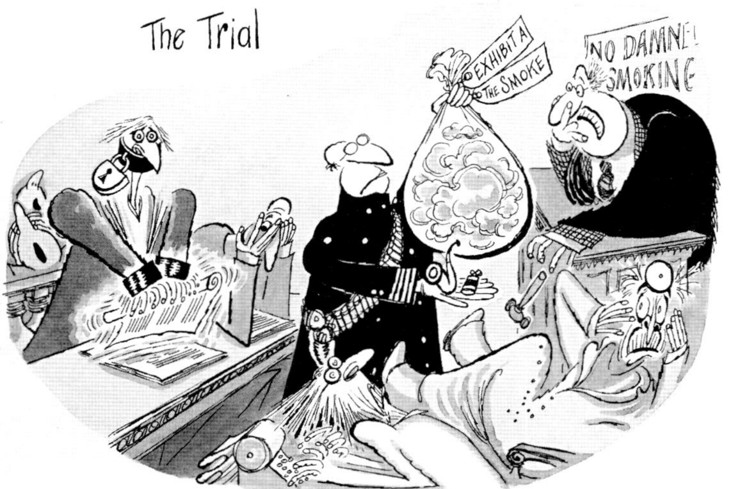

Rehabilitation

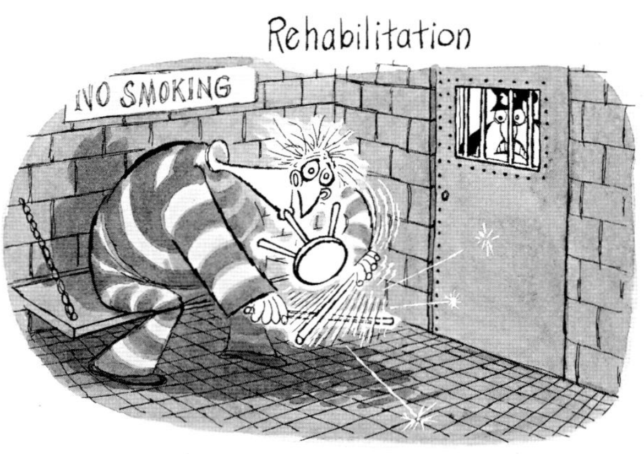

The Spy Who Came In From The Smoke

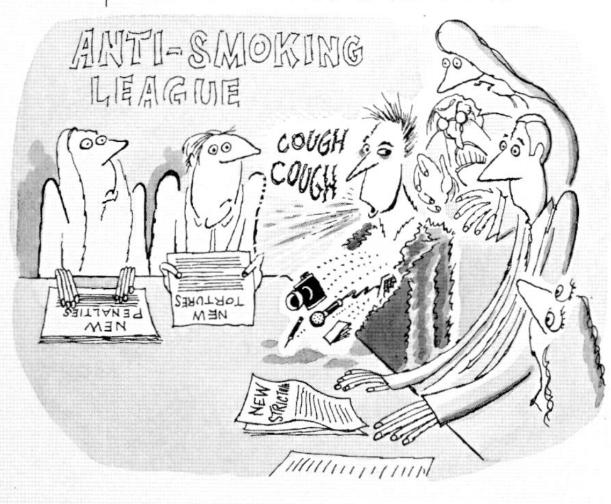

The Temptation of St. Oxygenia

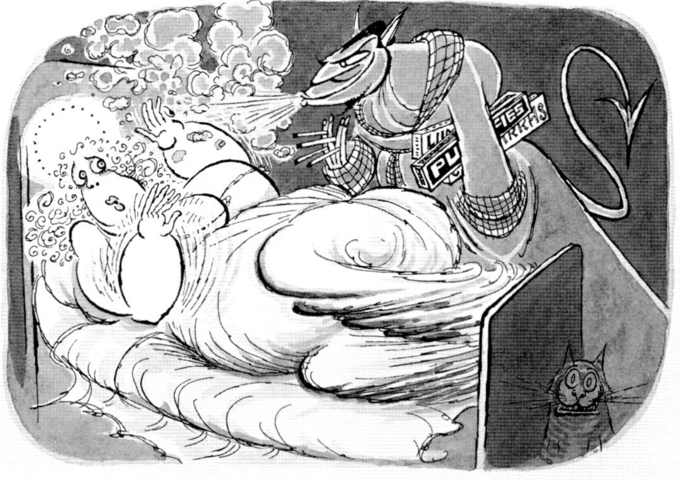

Above and opposite:
Figure 14
"The War Between the Non-Smokers & the Smokers"
Punch 1978

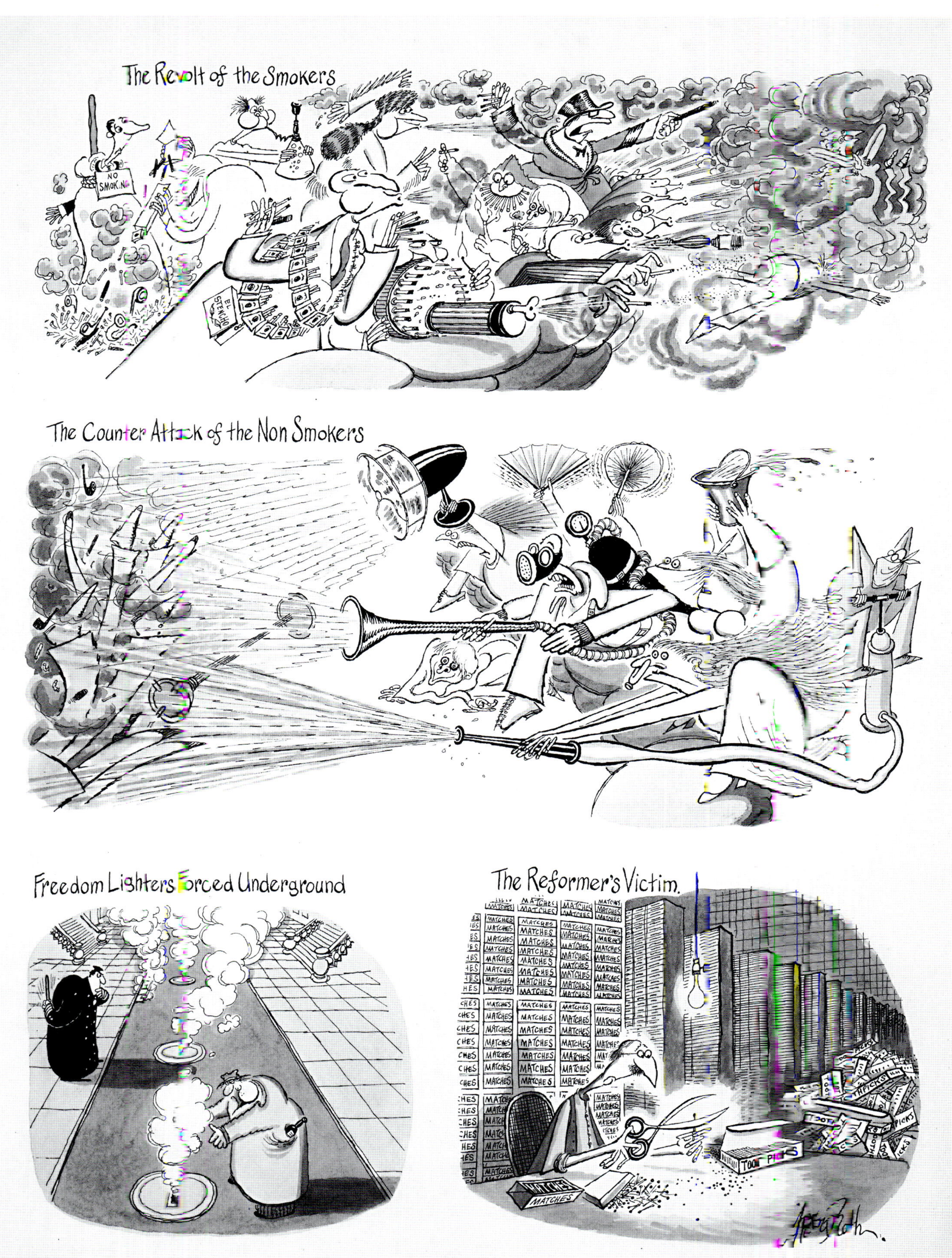
The Revolt of the Smokers
NO SMOKING
The Counter Attack of the Non Smokers
Freedom Lighters Forced Underground
The Reformer's Victim.
MATCHES
TOOTH PICKS

ASSERTIVE WOMAN
BY ARNOLD ROTH

Feel like telling your boss to "Go to hell and make your own coffee?" Want to tell your husband to "Go to hell and make your own bed?" If you THINK of saying these things, you are on your way to becoming Assertive Woman. If you HAVE said these things, you already are Assertive Woman . . . and you are probably on your way to being fired and single again.

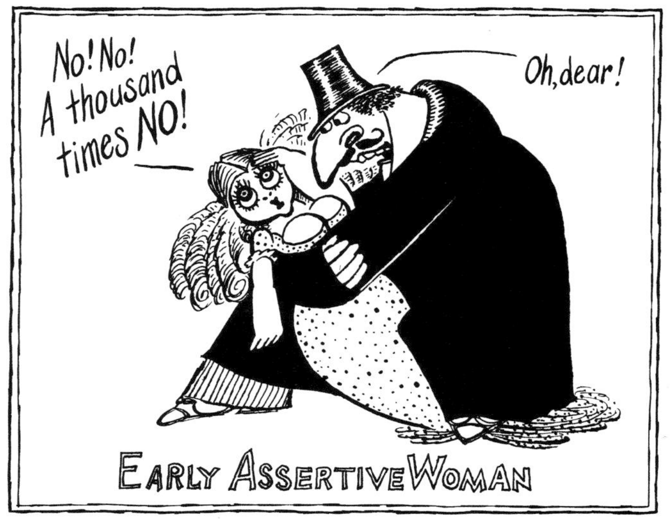

EARLY ASSERTIVE WOMAN

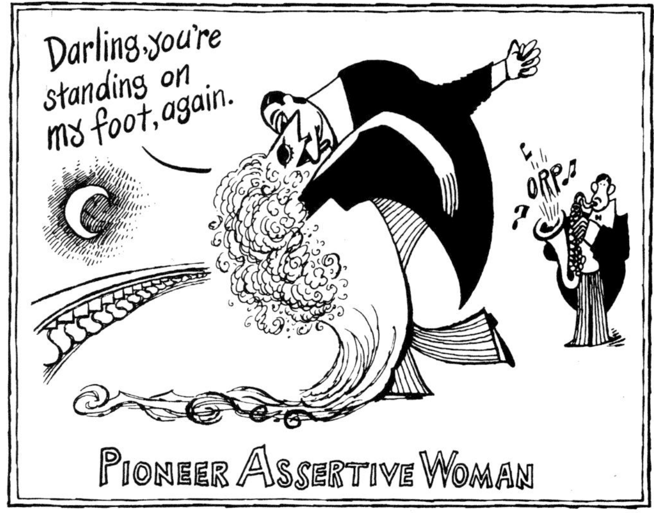

PIONEER ASSERTIVE WOMAN

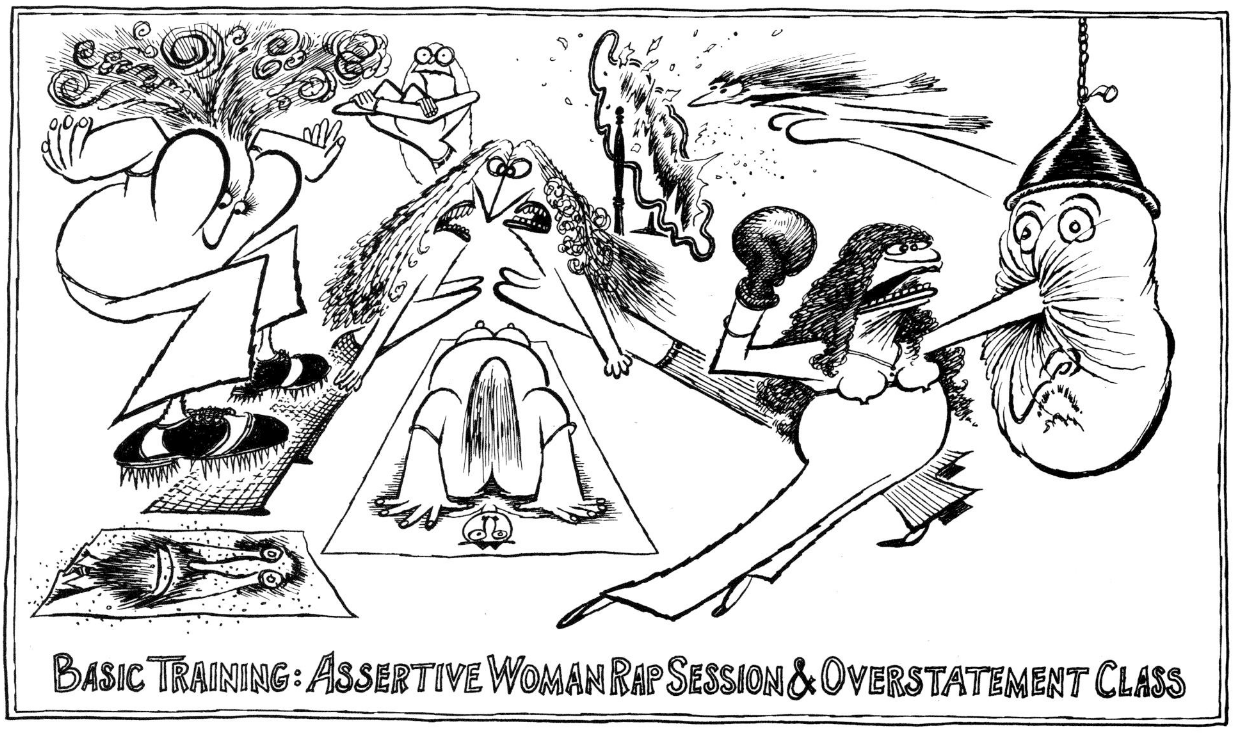
BASIC TRAINING: ASSERTIVE WOMAN RAP SESSION & OVERSTATEMENT CLASS

Above and opposite:
Figure 15
"Assertive Woman"
Punch 1977

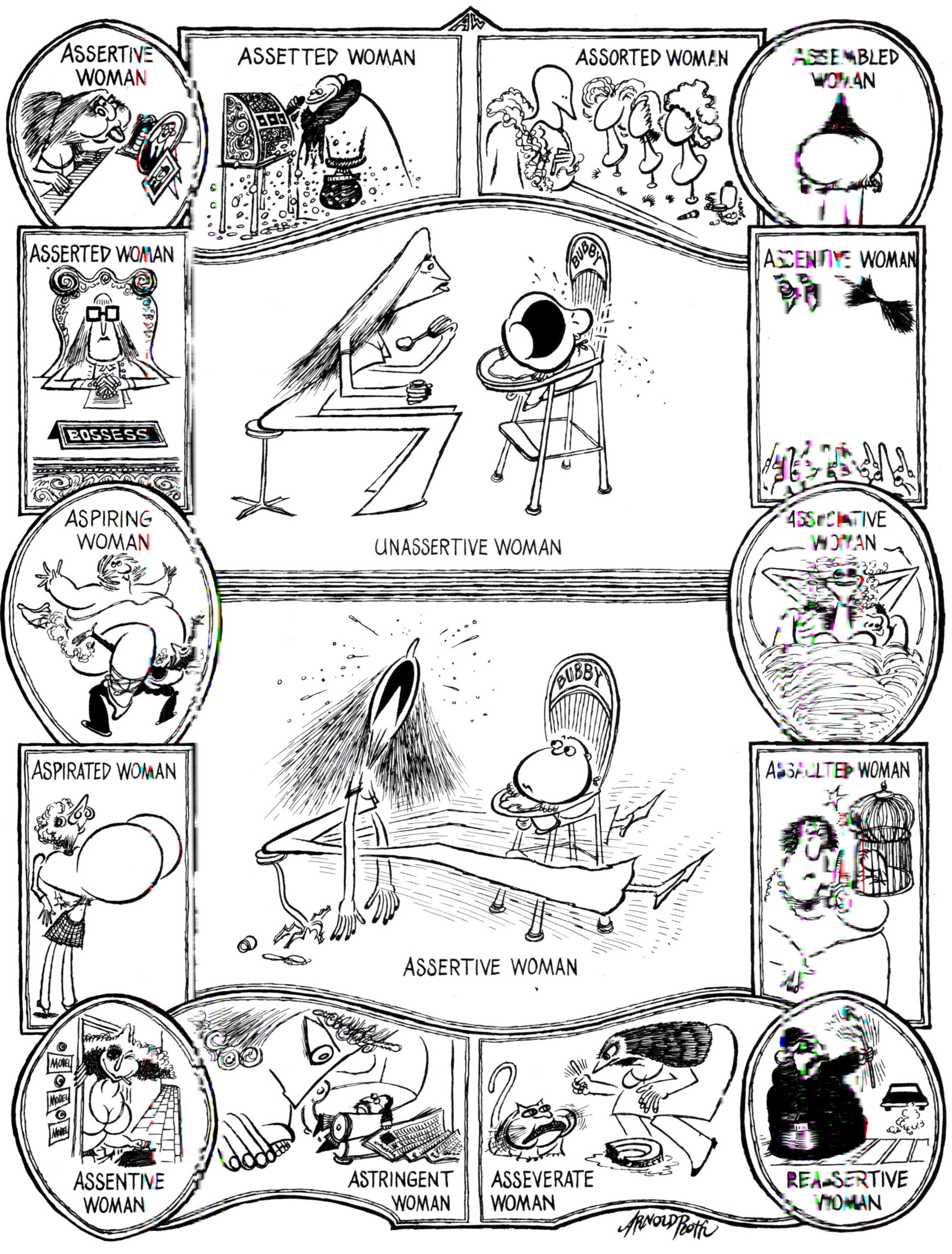
ASSERTIVE WOMAN
ASSETTED WOMAN
ASSORTED WOMAN
ASSEMBLED WOMAN
ASSERTED WOMAN
BOSSESS
ASCENTIVE WOMAN
BUBBY
UNASSERTIVE WOMAN
ASPIRING WOMAN
ASSOCIATIVE WOMAN
BUBBY
ASPIRATED WOMAN
ASSAULTED WOMAN
ASSERTIVE WOMAN
MOTEL
MOTEL
MOTEL
ASSENTIVE WOMAN
ASTRINGENT WOMAN
ASSEVERATE WOMAN
REASSERTIVE WOMAN
ARNOLD ROTH

ALL JOGGING ASIDE...

Every American is ~~Everybody's~~ on a jog jag...

...except ARNOLD ROTH

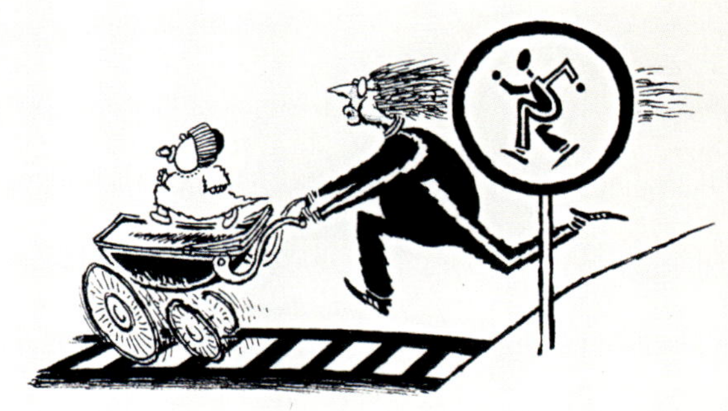

Hidden camera proves that jogging is faster, though different, than walking.

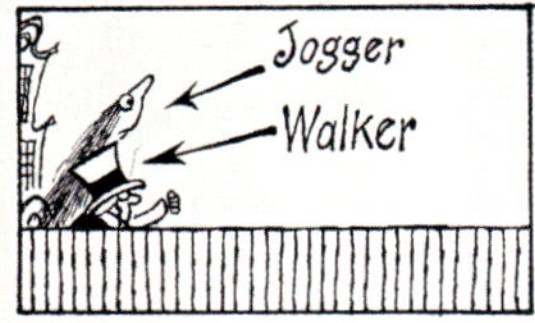

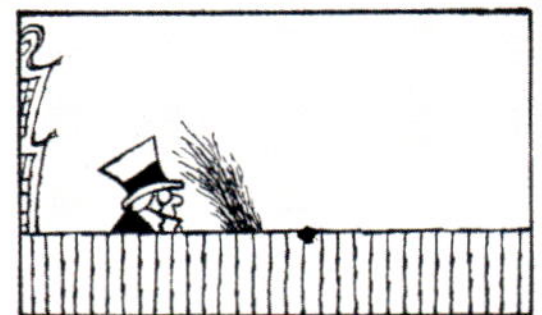

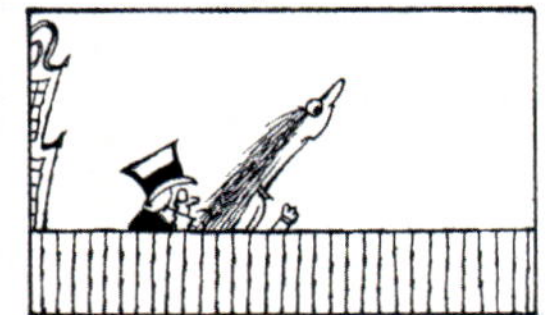

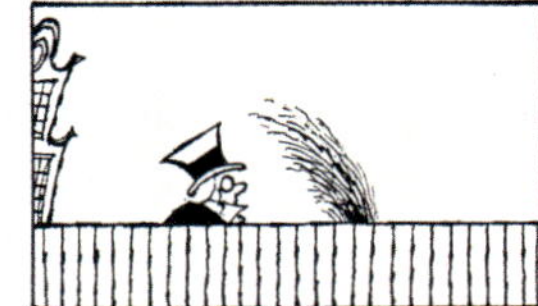

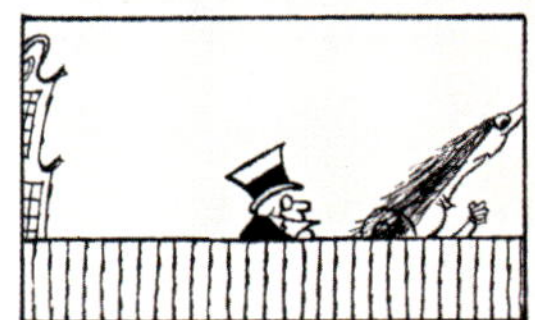

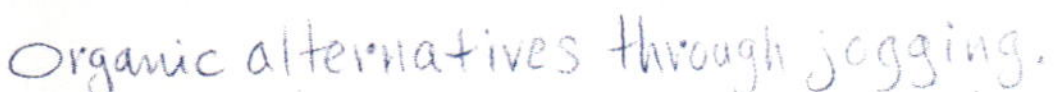

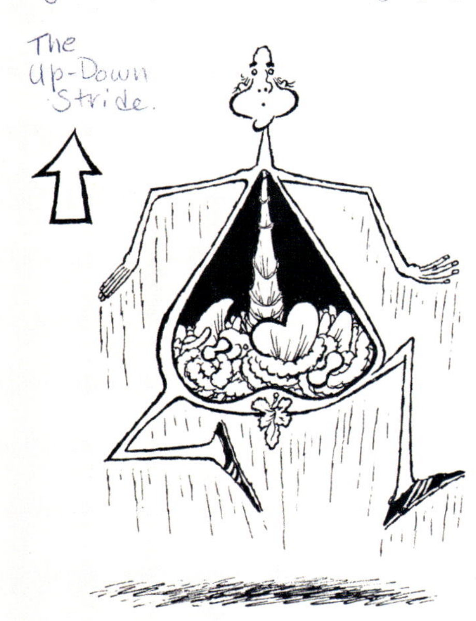

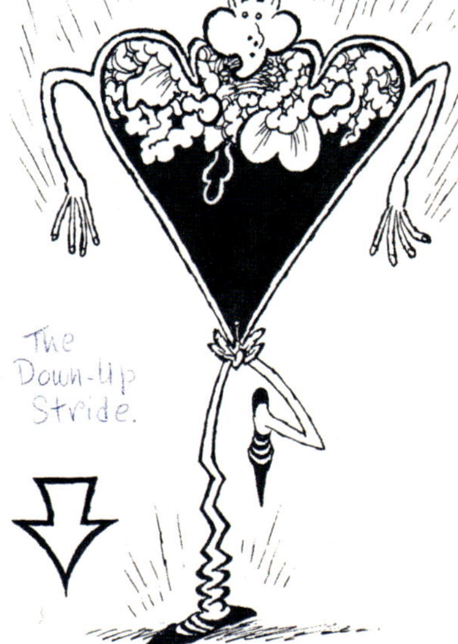

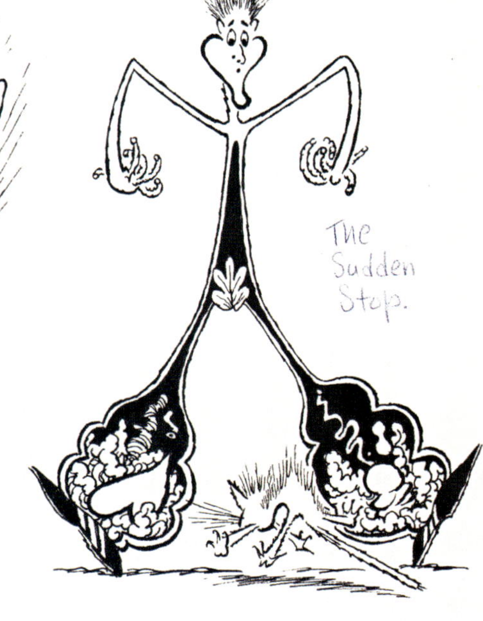

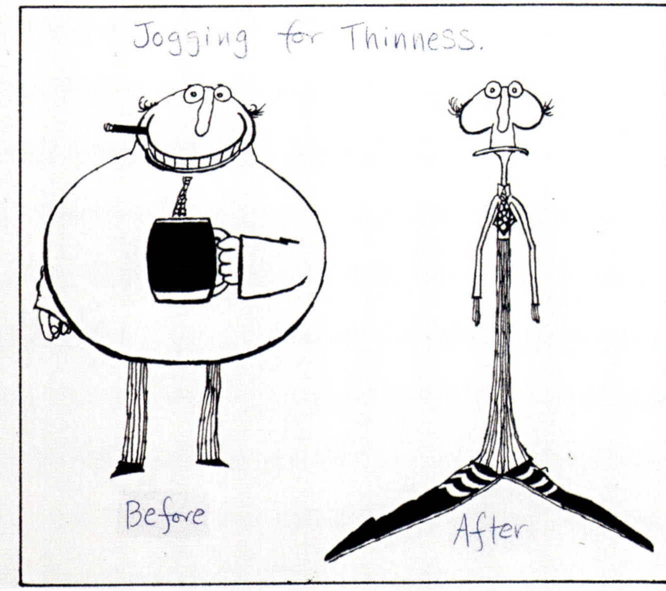

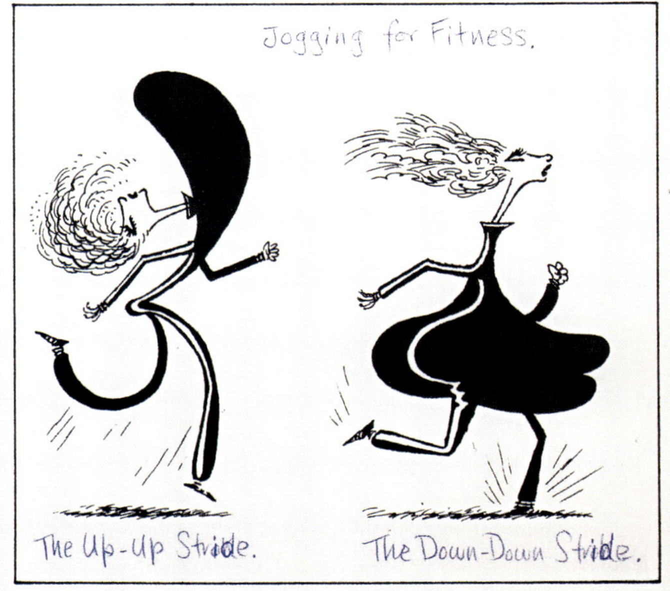

Above and opposite:
Figure 16
"All Jogging Aside"
Punch 1978

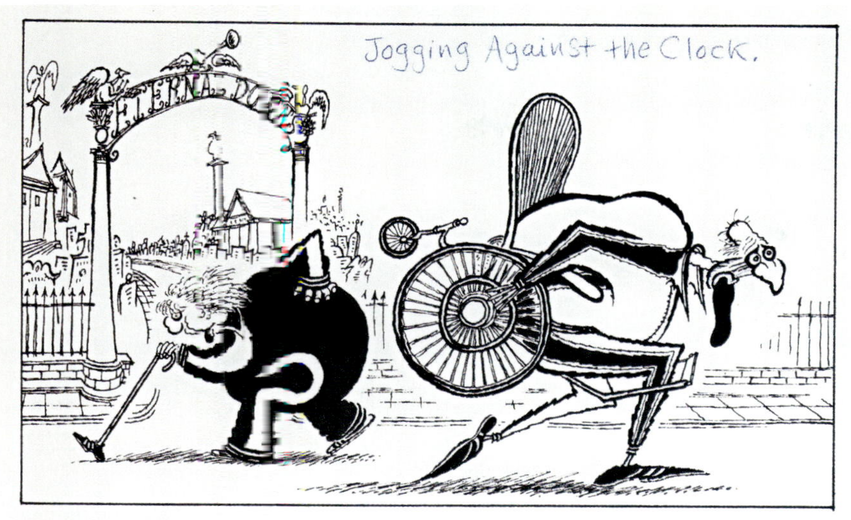
Jogging Against the Clock.

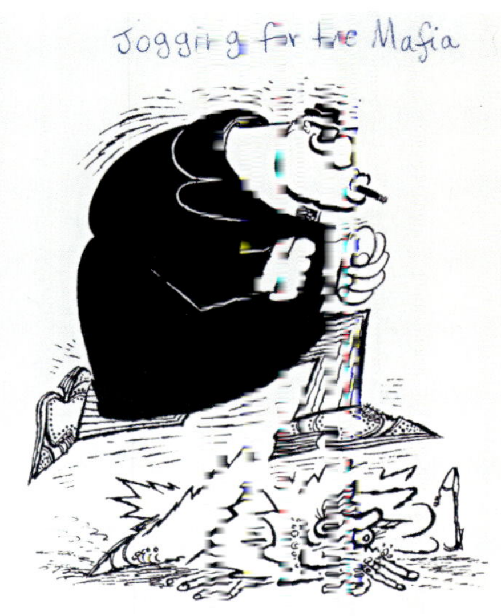
Jogging for the Mafia

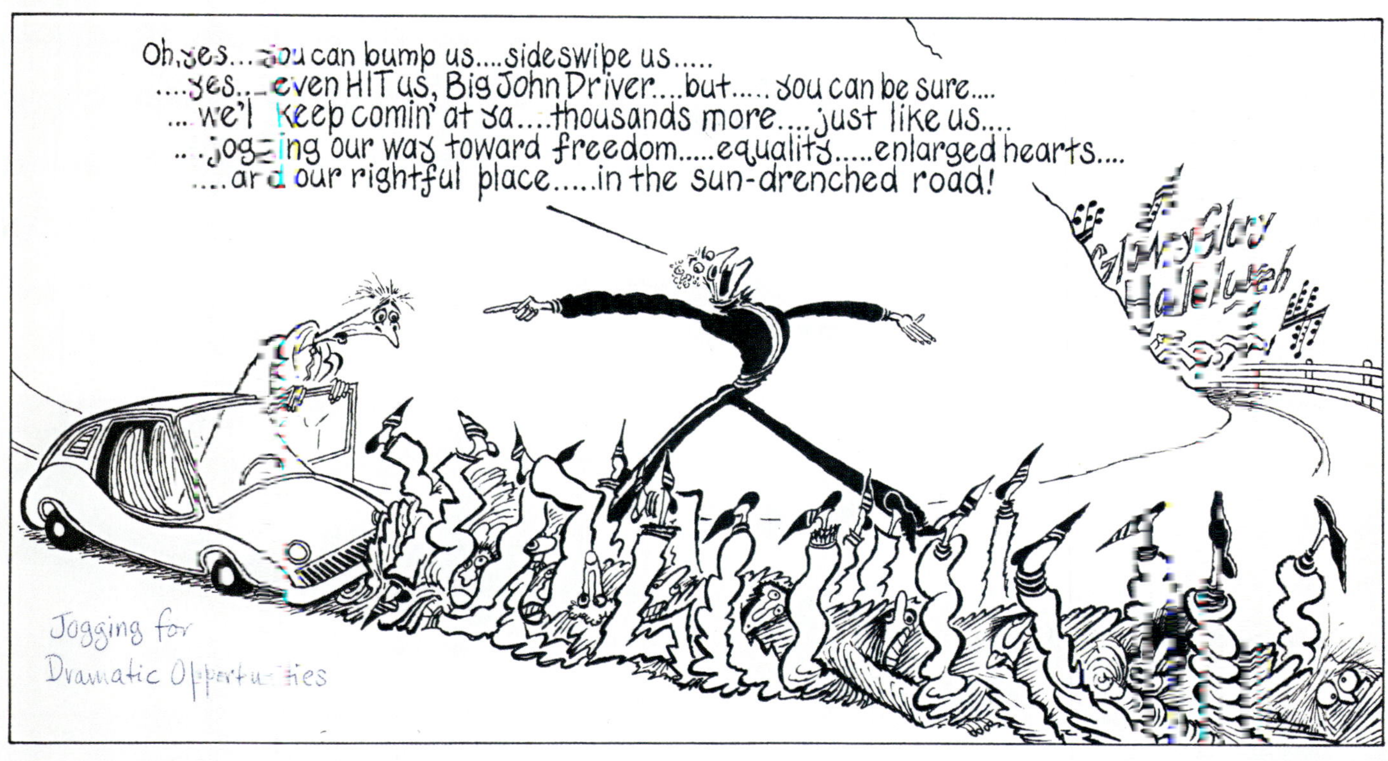
Oh, yes... you can bump us....sideswipe us.....
....yes... even HIT us, Big John Driver....but..... you can be sure....
...we'll keep comin' at ya....thousands more....just like us....
...jogging our way toward freedom.....equality.....enlarged hearts....
....and our rightful place.....in the sun-drenched road!
Jogging for Dramatic Opportunities

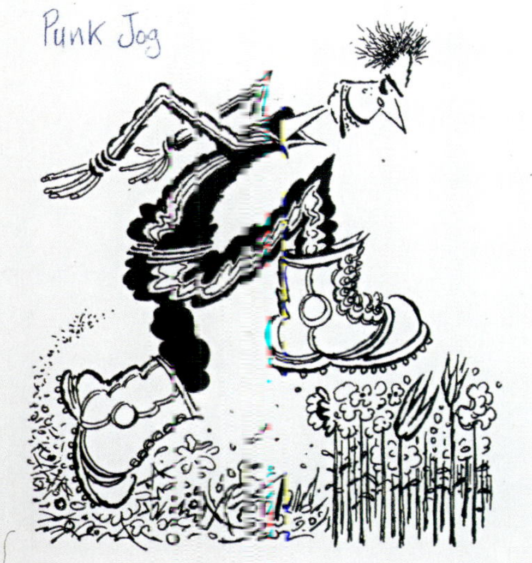
Punk Jog

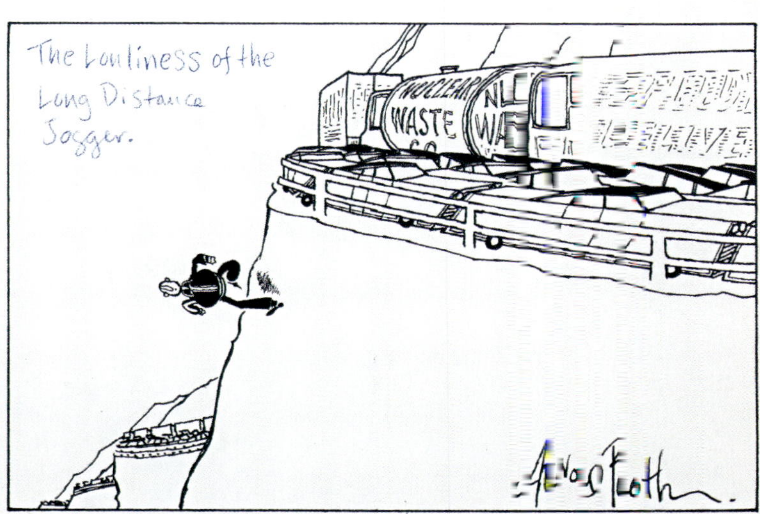
The Loneliness of the Long Distance Jogger.
WASTE
Arnold Roth

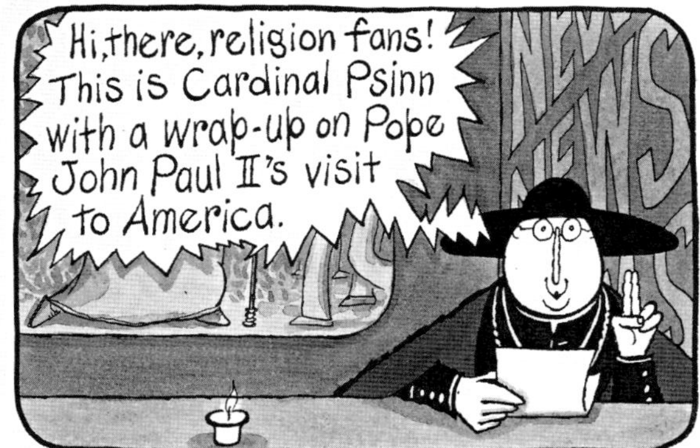

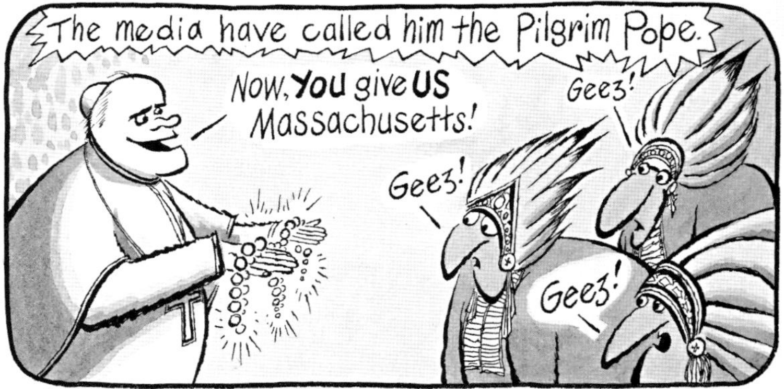

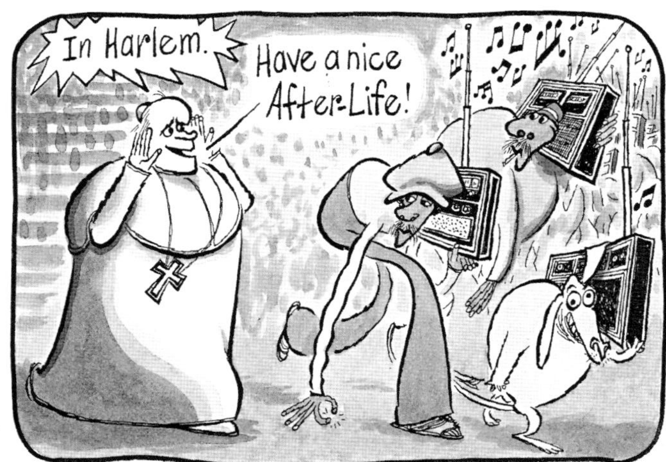

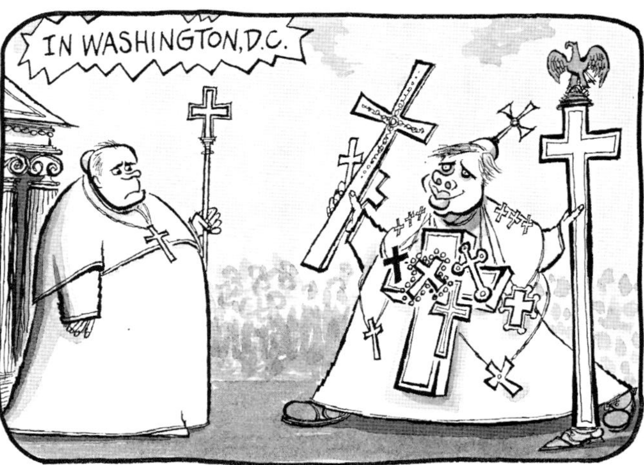

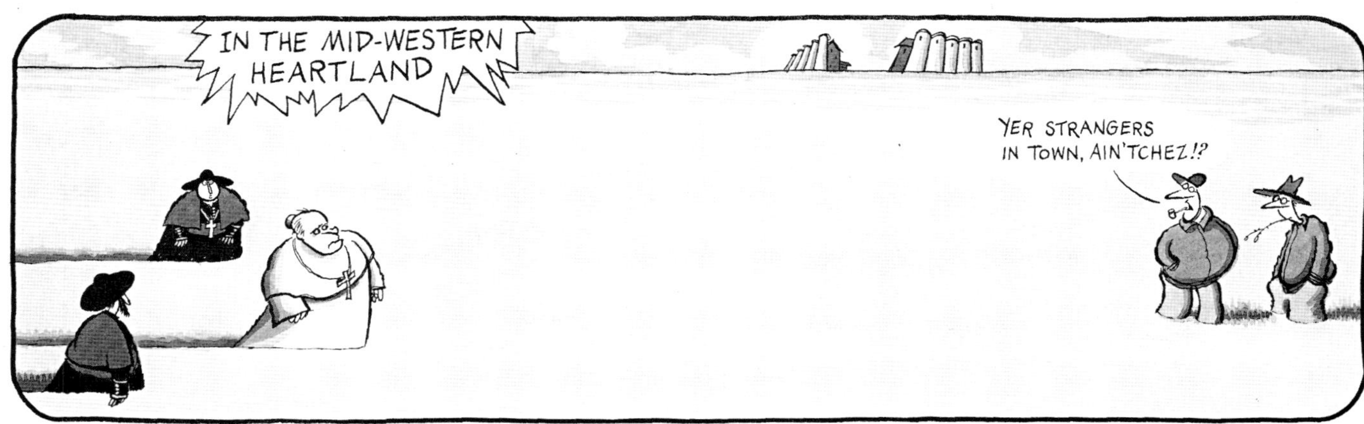

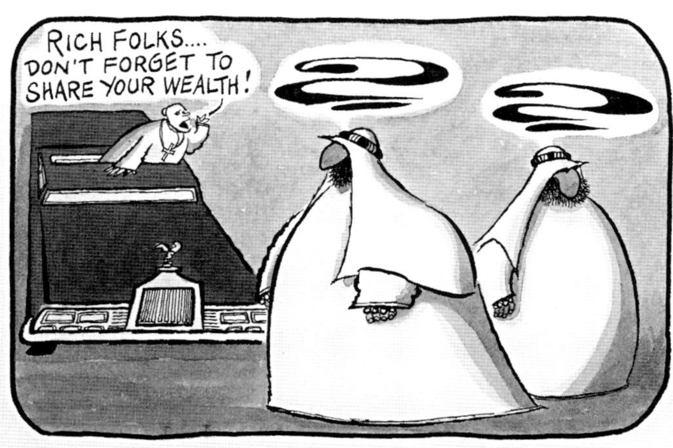

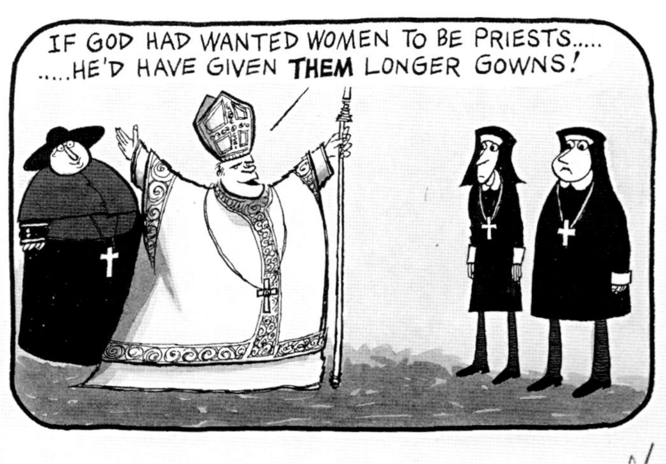

Above and opposite:
Figure 17
"Papal Bull"
Punch 1979

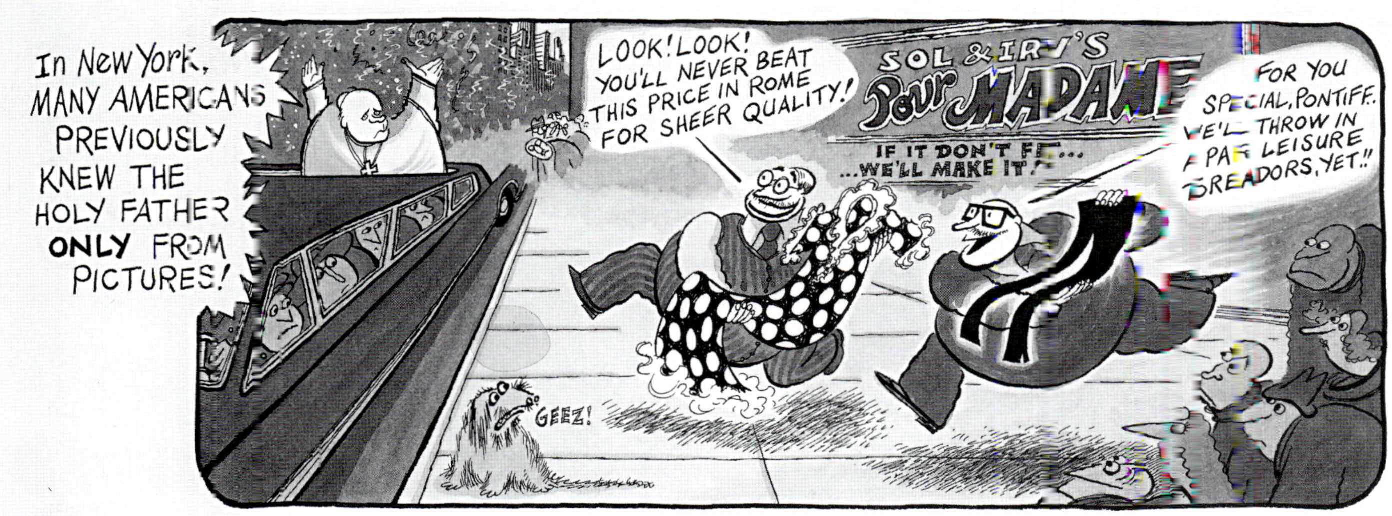
In New York, MANY AMERICANS PREVIOUSLY KNEW THE HOLY FATHER ONLY FROM PICTURES!
LOOK! LOOK! YOU'LL NEVER BEAT THIS PRICE IN ROME FOR SHEER QUALITY!
SOL & IRV'S Pour MADAME
IF IT DON'T FIT... ...WE'LL MAKE IT!
FOR YOU SPECIAL, PONTIFF. WE'LL THROW IN A PAIR LEISURE TOREADORS, YET.!!
GEEZ!

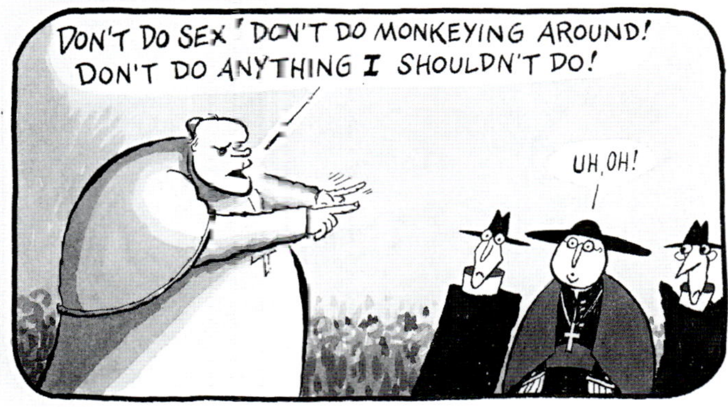
DON'T DO SEX! DON'T DO MONKEYING AROUND! DON'T DO ANYTHING I SHOULDN'T DO!
UH, OH!

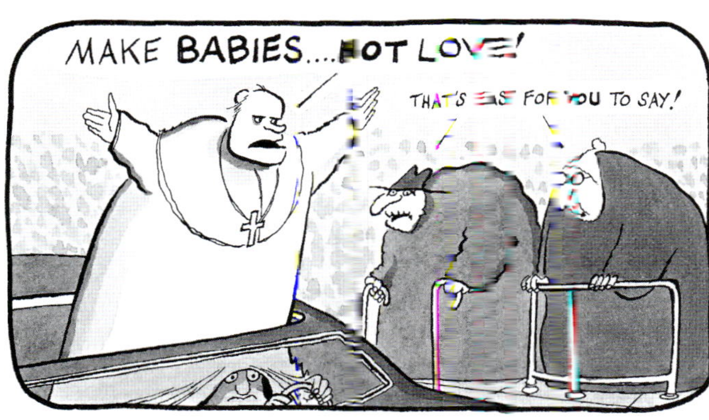
MAKE BABIES....NOT LOVE!
THAT'S EASY FOR YOU TO SAY!

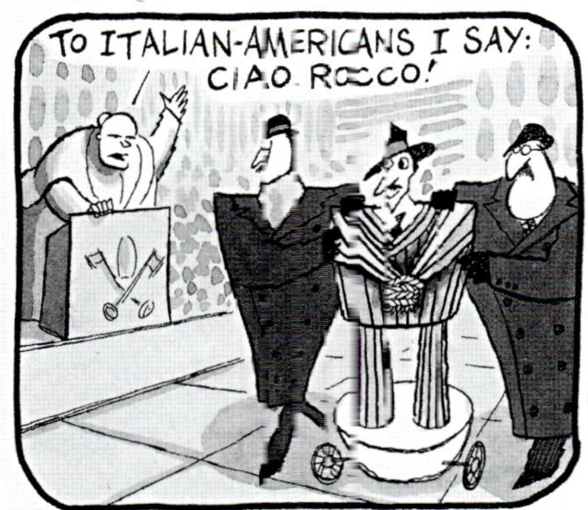
TO ITALIAN-AMERICANS I SAY: CIAO ROCCO!

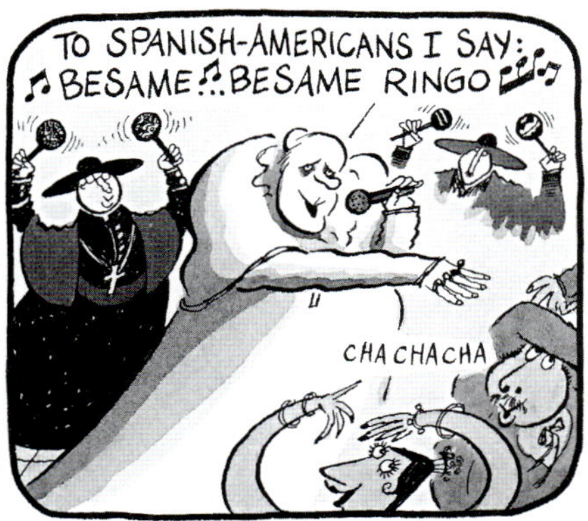
TO SPANISH-AMERICANS I SAY: ♫ BESAME ♫ BESAME RINGO ♫
CHA CHA CHA

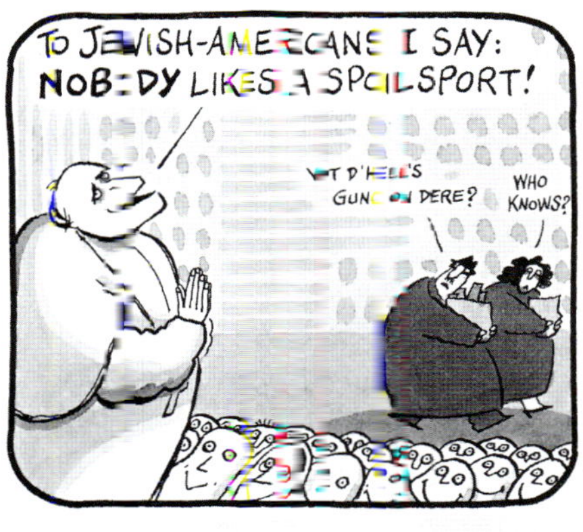
TO JEWISH-AMERICANS I SAY: NOBODY LIKES A SPOILSPORT!
WOT D'HELL'S GUING ON DERE?
WHO KNOWS?

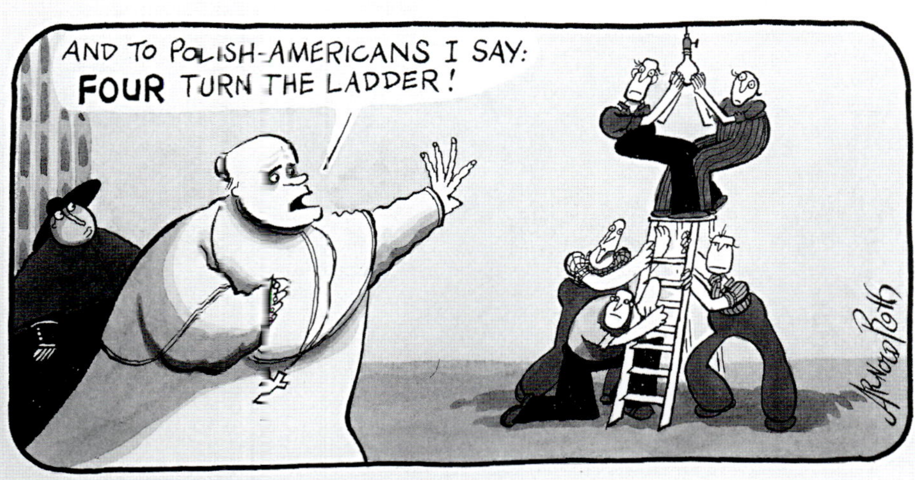
AND TO POLISH-AMERICANS I SAY: FOUR TURN THE LADDER!
Arnold Roth

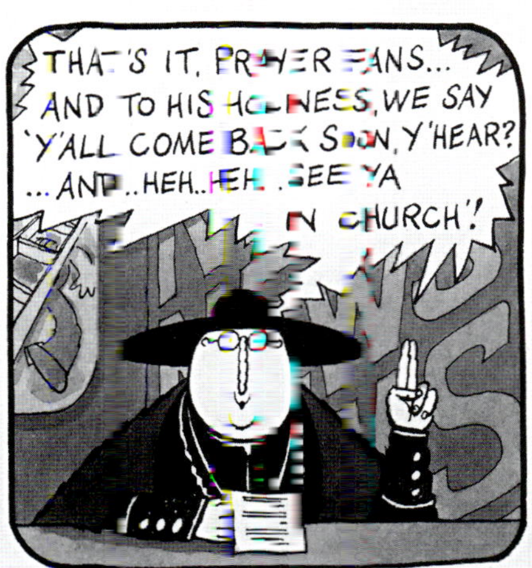
THAT'S IT, PRAYER FANS... AND TO HIS HOLINESS, WE SAY 'Y'ALL COME BACK SOON, Y'HEAR? ...AND...HEH...HEH...SEE YA IN CHURCH'!

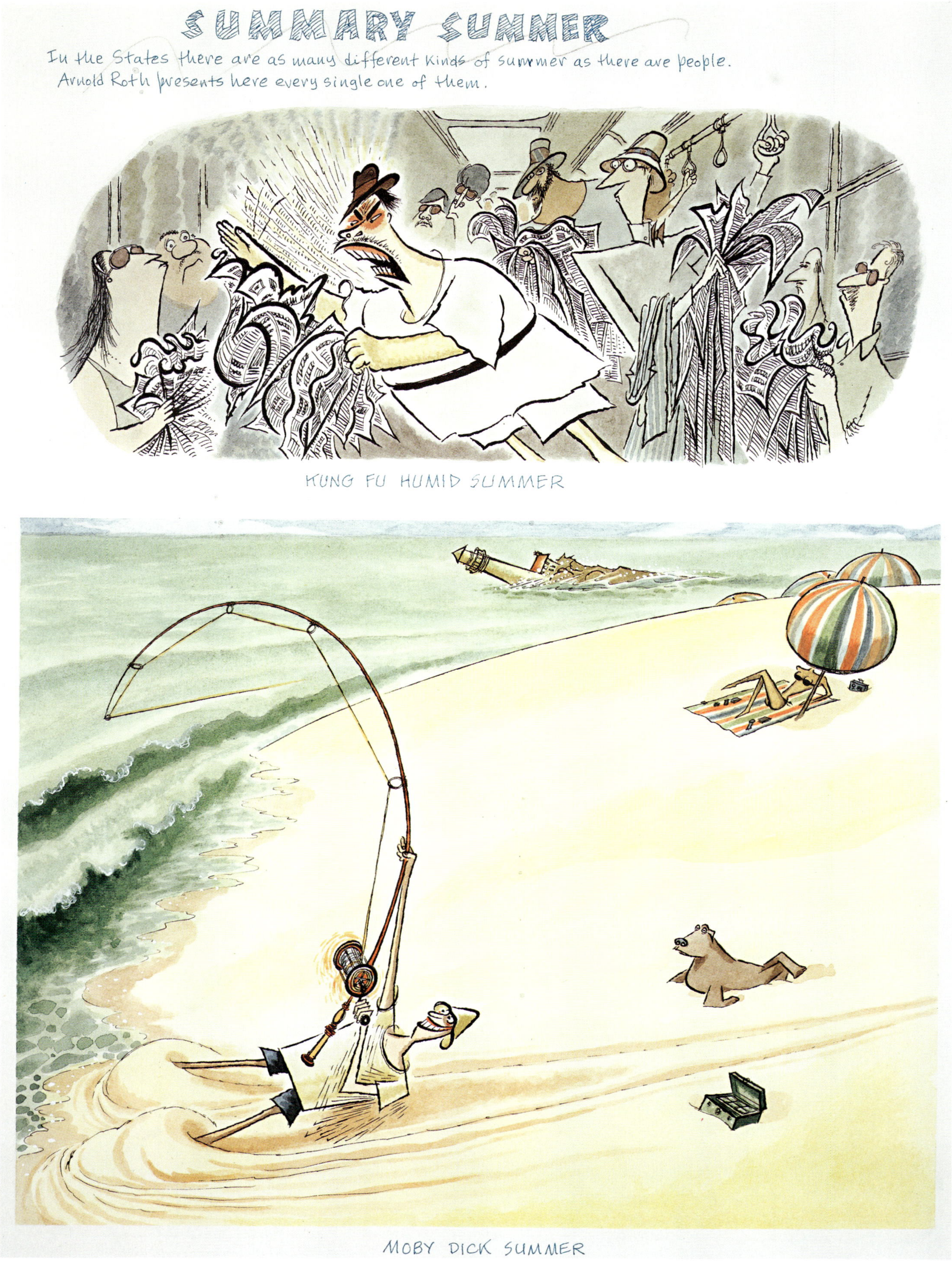

SUMMARY SUMMER

In the States there are as many different kinds of summer as there are people. Arnold Roth presents here every single one of them.

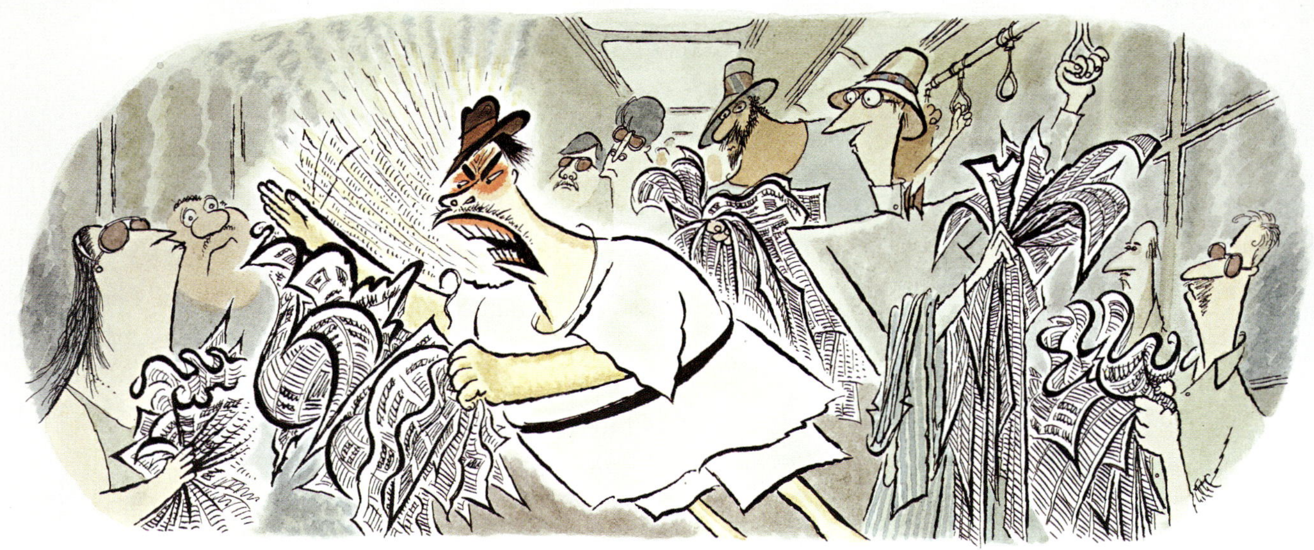

KUNG FU HUMID SUMMER

MOBY DICK SUMMER

Above and opposite:
Figure 18
"Summary Summer"
Punch 1987

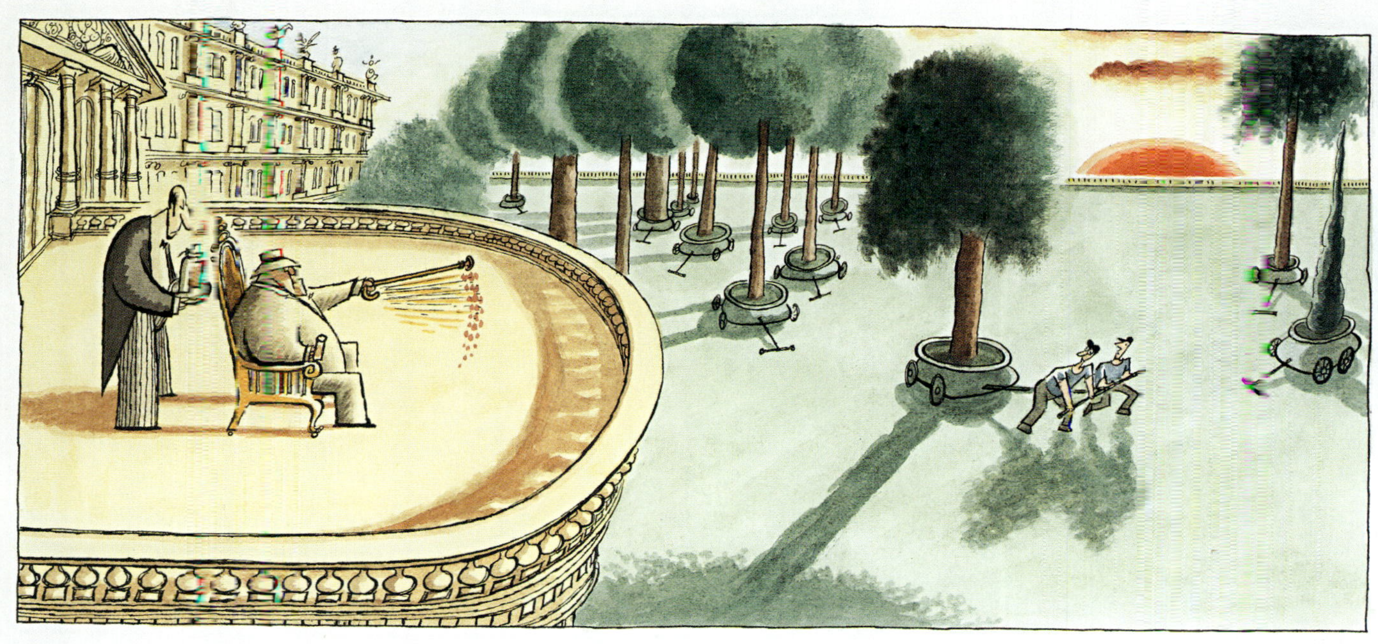

PERFECT SUMMER

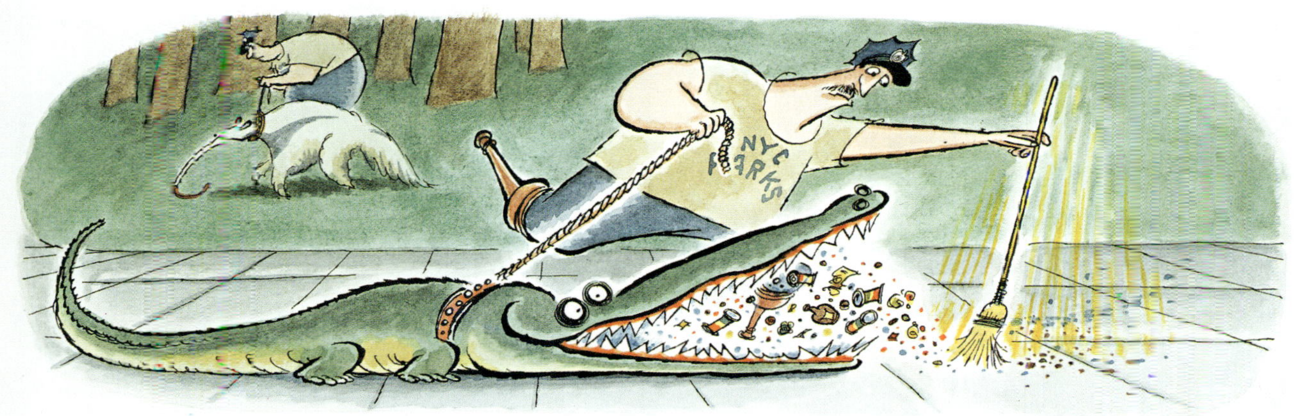

ECOLOGICAL SUMMER

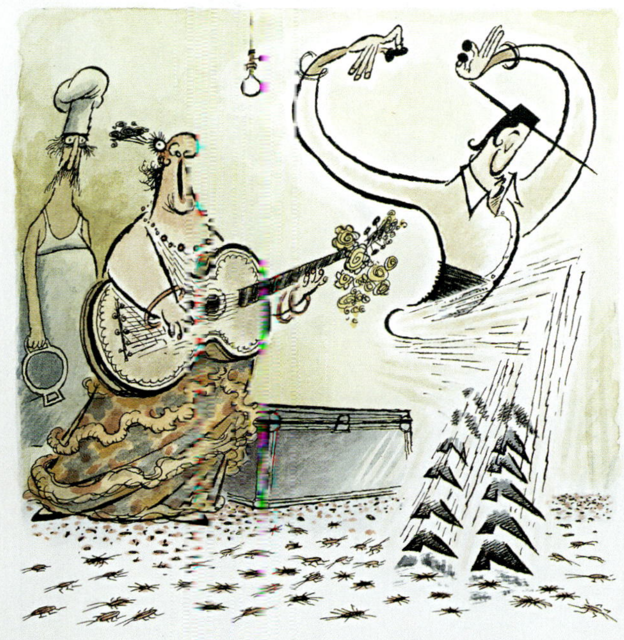

SUMMER KITCHEN

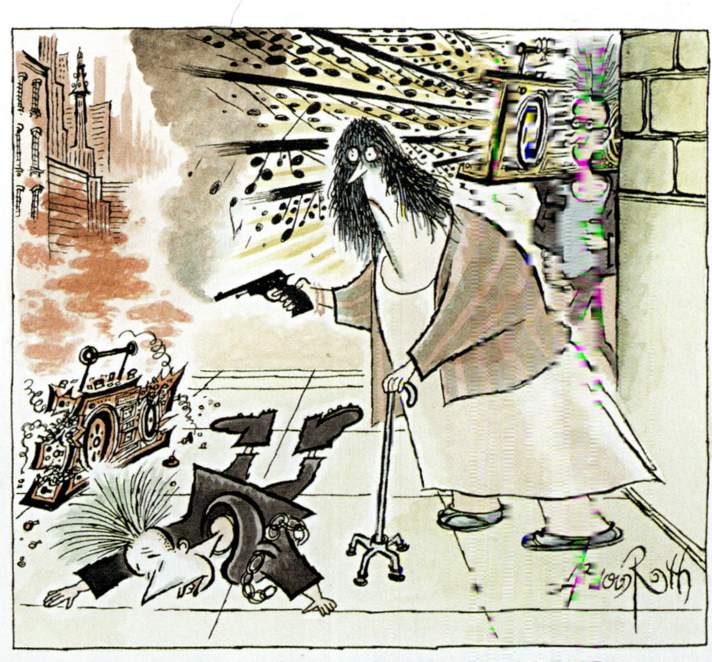

ROCK'N'ROLL-WILL-NEVER-DIE SUMMER

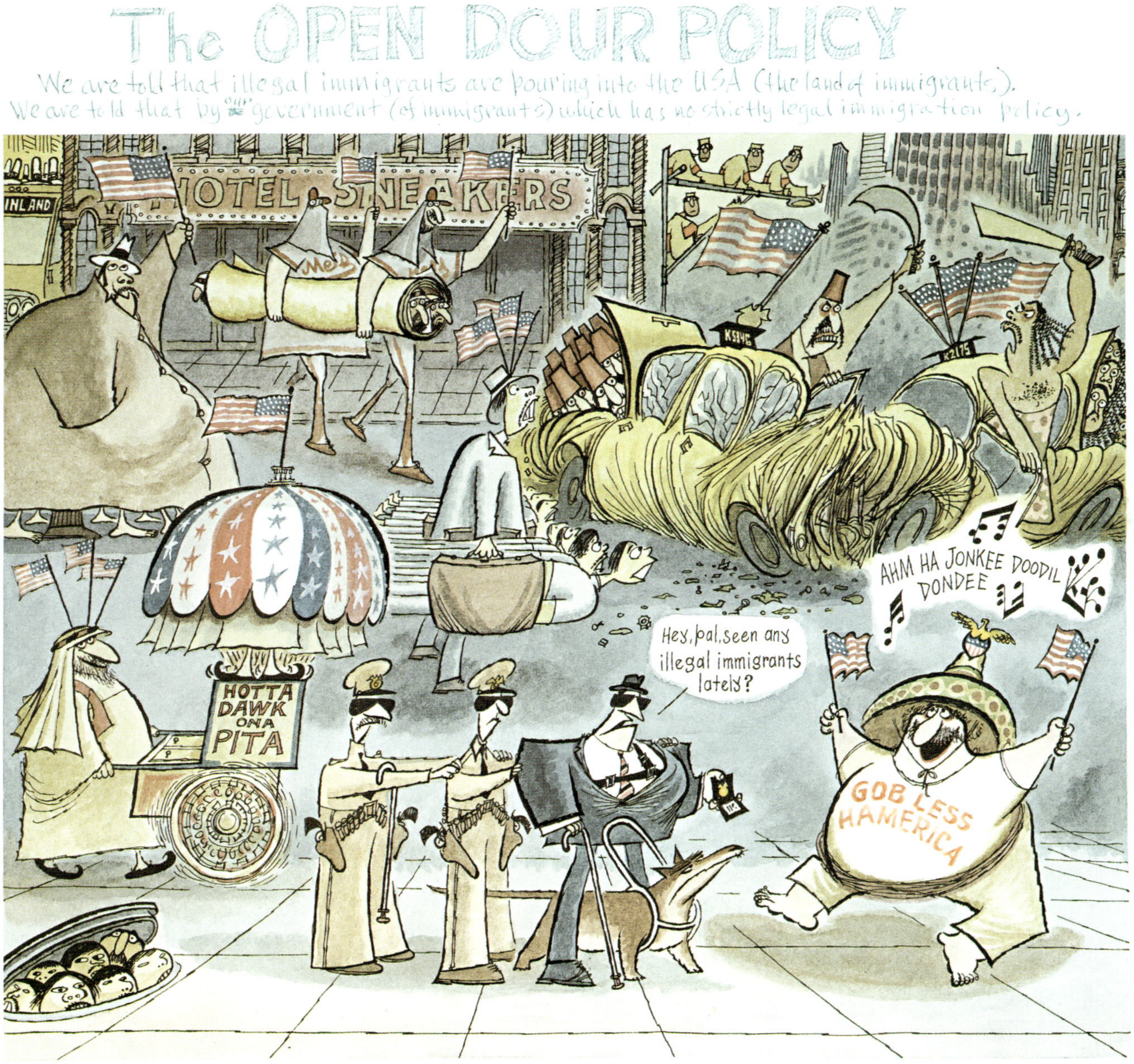

The OPEN DOUR POLICY

We are told that illegal immigrants are pouring into the USA (the land of immigrants).
We are told that by our government (of immigrants) which has no strictly legal immigration policy.

HOTEL SNEAKERS

HOTTA DAWK ONA PITA

AHM HA JONKEE DOODIL DONDEE

Hey, pal, seen any illegal immigrants lately?

GOB LESS HAMERICA

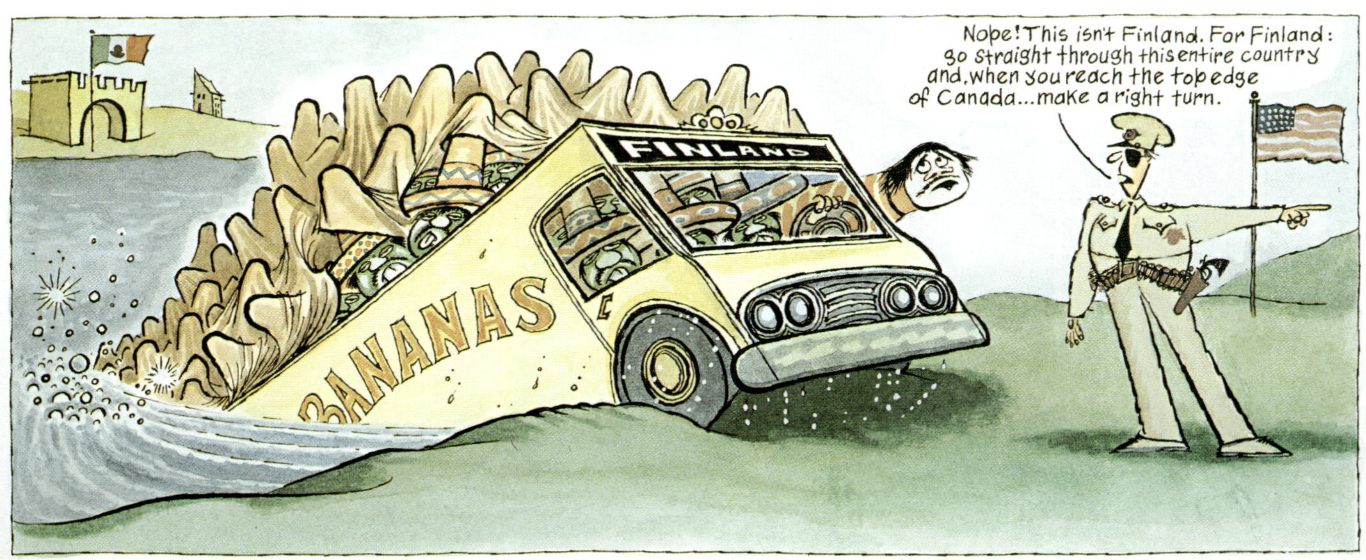

Above and opposite:
Figure 19
"The Open Dour Policy"
Punch 1986

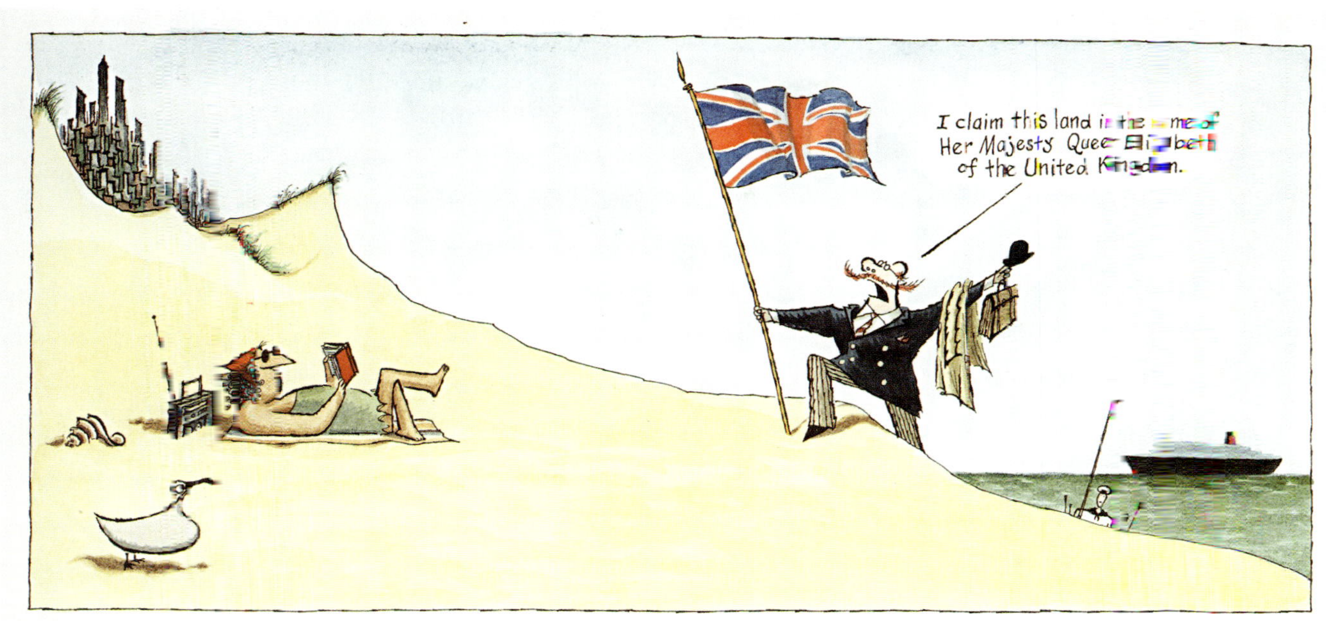
I claim this land in the name of Her Majesty Queen Elizabeth of the United Kingdom.

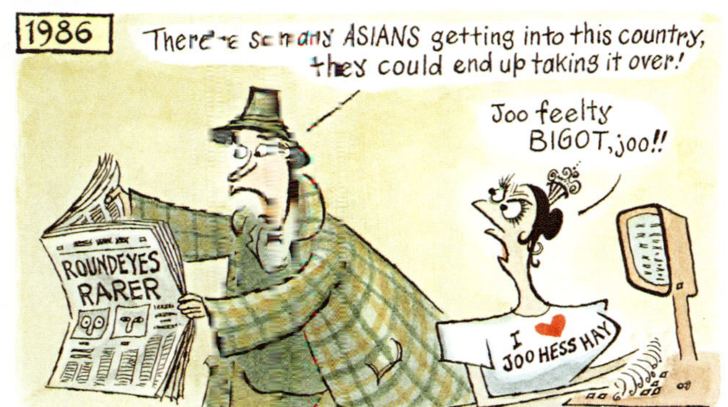
1986
There're so many ASIANS getting into this country, they could end up taking it over!
Joo feelty BIGOT, joo!!
ROUNDEYES RARER
I ♥ JOO HESS HAY

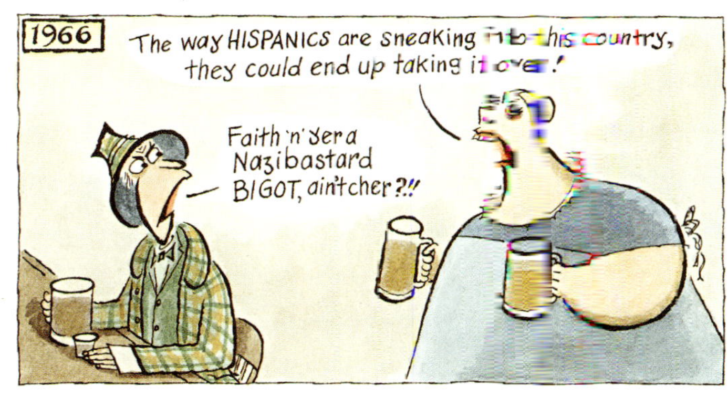
1966
The way HISPANICS are sneaking into this country, they could end up taking it over!
Faith 'n' yer a Nazibastard BIGOT, ain'tcher?!!

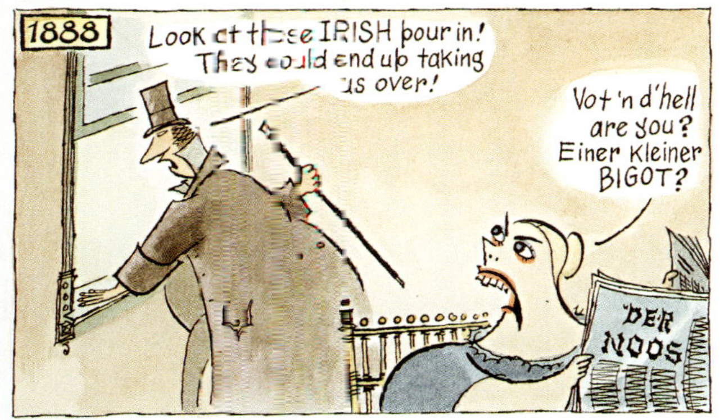
1888
Look at those IRISH pour in! They could end up taking us over!
Vot 'n d'hell are you? Einer Kleiner BIGOT?
DER NOOS

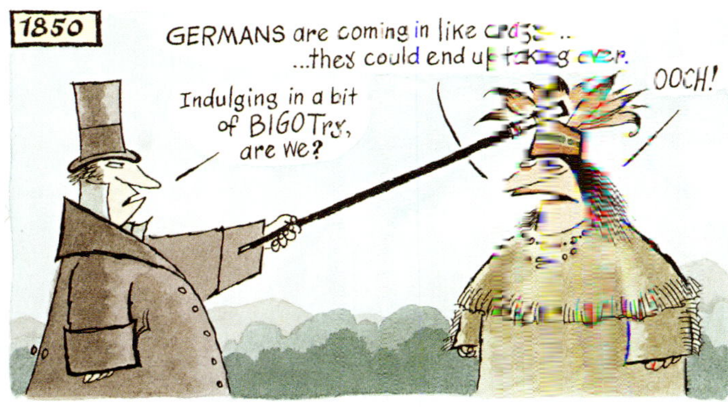
1850
GERMANS are coming in like crazy.. ...they could end up taking over.
Indulging in a bit of BIGOTry, are we?
OOCH!

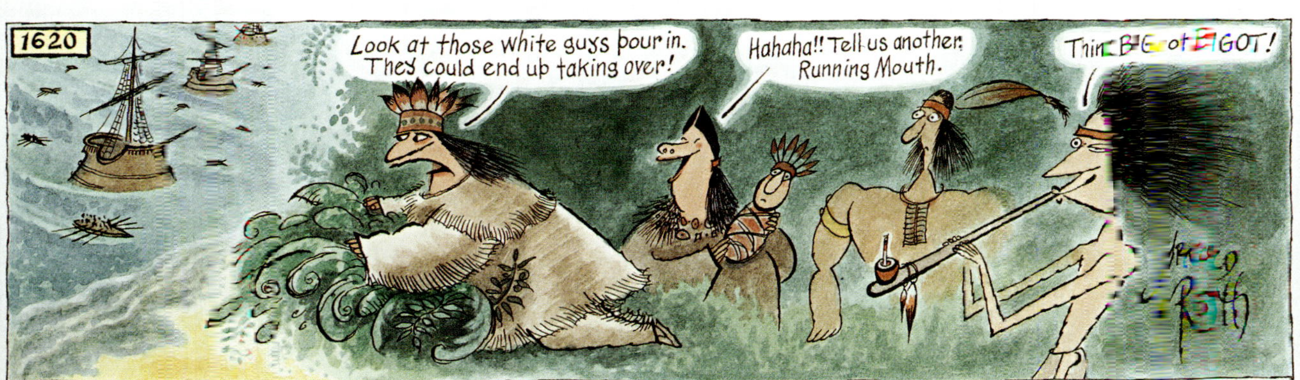
1620
Look at those white guys pour in. They could end up taking over!
Hahaha!! Tell us another, Running Mouth.
Think BIG, not BIGOT!

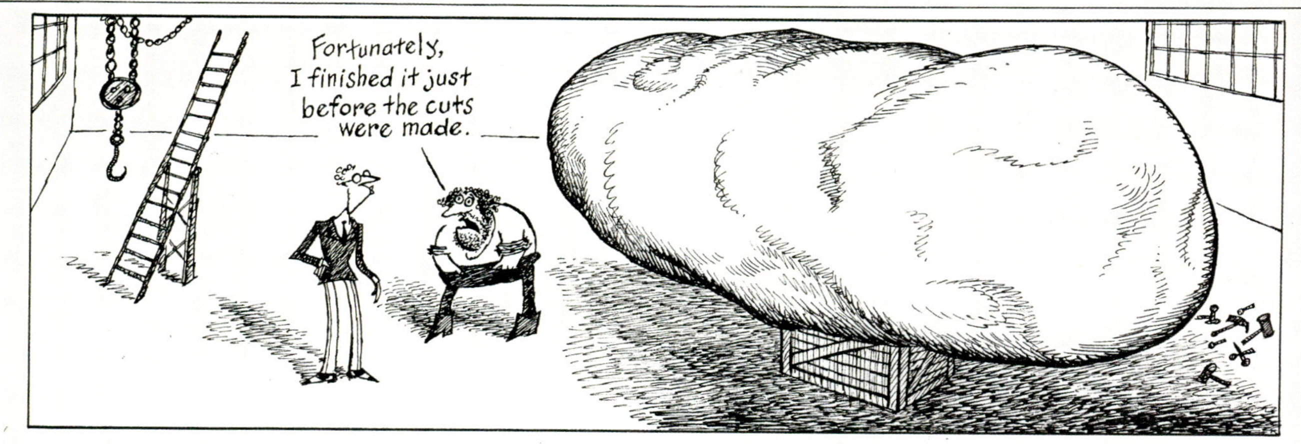

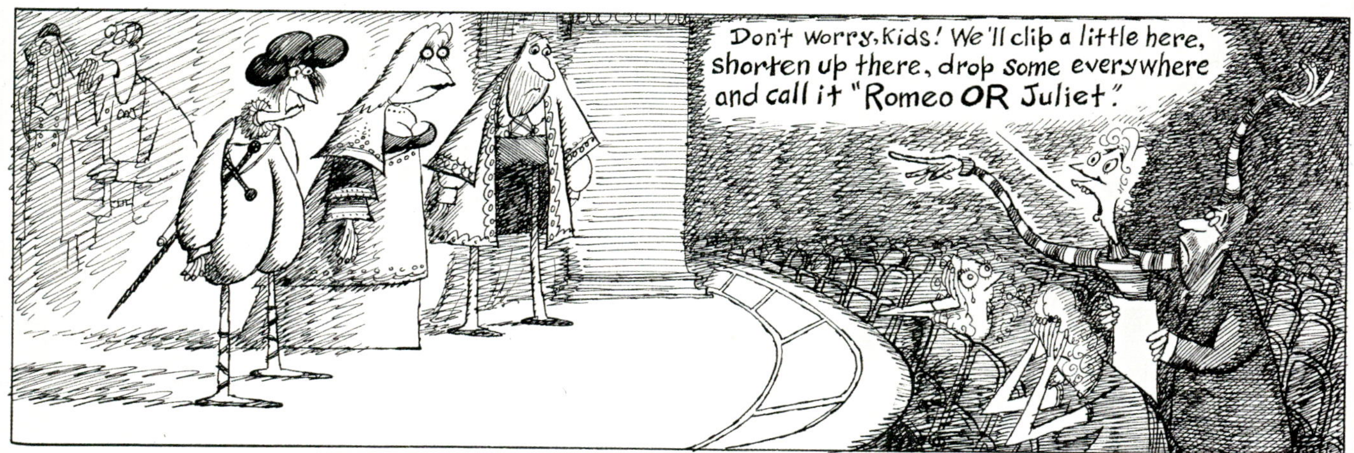

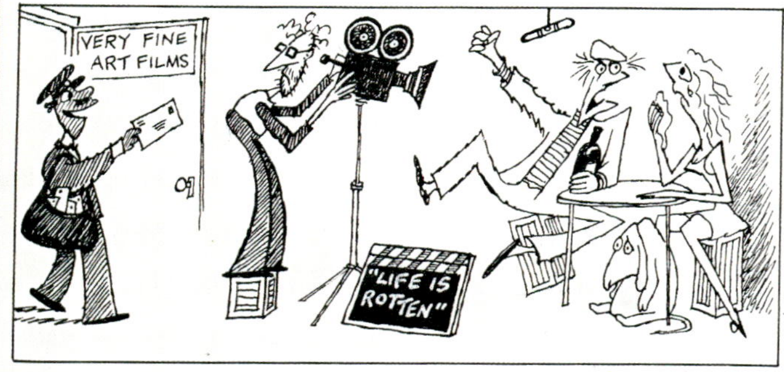

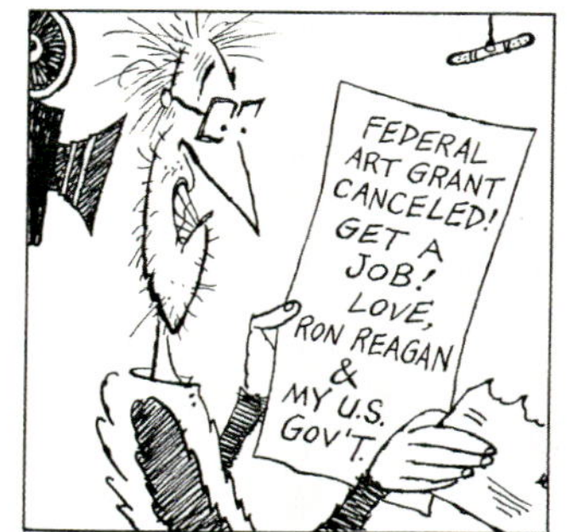

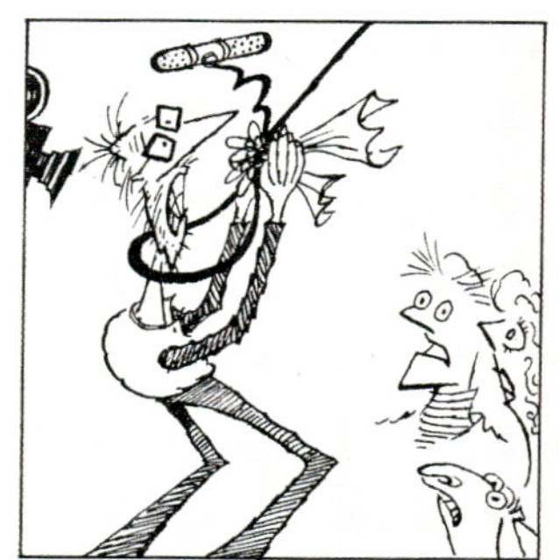

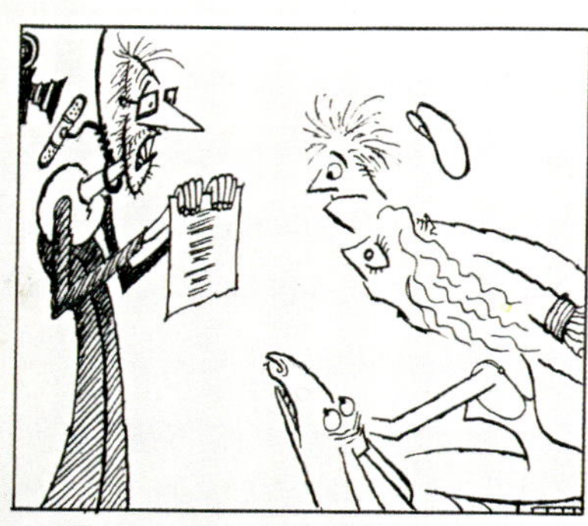

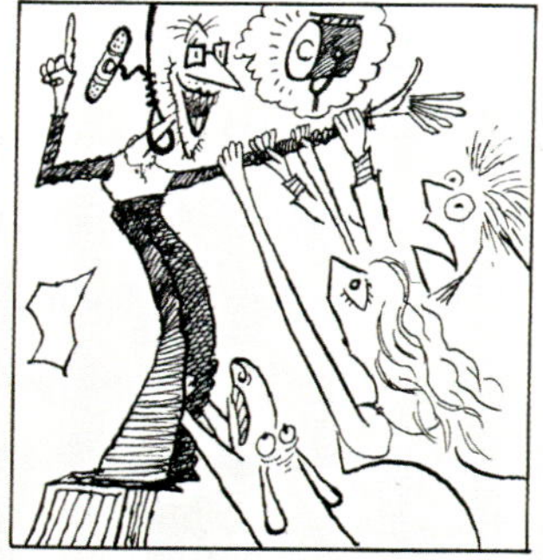

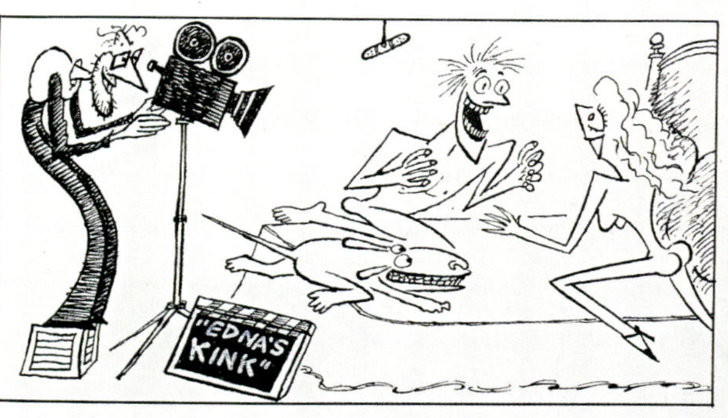

Above and opposite:
Figure 20
"Ars Shorta"
Punch 1982

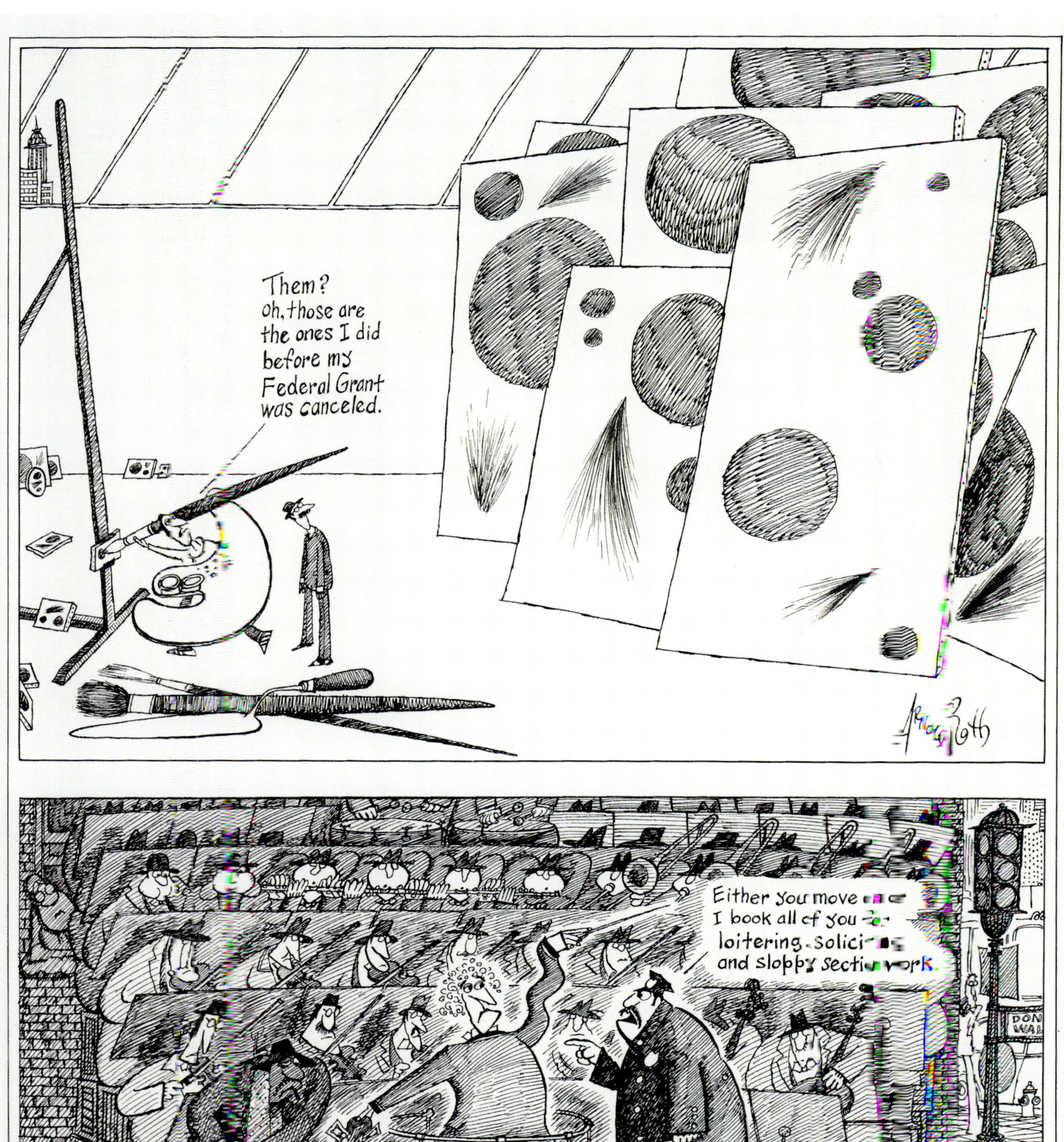
Them?
oh, those are
the ones I did
before my
Federal Grant
was canceled.
Either you move
I book all of you
loitering, Solici
and sloppy Secti ork.

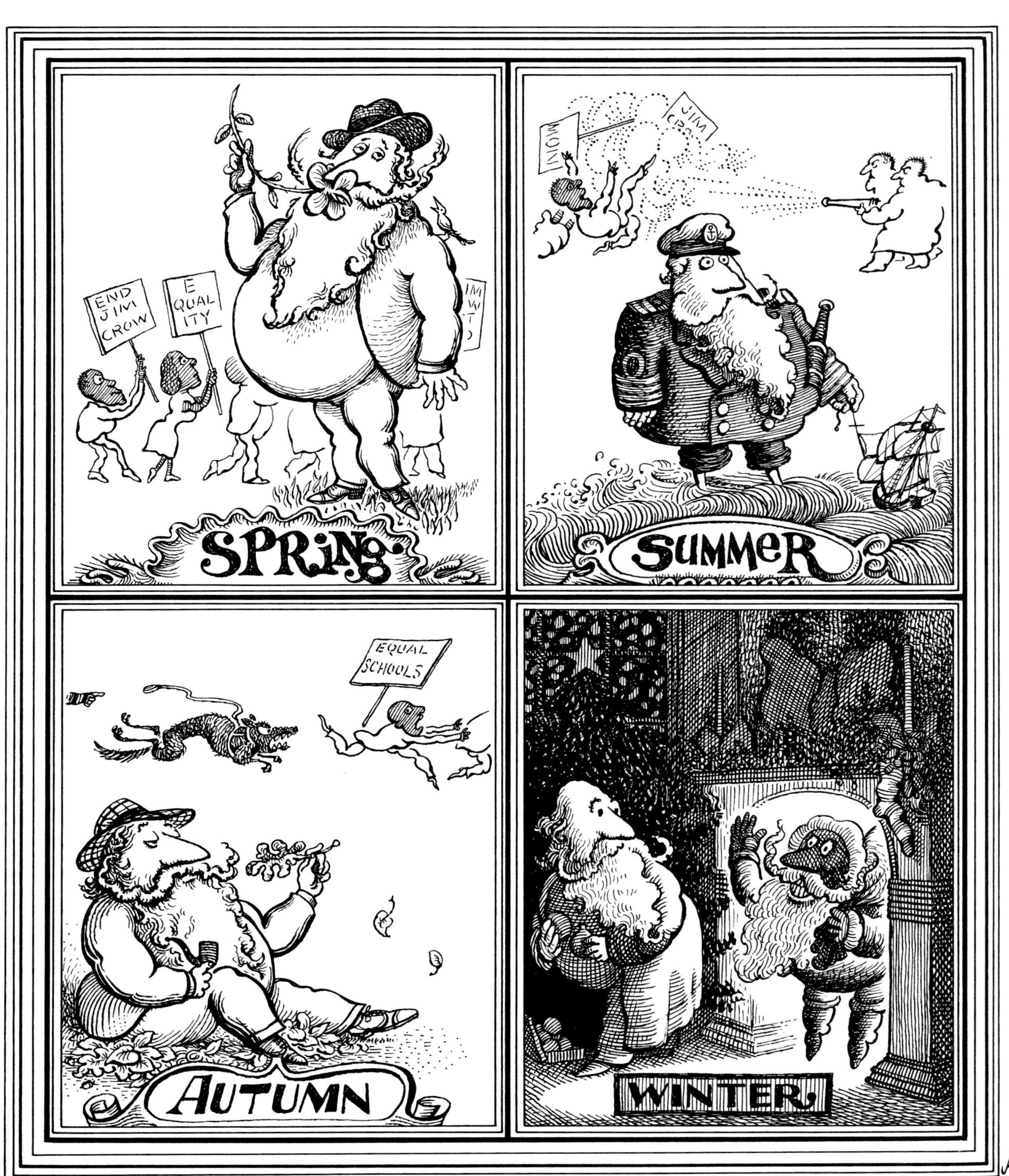

Figure 21
"Merry Christmas"
circa 1963

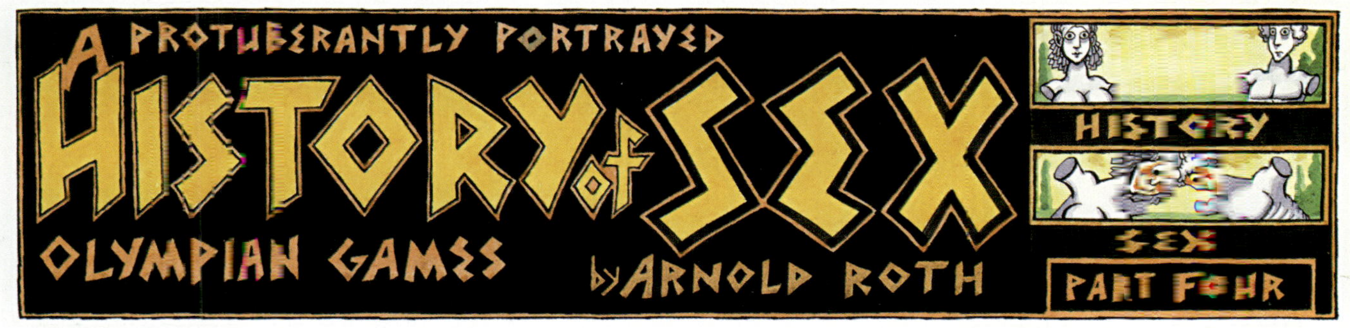

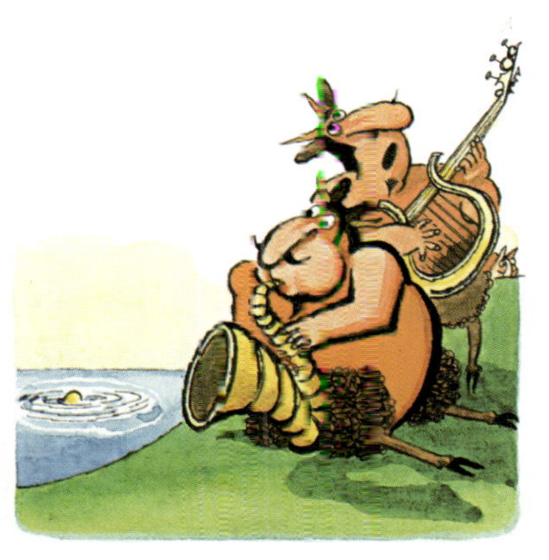

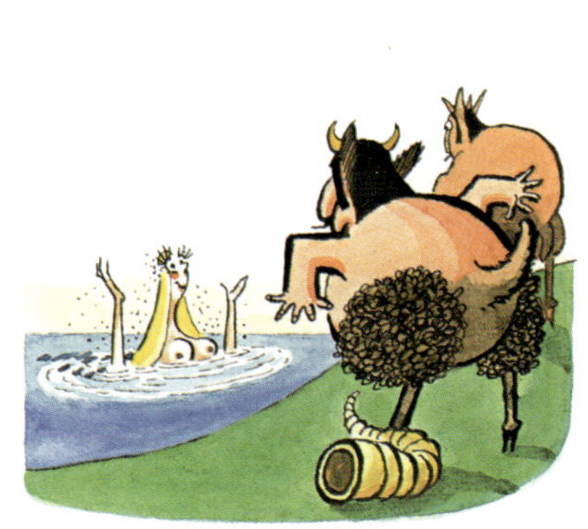

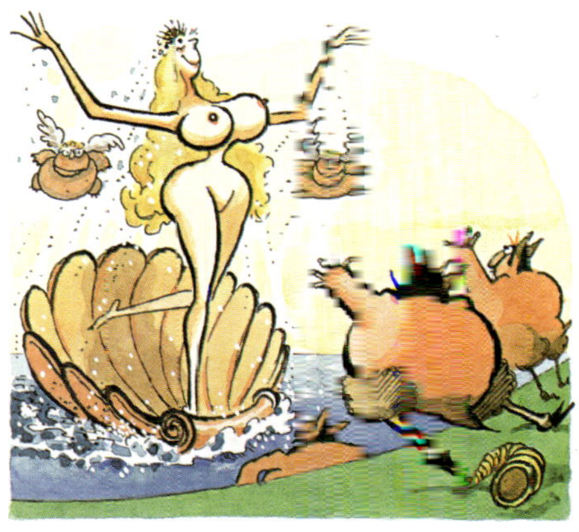

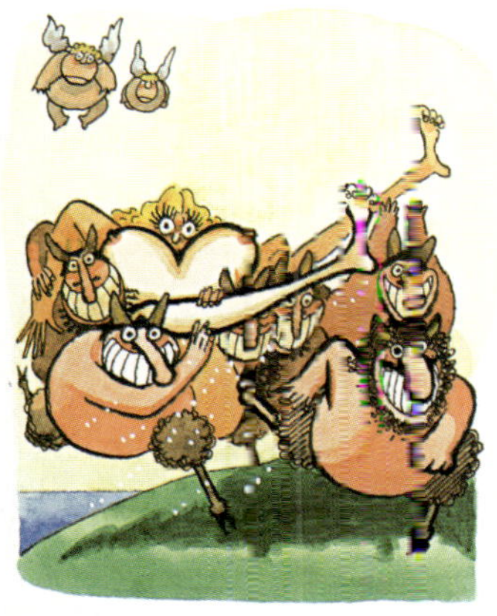

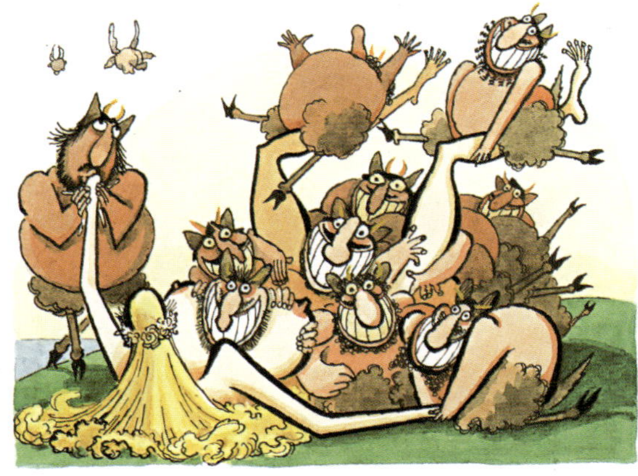

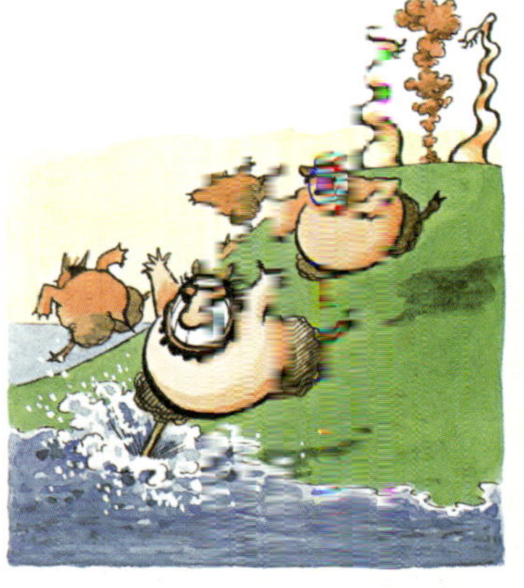

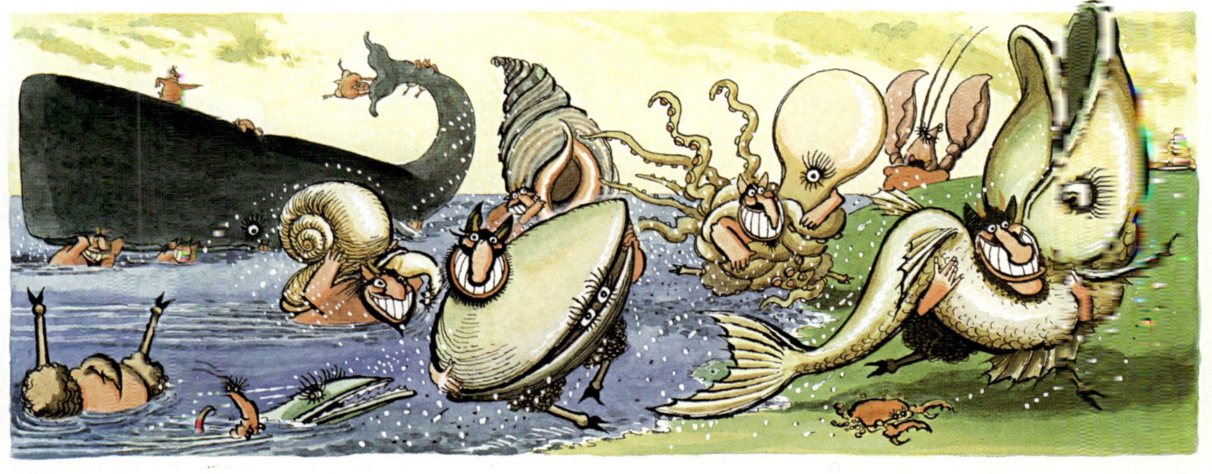

Above and two following pages:
Figure 22
"A History of Sex Part Four: Olympic Games"
Playboy 1975

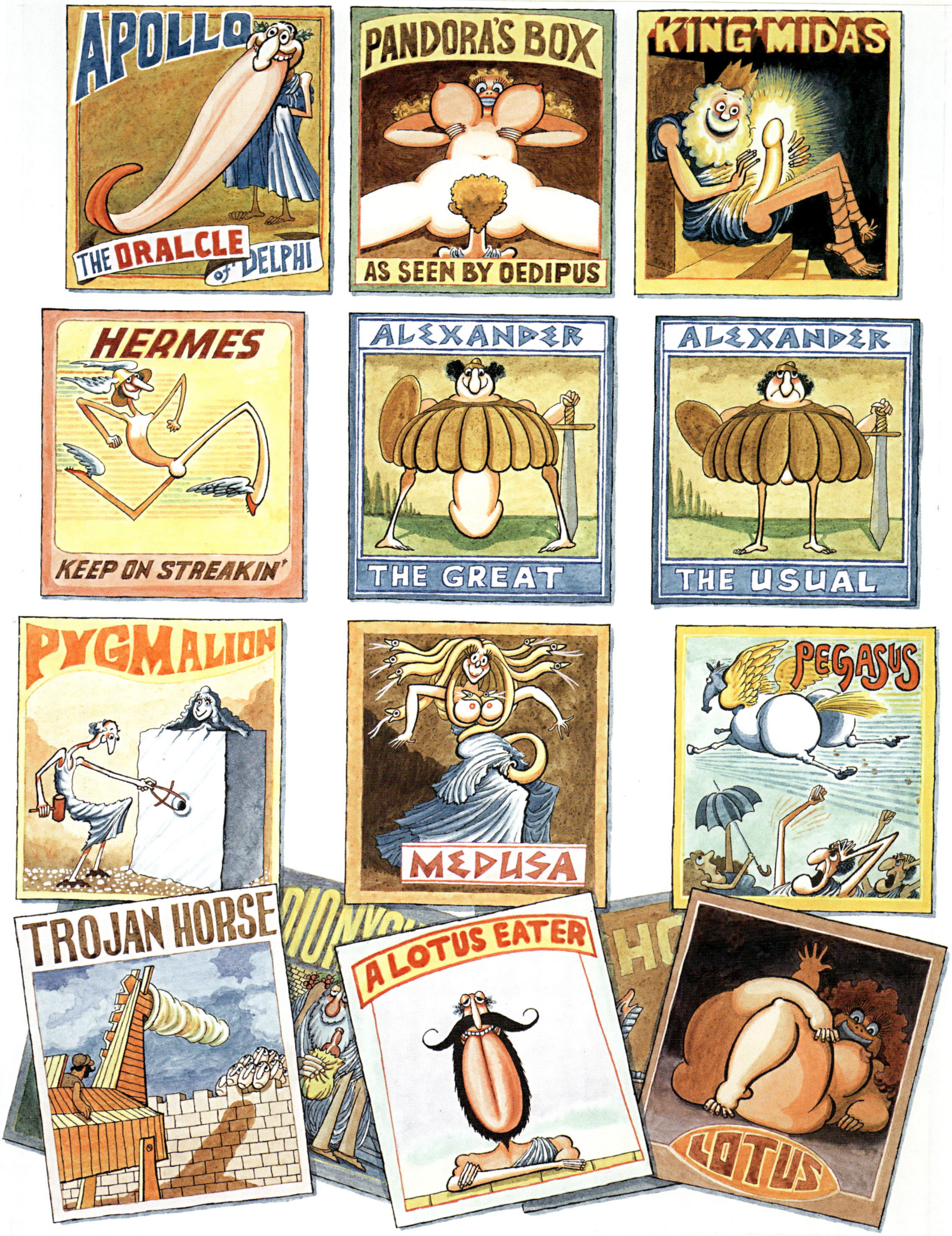

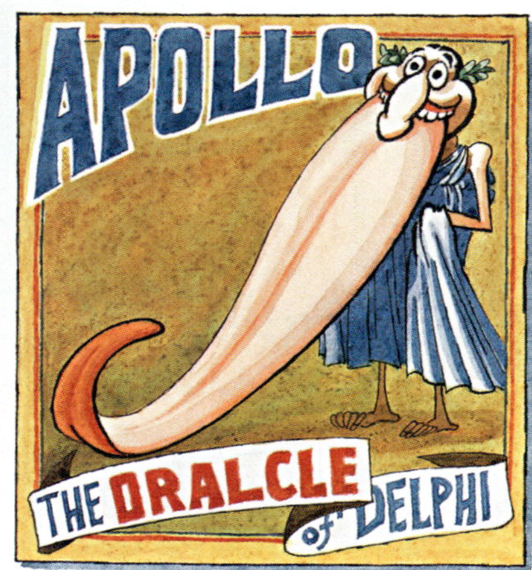
APOLLO
THE ORALCLE of DELPHI

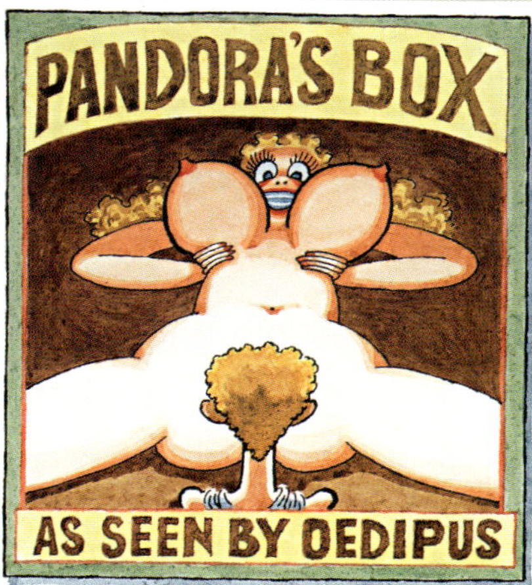
PANDORA'S BOX
AS SEEN BY OEDIPUS

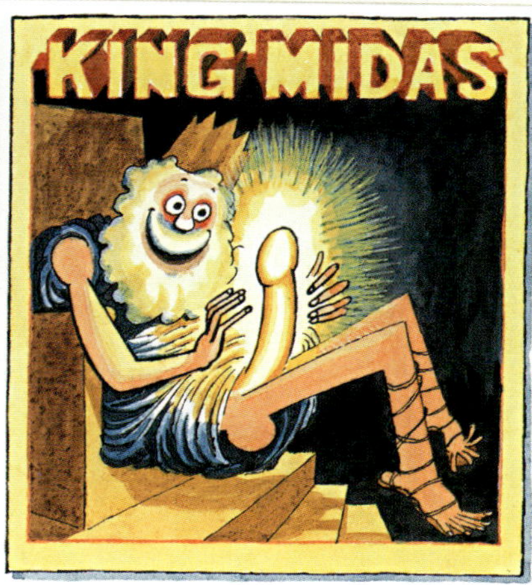
KING MIDAS

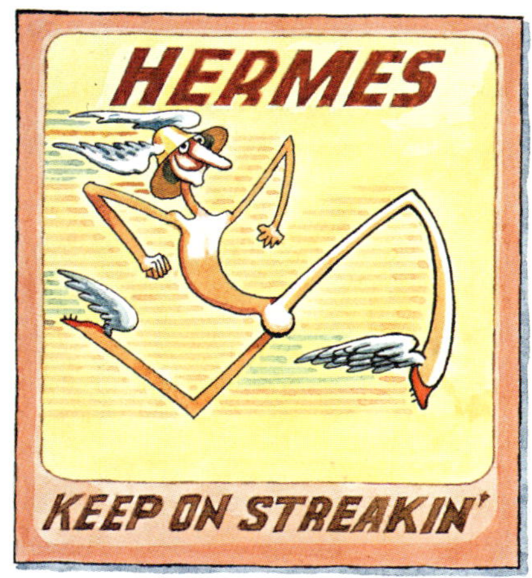
HERMES
KEEP ON STREAKIN'

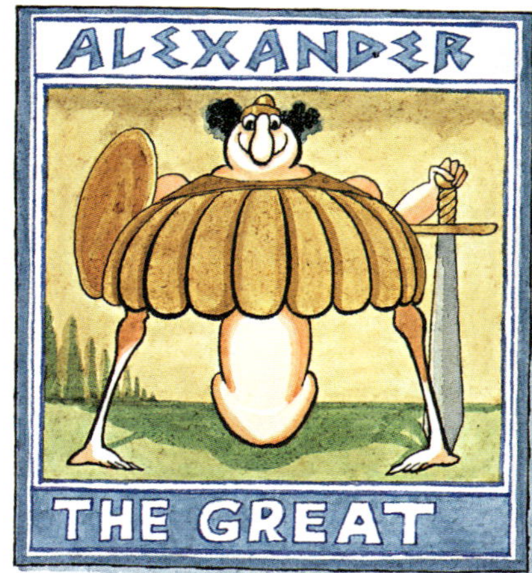
ALEXANDER
THE GREAT

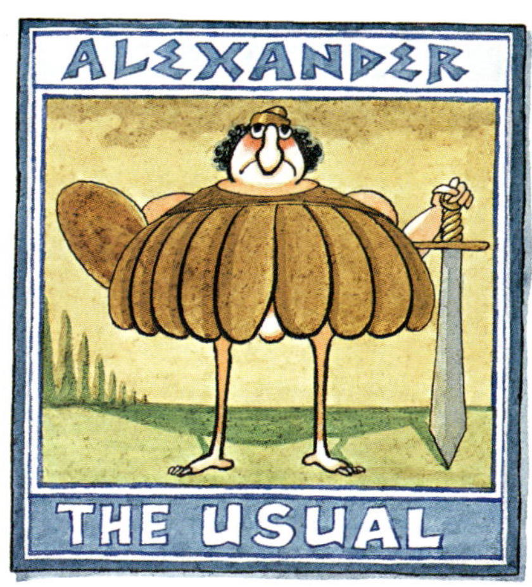
ALEXANDER
THE USUAL

PYGMALION
MEDUSA
PEGASUS
TROJAN HORSE
A LOTUS EATER
LOTUS

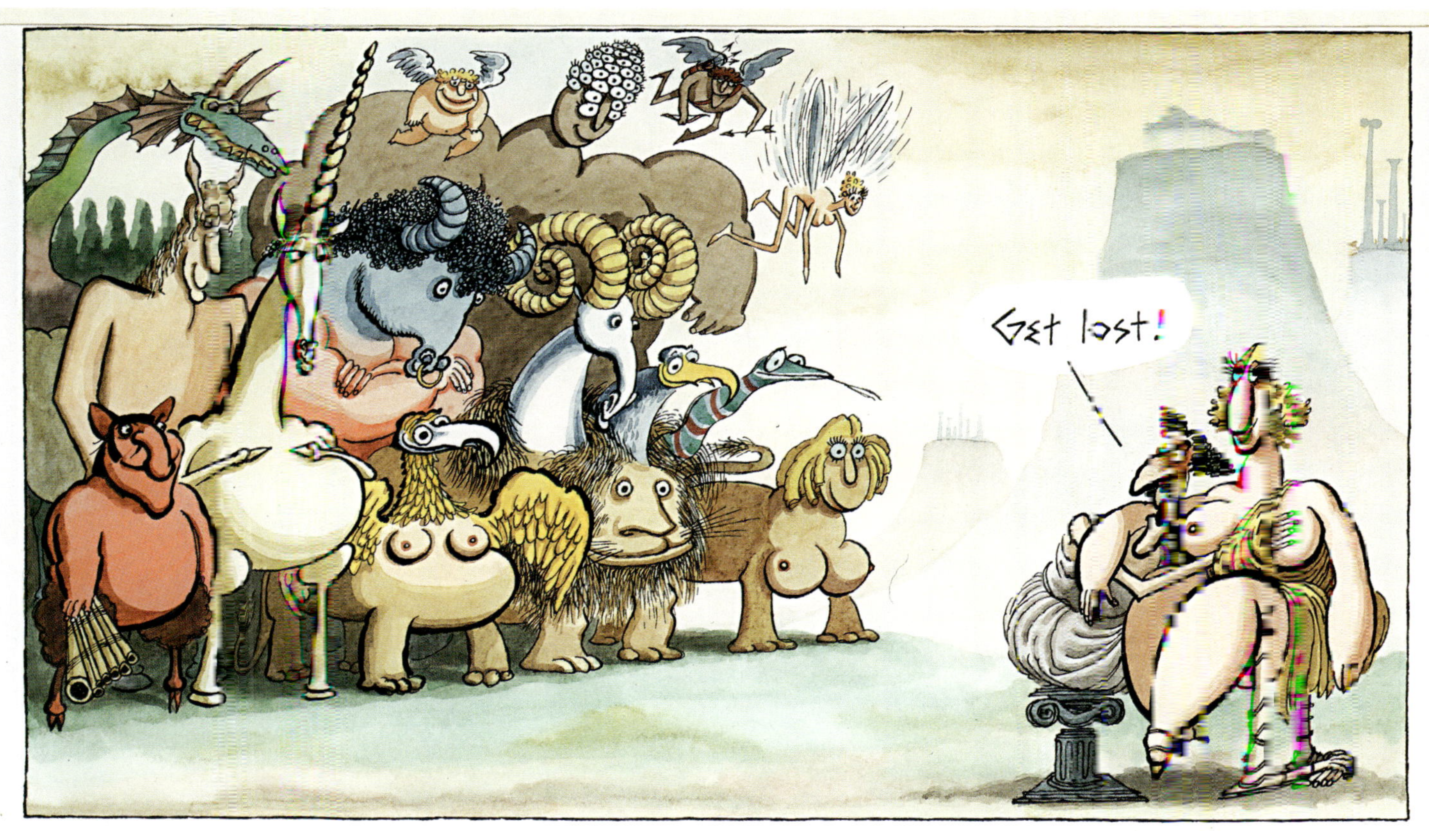
Get lost!

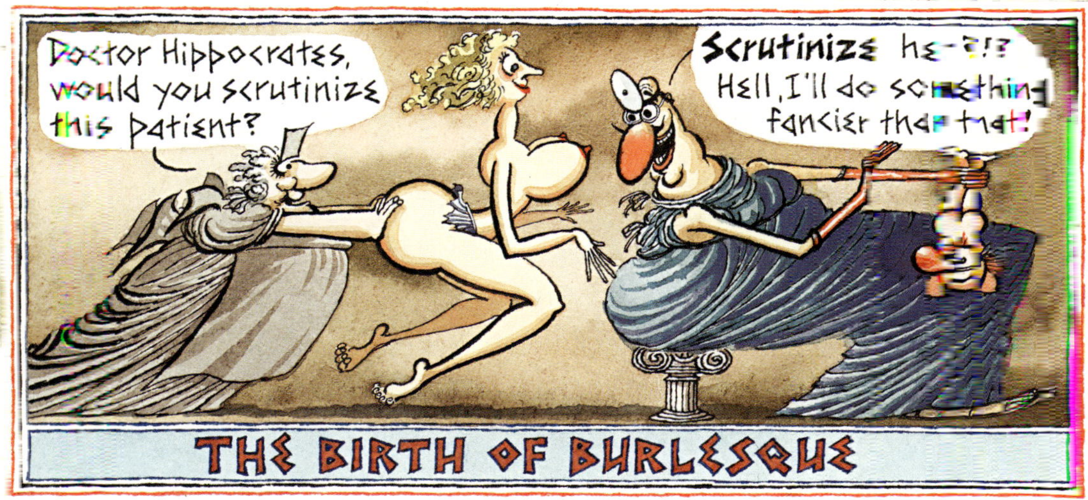
Doctor Hippocrates, would you scrutinize this patient?
Scrutinize her?!? Hell, I'll do something fancier than that!
THE BIRTH OF BURLESQUE

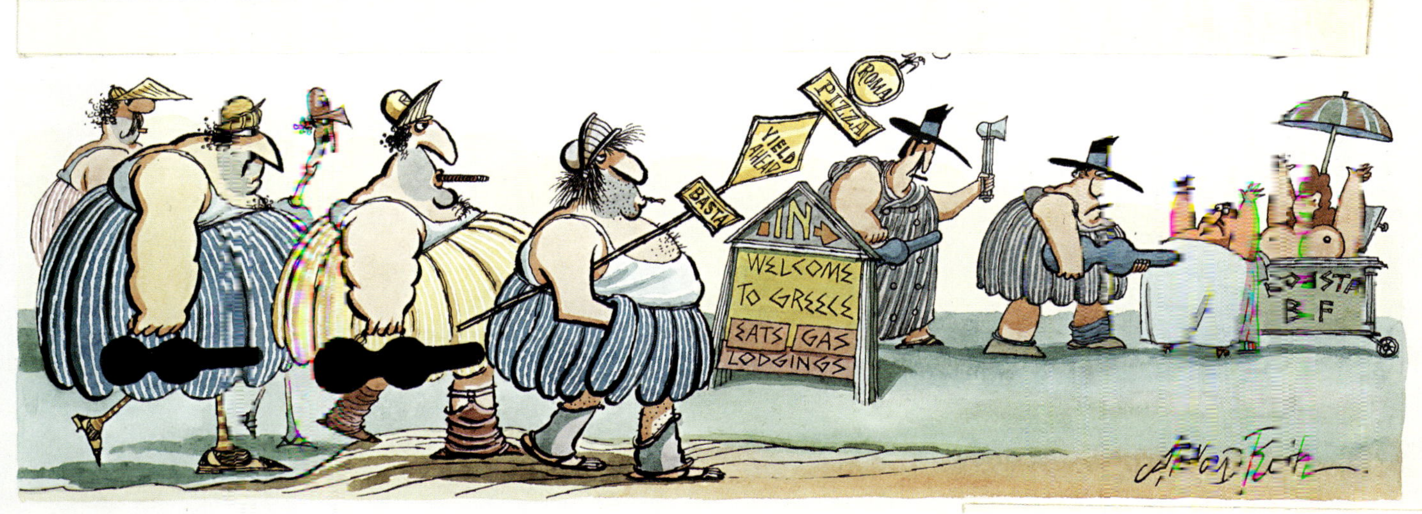
ROMA
PIZZA
YIELD AHEAD
BASTA
IN
WELCOME TO GREECE
EATS
GAS
LODGINGS

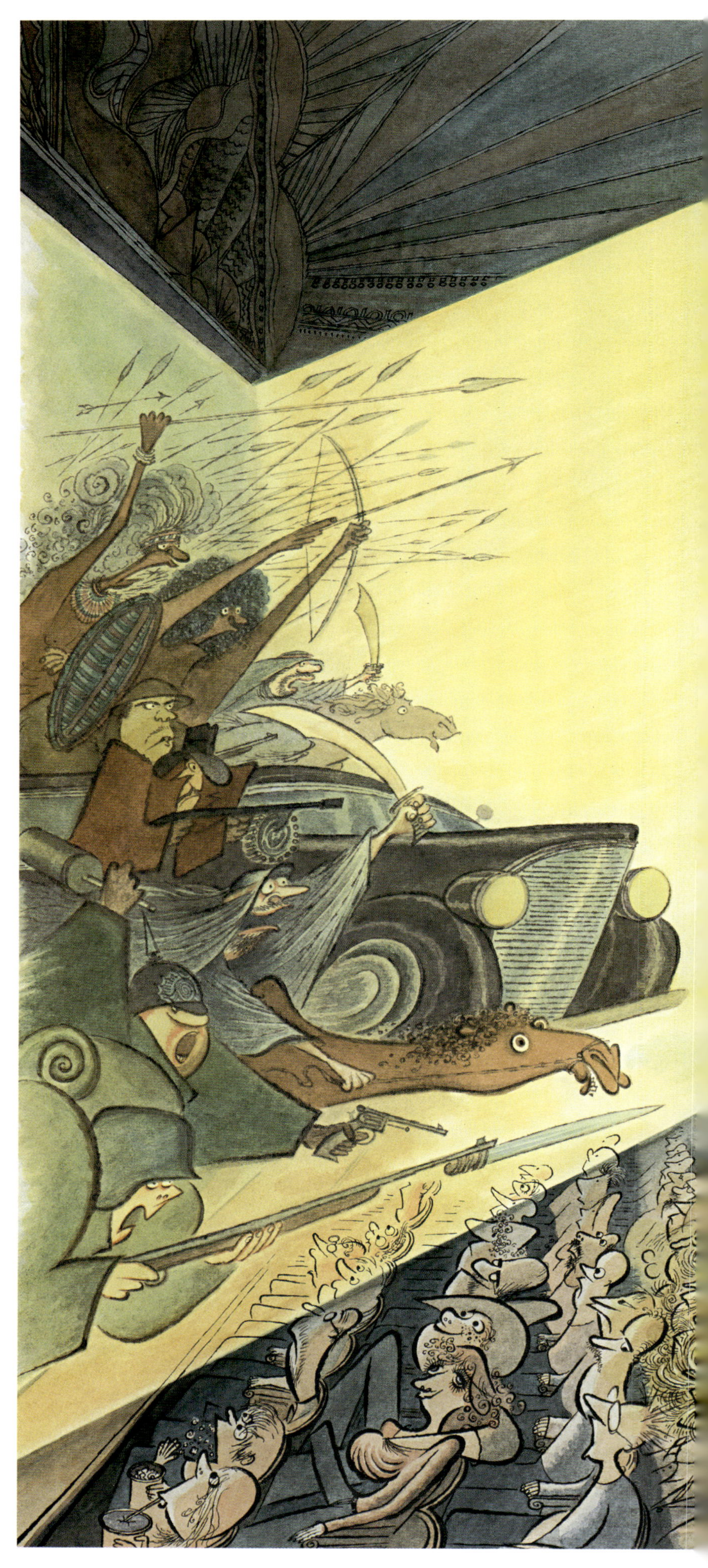

Figure 23
"Intermission"
Playboy 1987

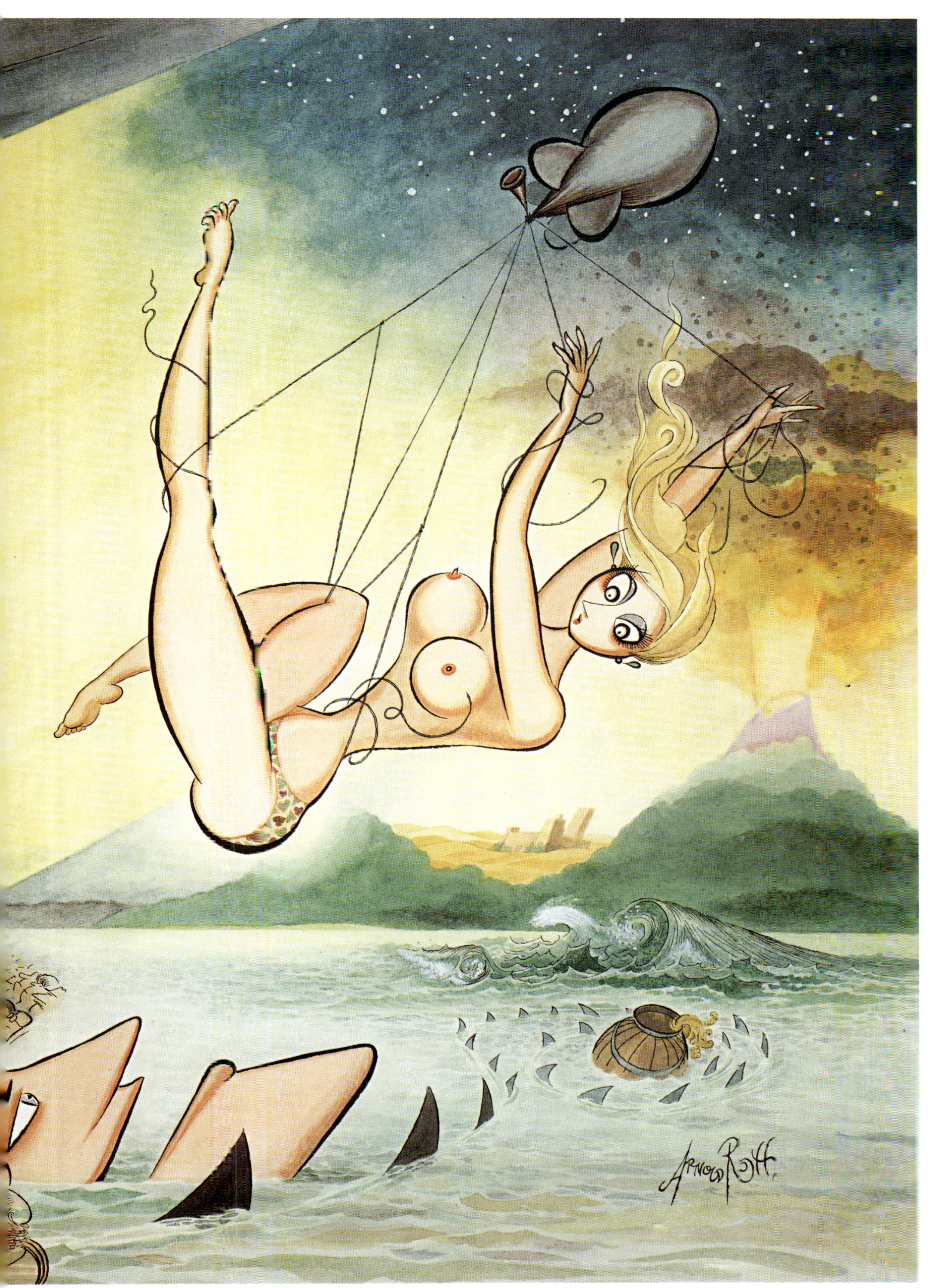

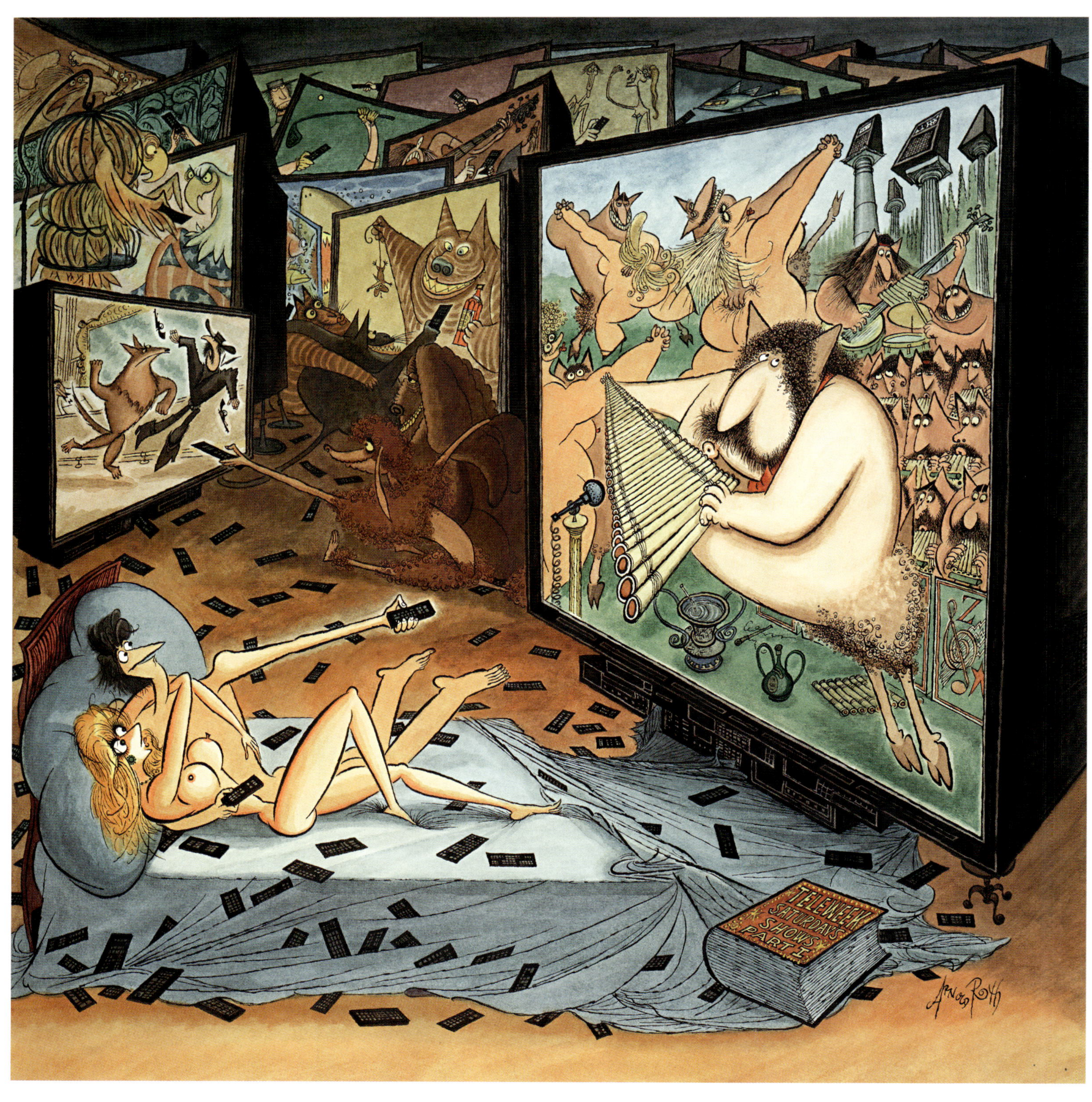

Figure 24
"500 Channels"
Playboy 1993

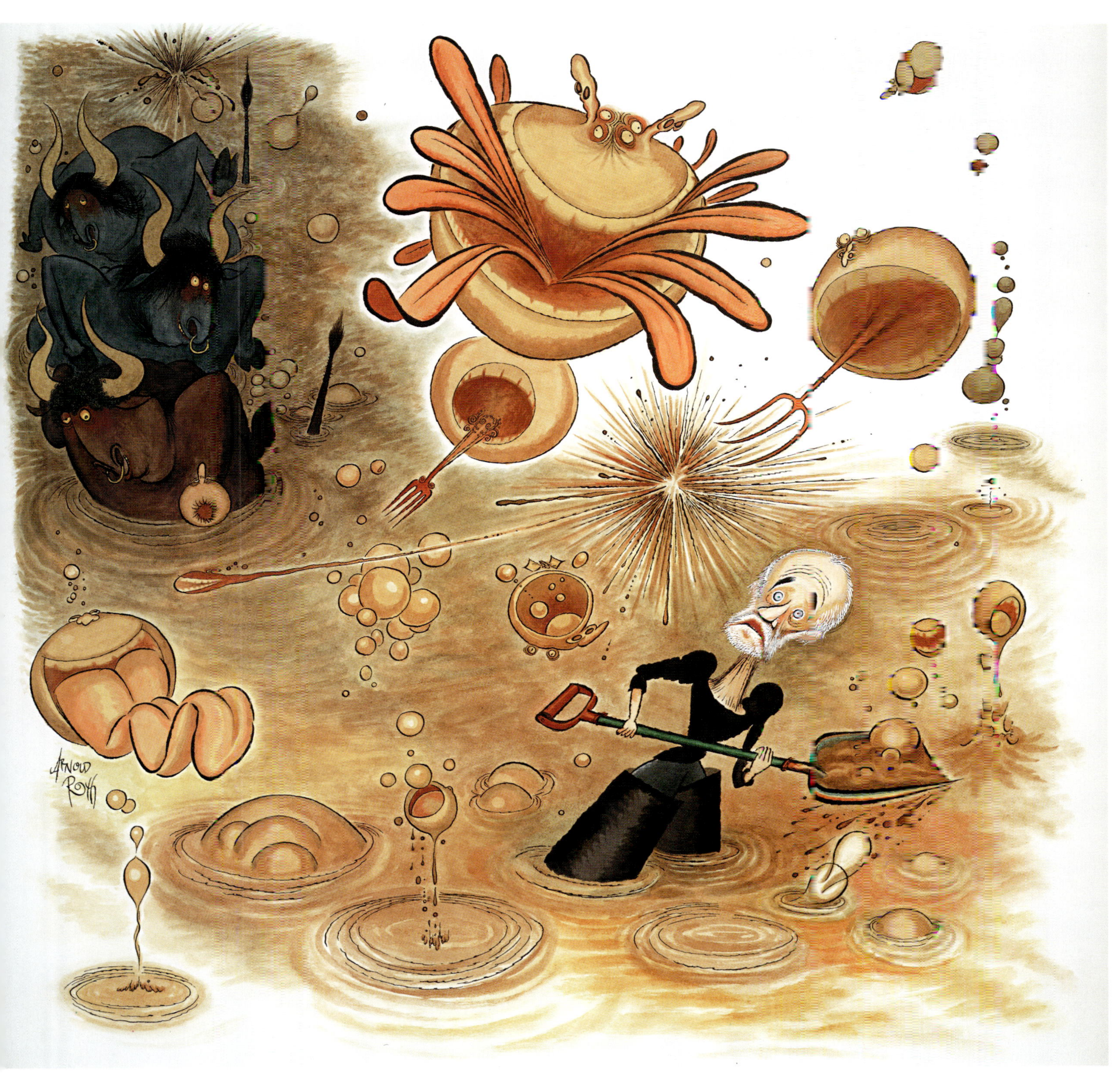

Figure 25
"Euphemisms"
Playboy 1997

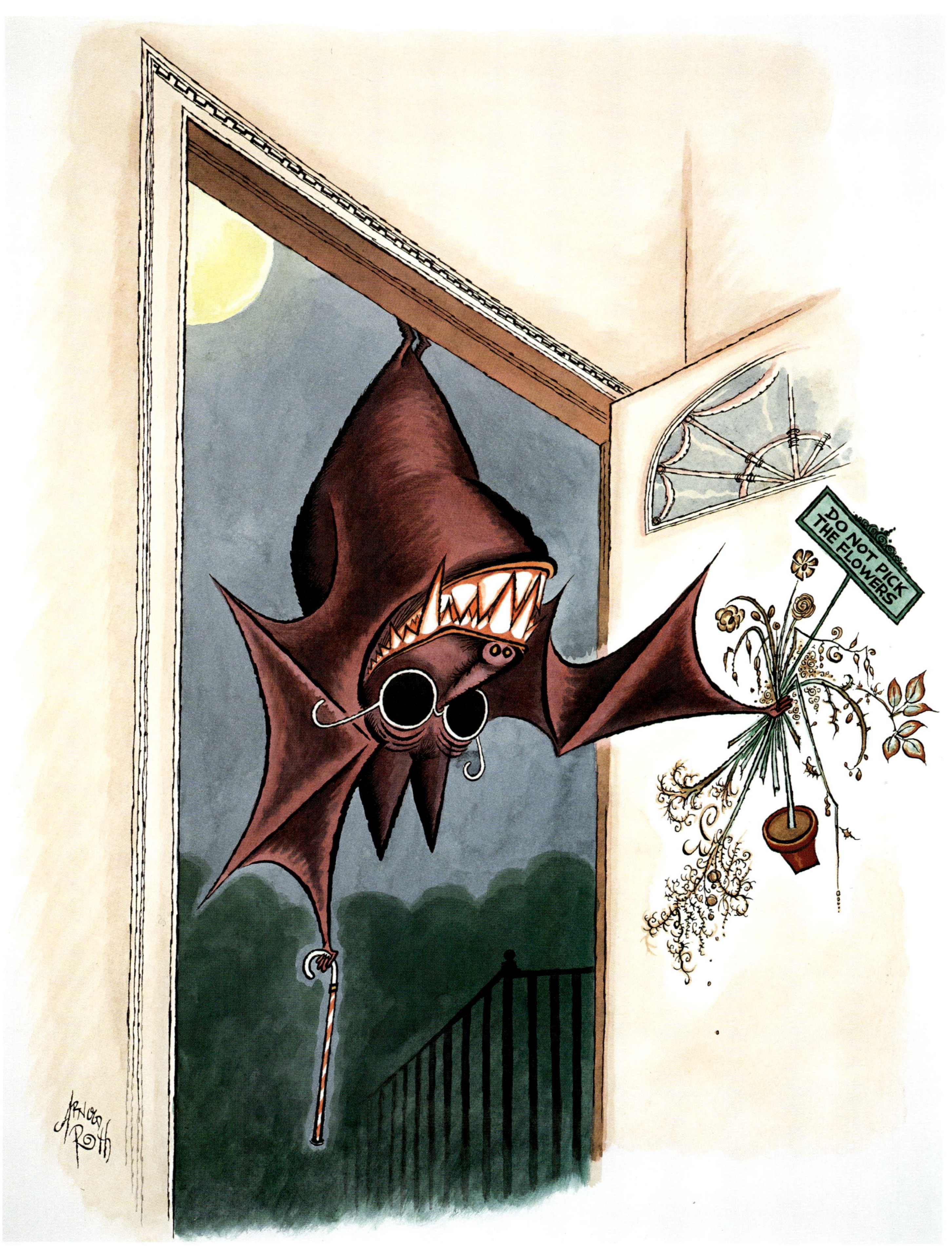

Figure 26
"Blind Date"
Playboy 1997

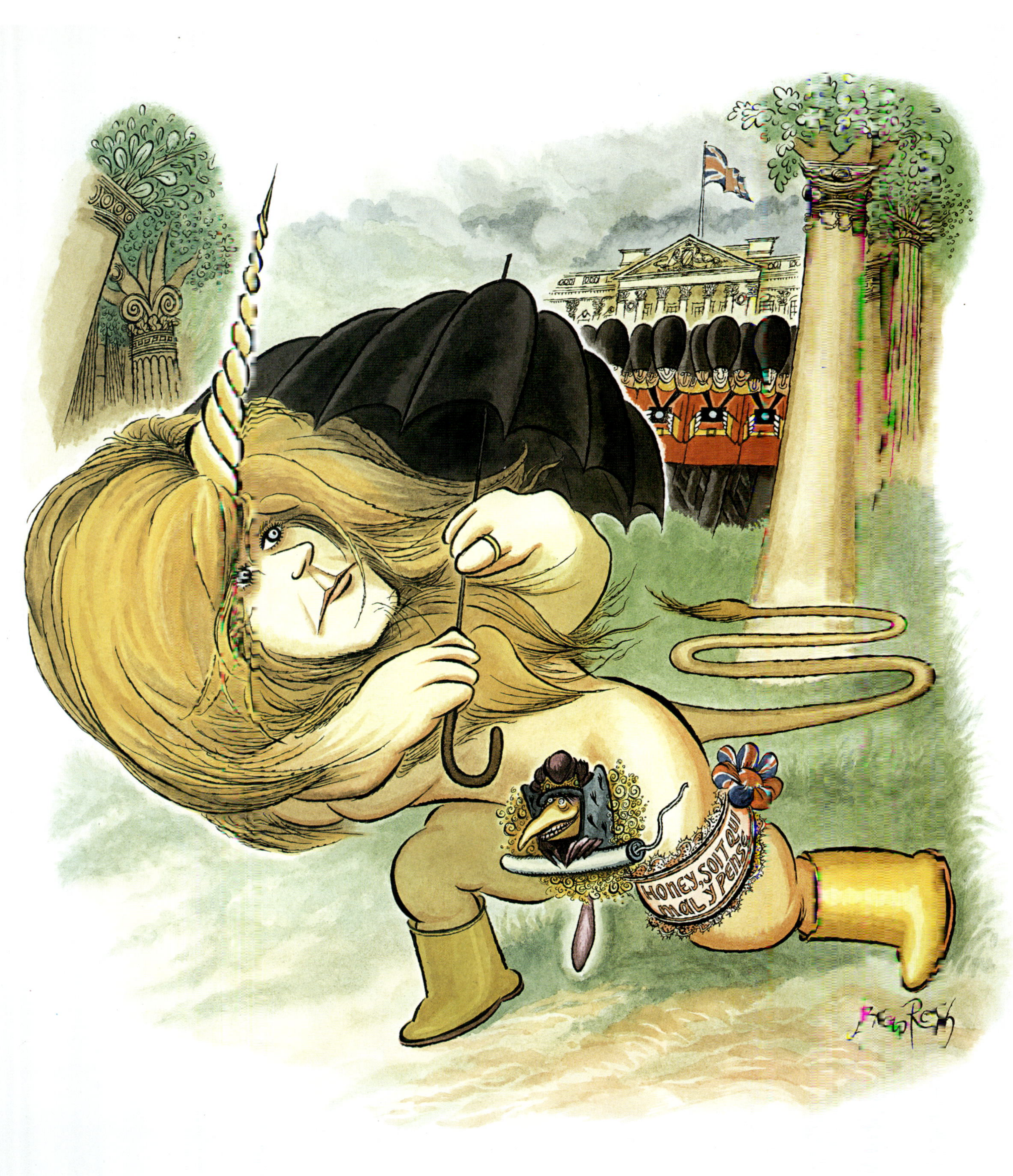

Figure 27
"Camilla Parker Bowles"
Playboy 1997

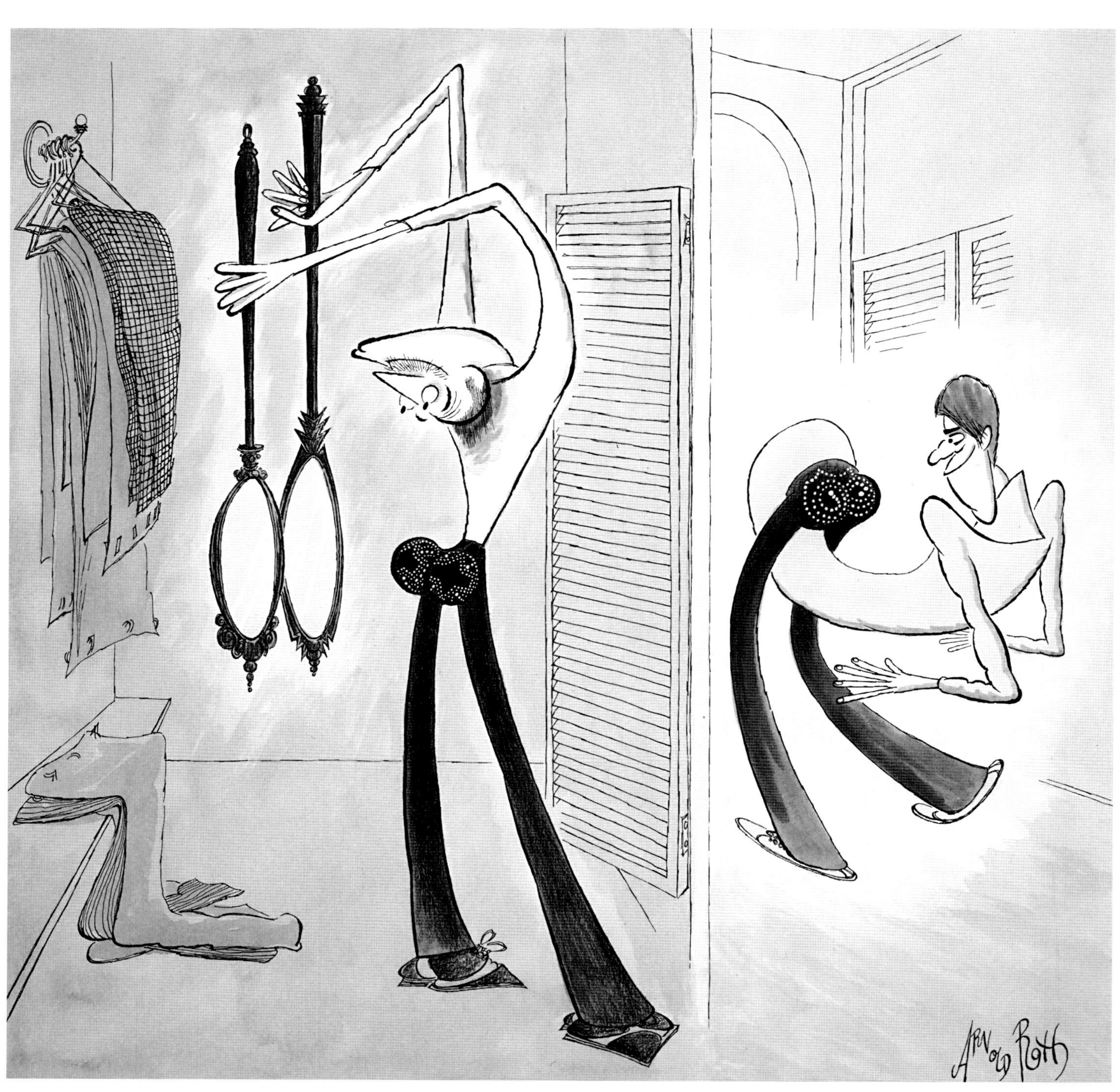

Figure 28
"For Your Two Legs Only"
Esquire 1981

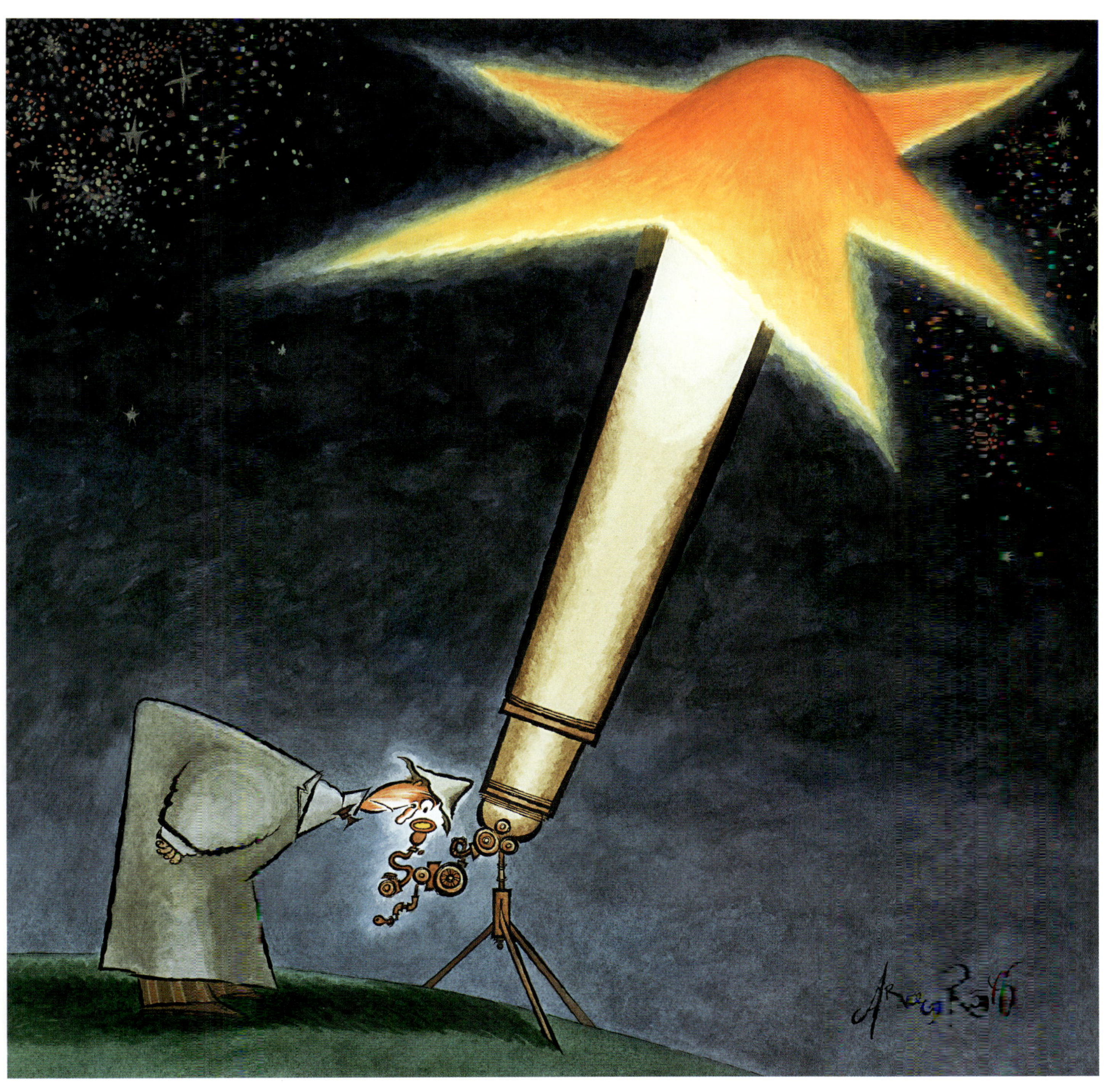

Figure 29
"First Rate Telescopes"
Esquire 1987

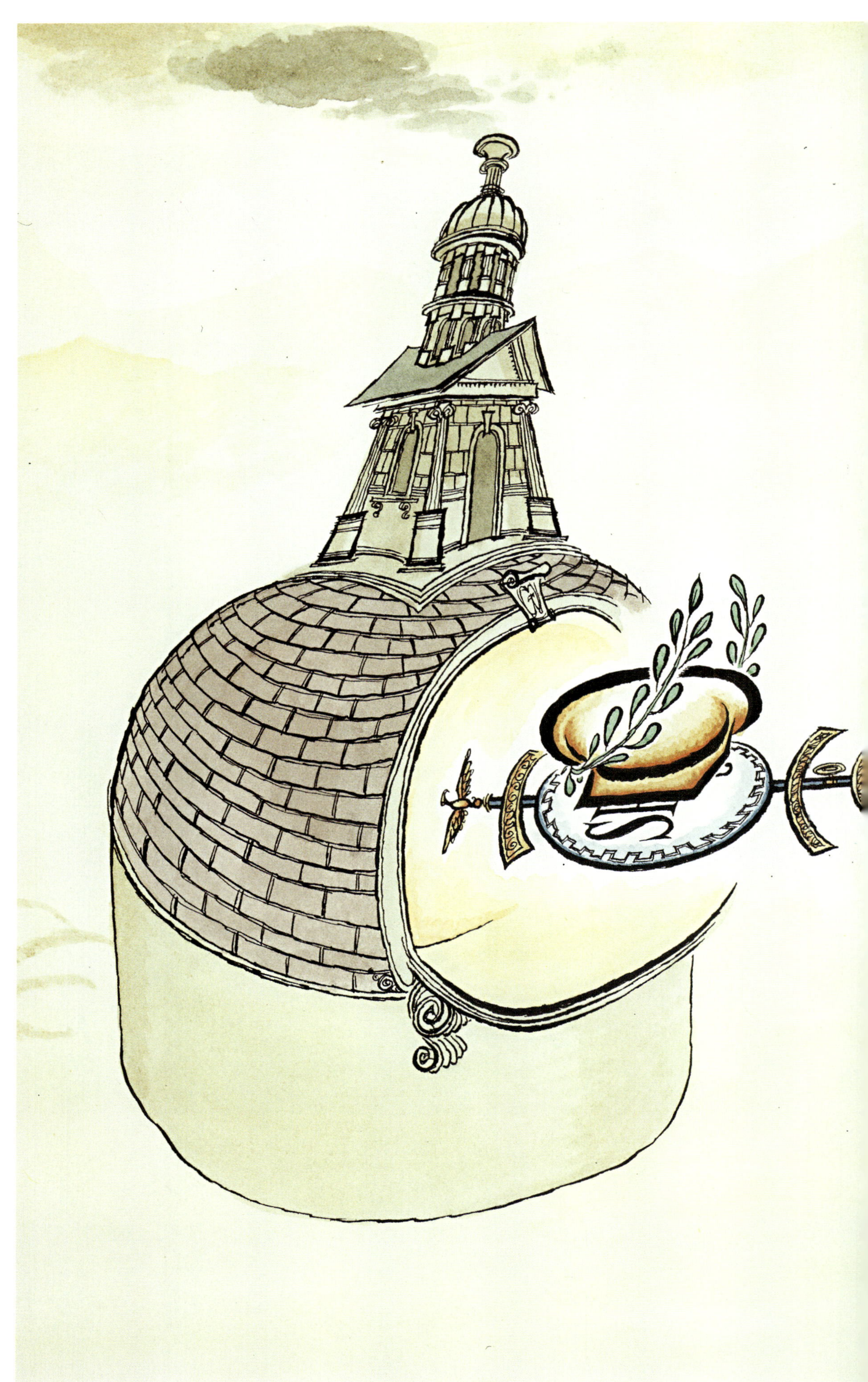

Figure 30
"Seasoned Cook:
Tuscan Bread"
Esquire 1987

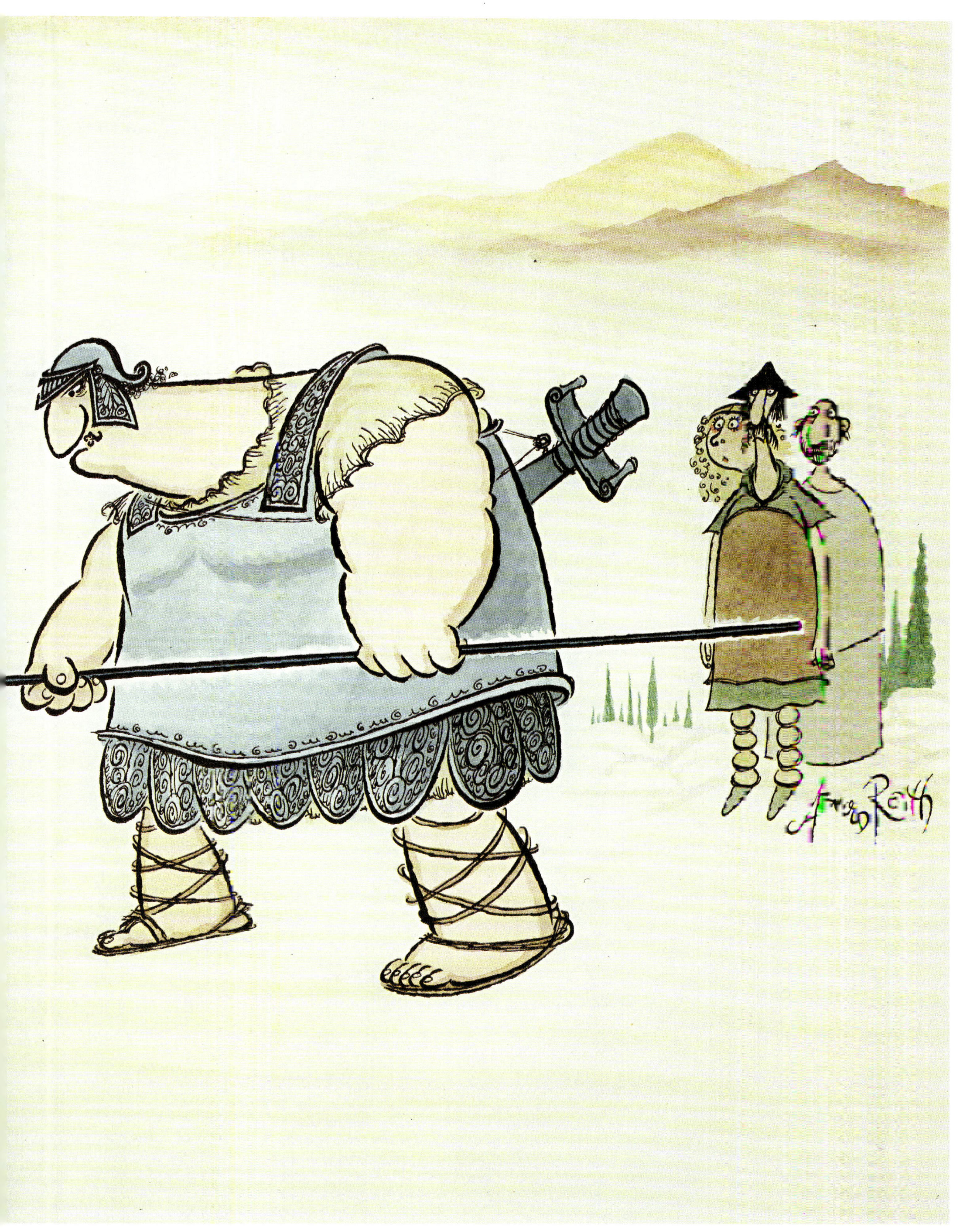

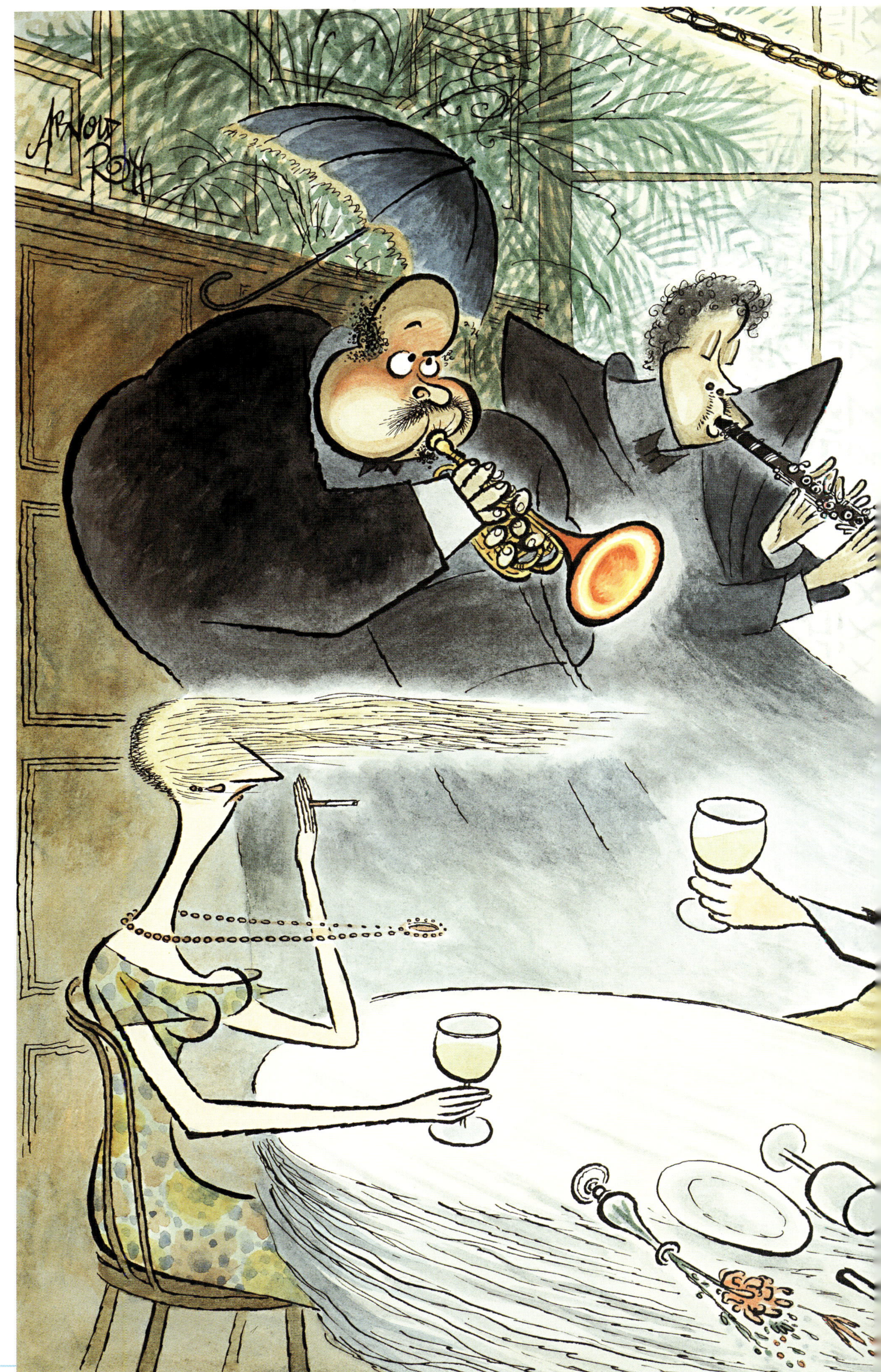

Figure 31
"Seasoned Cook: New Orleans"
Esquire 1985

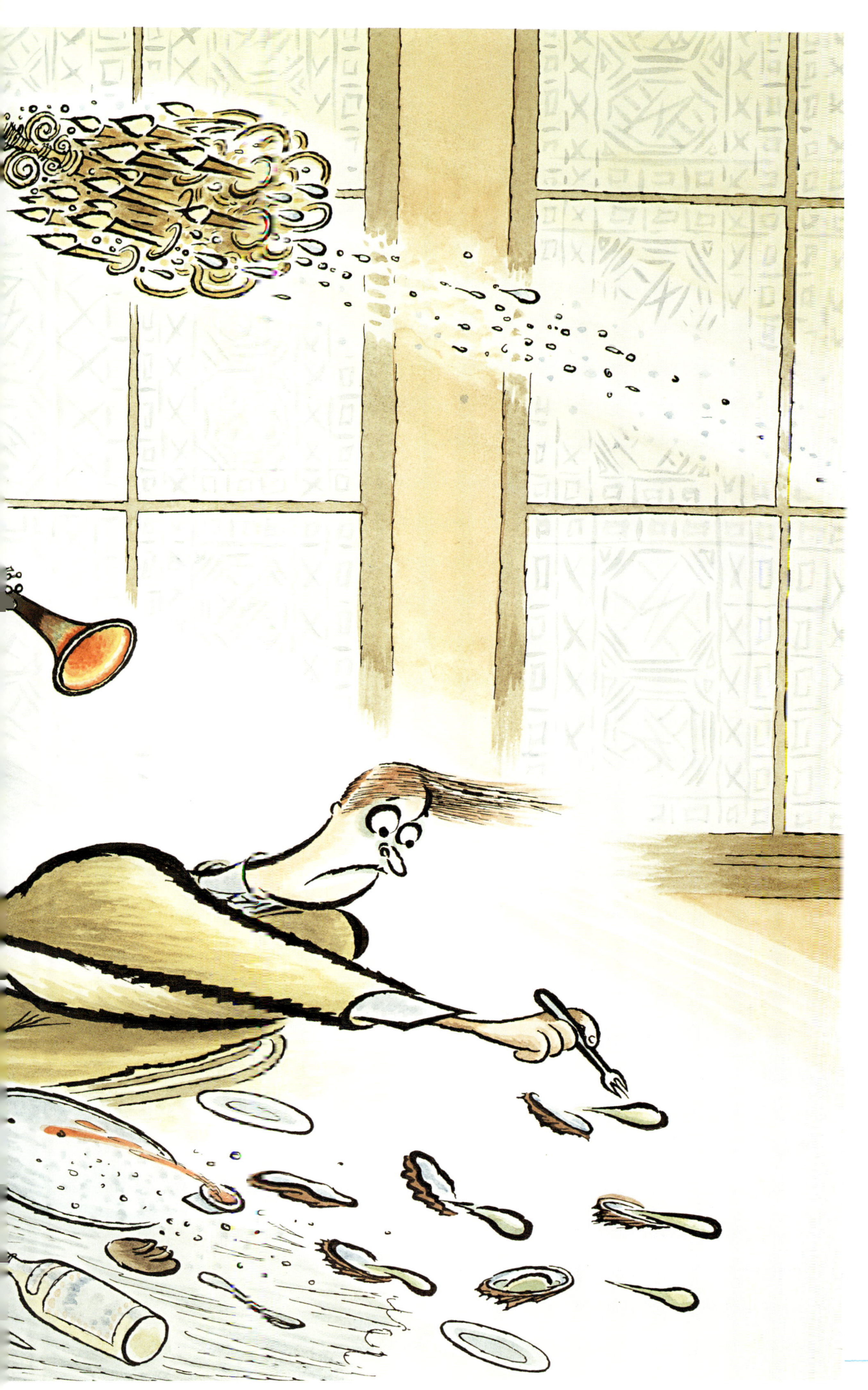

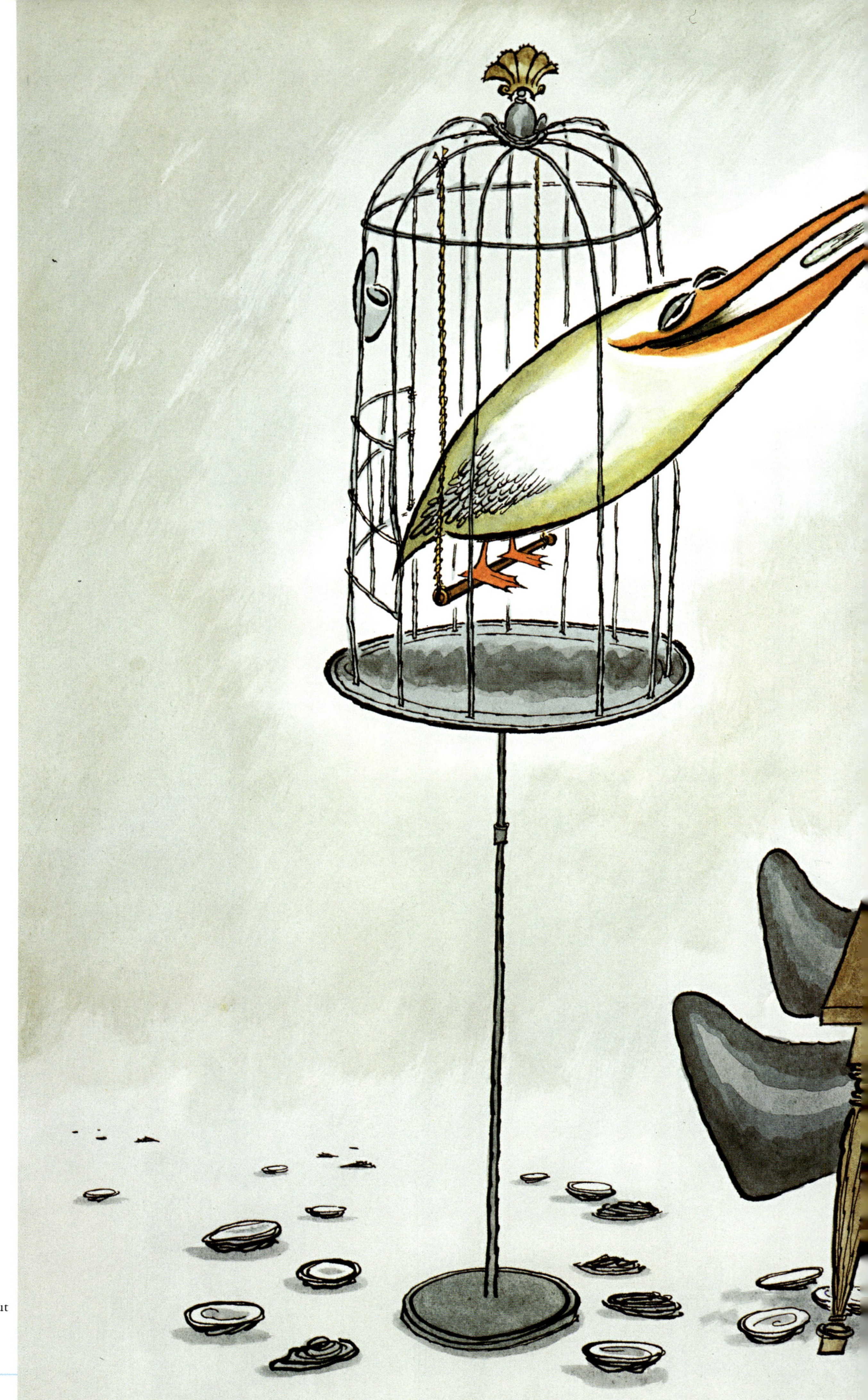

Figure 32
"What Every Man Should Know About Opening Oysters"
Esquire 1983

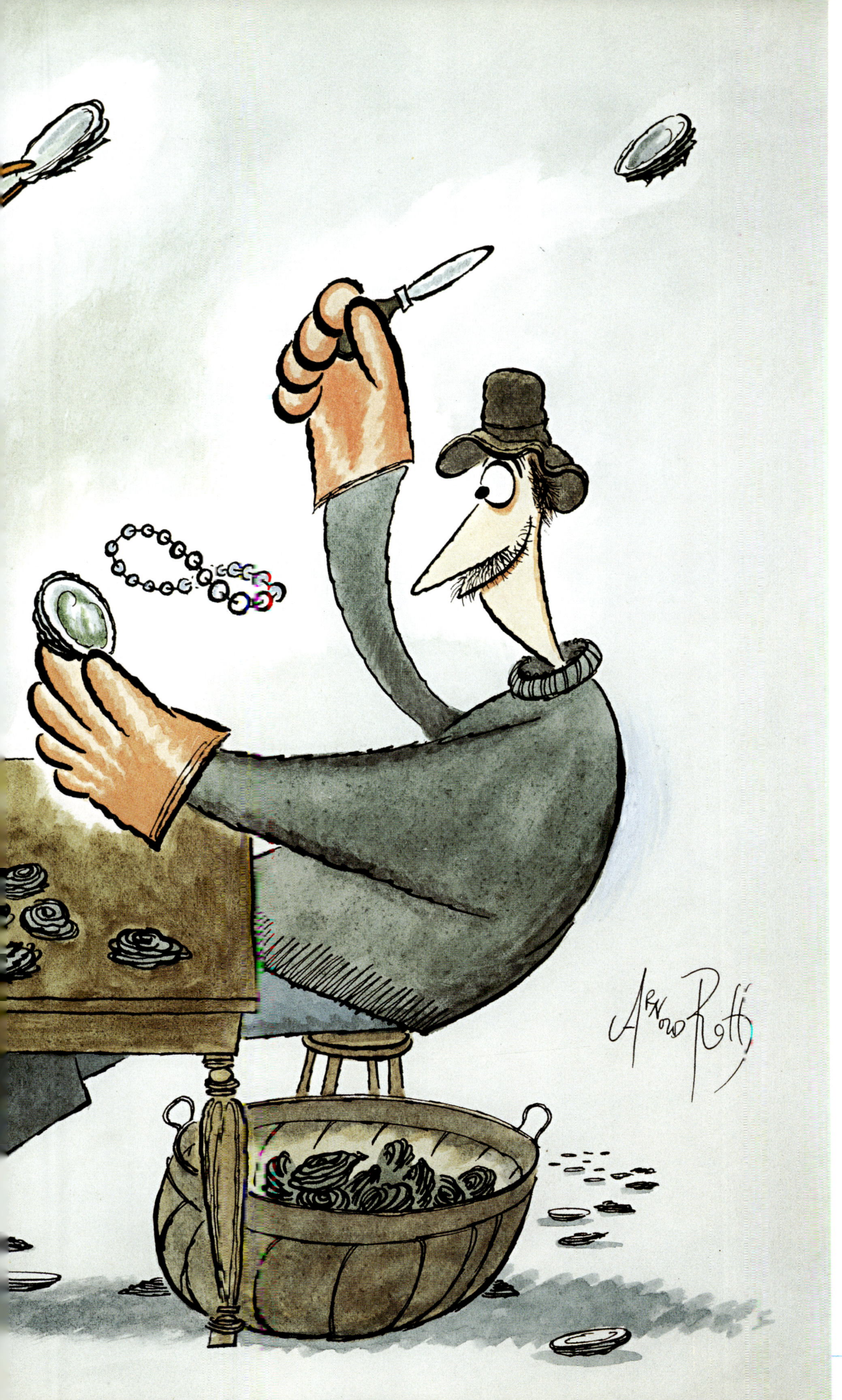

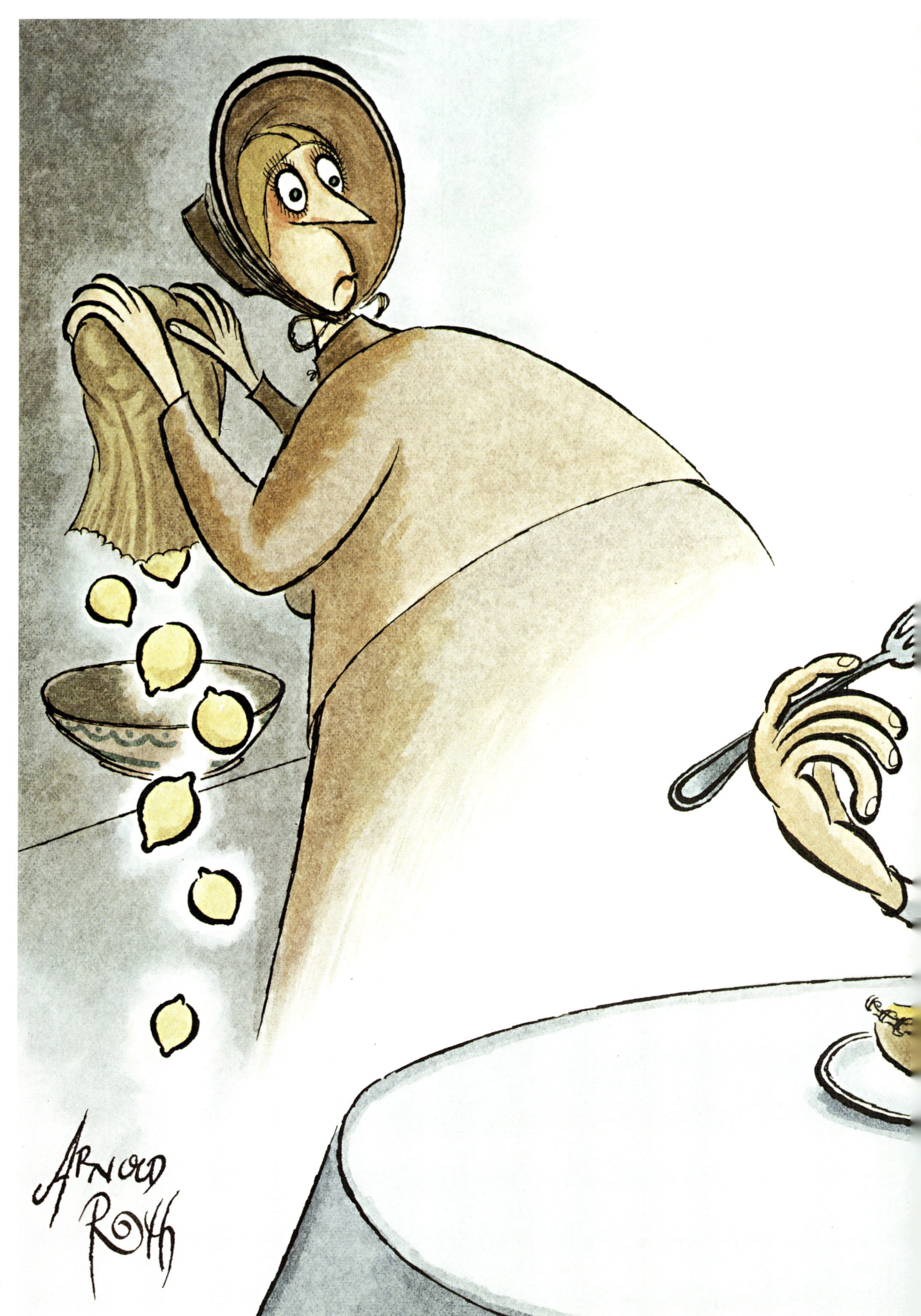

Figure 33
"Seasoned Cook: Lemon Pie"
Esquire 1984

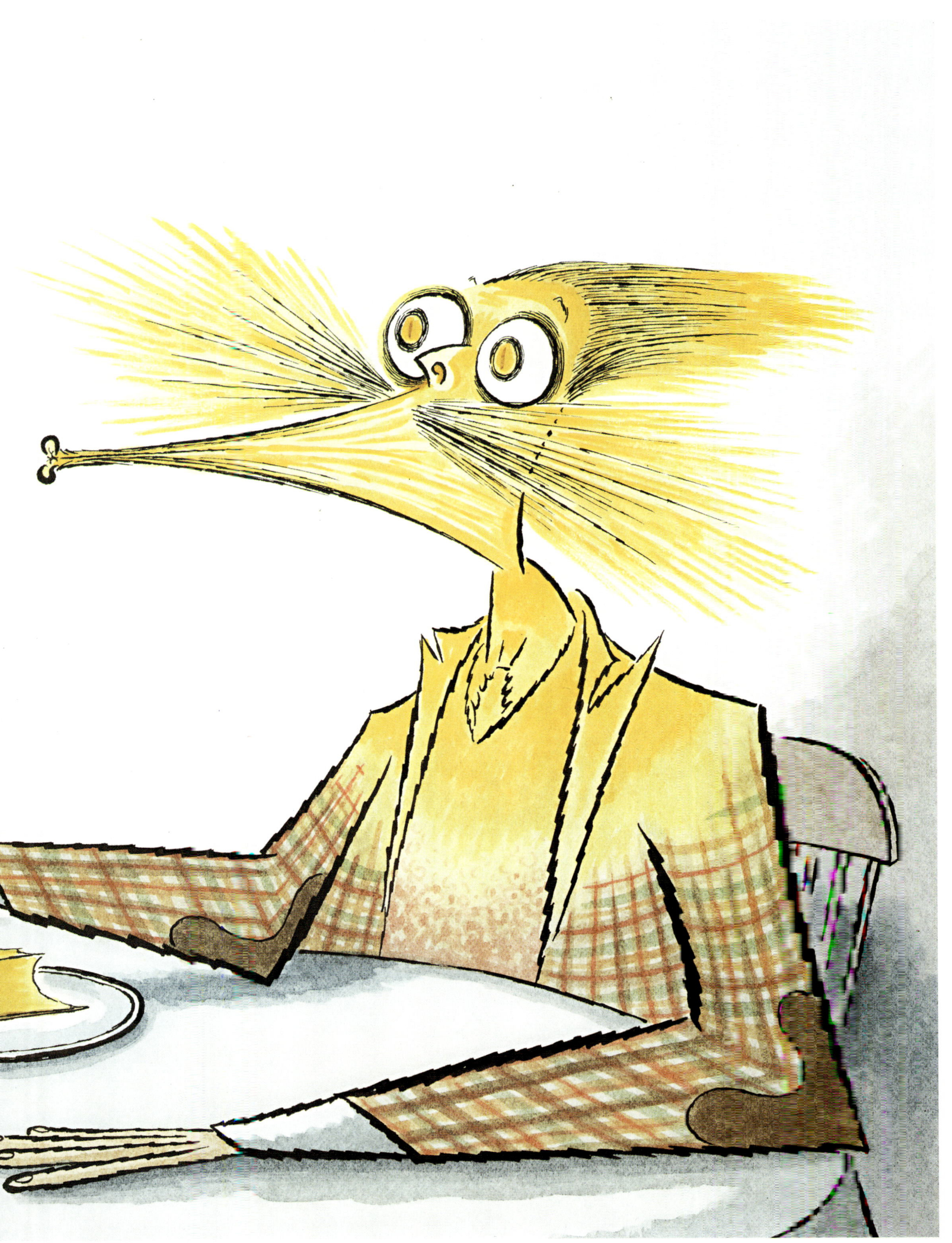

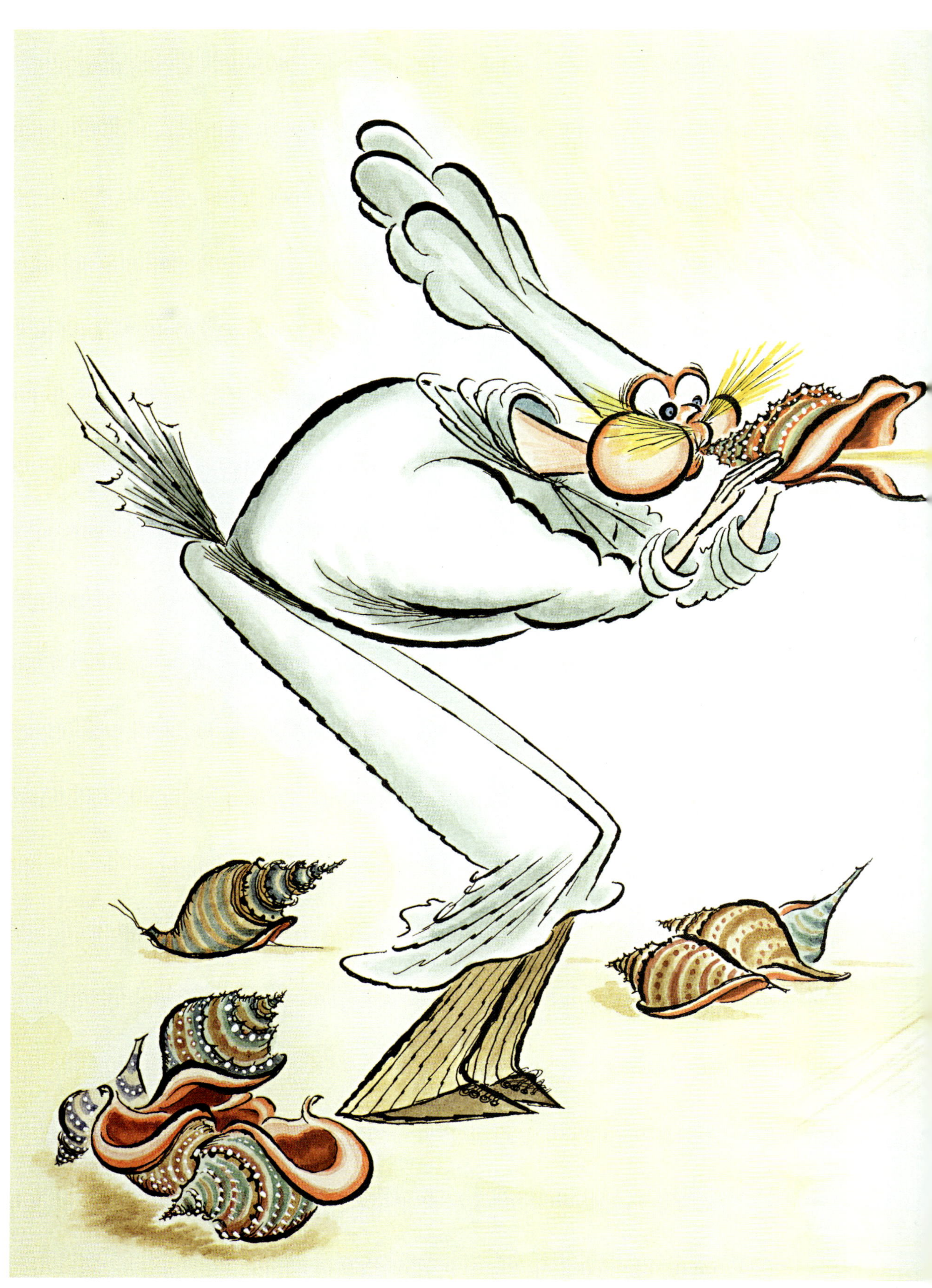

Figure 34
"Seasoned Cook: Conch"
Esquire 1985

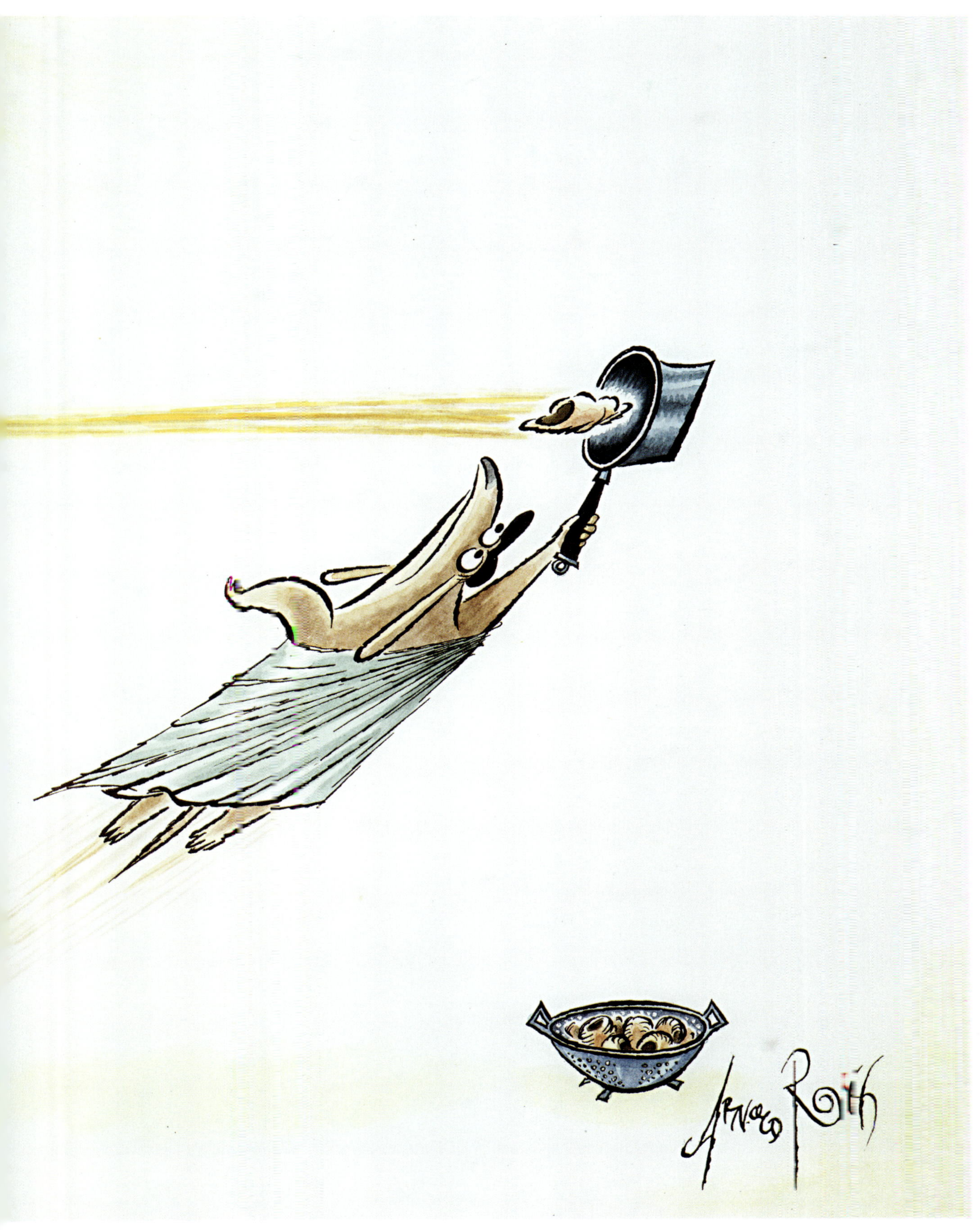
Arnold Roth

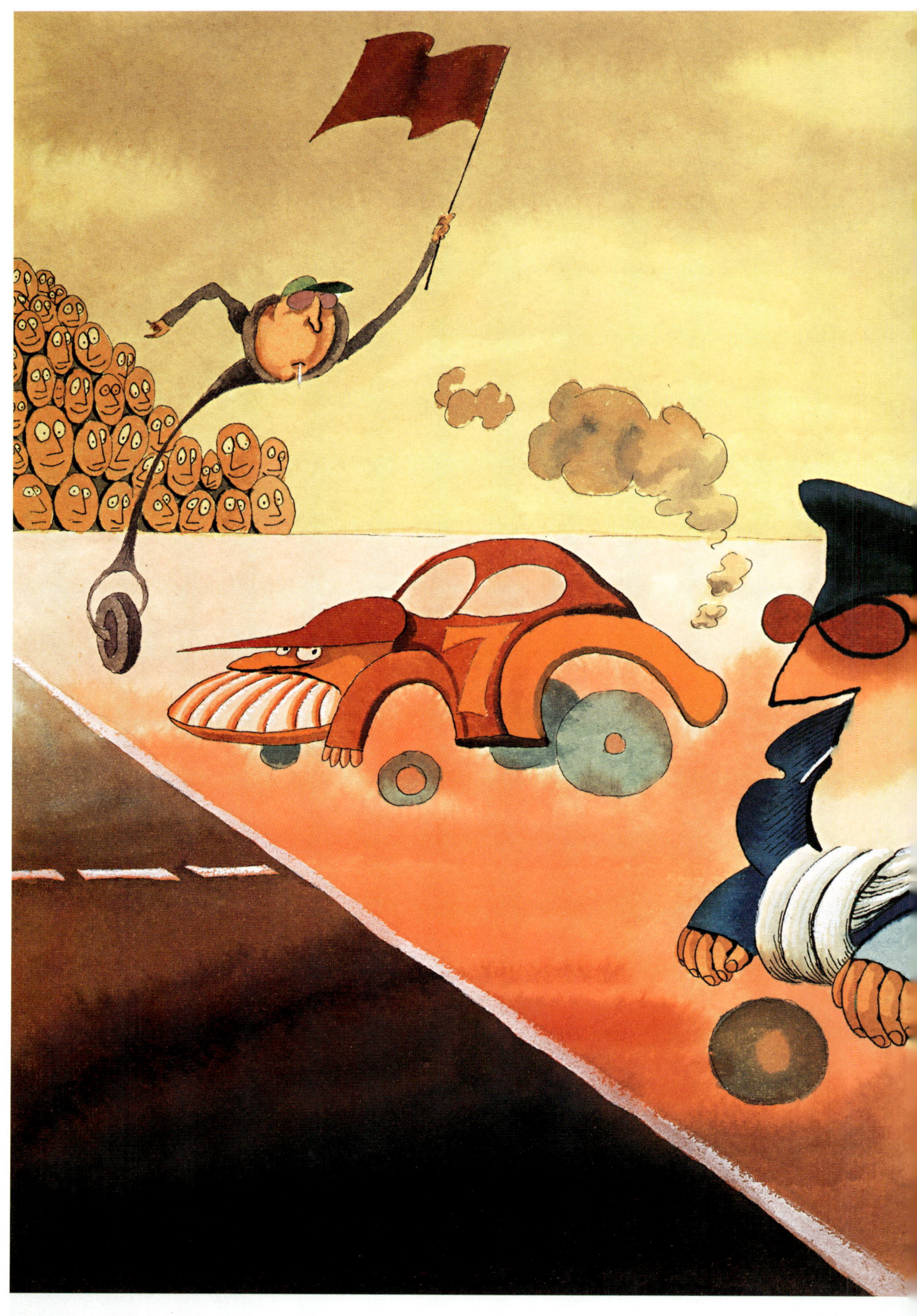

In drag racing the machine is the man and vi
represents an awful lot of ego pla

Figure 35
"In Drag Racing, the Machine Is the Man and Vice Versa"
Sports Illustrated 1968

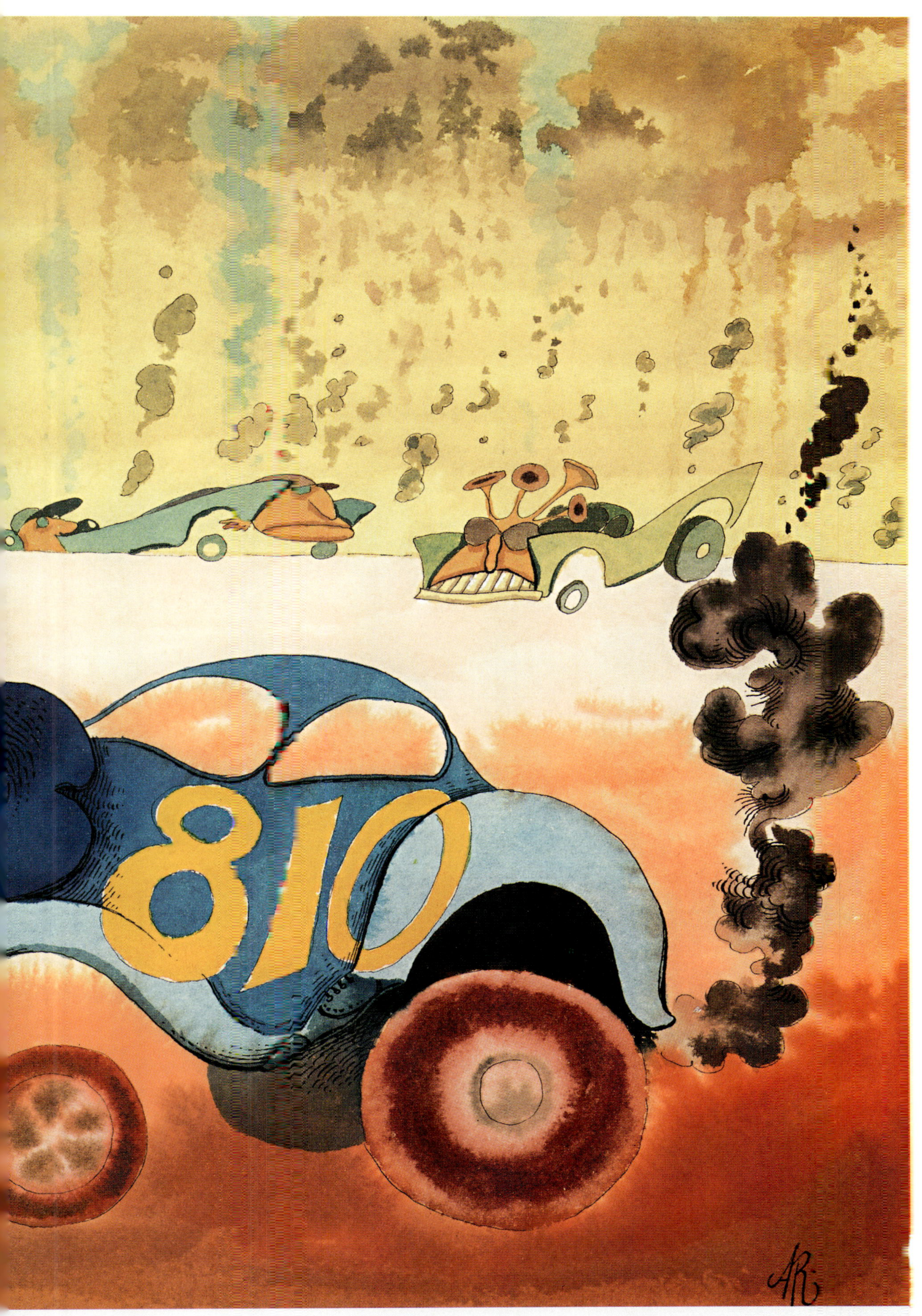

ersa. The ton-pins of powered metal
n the line.

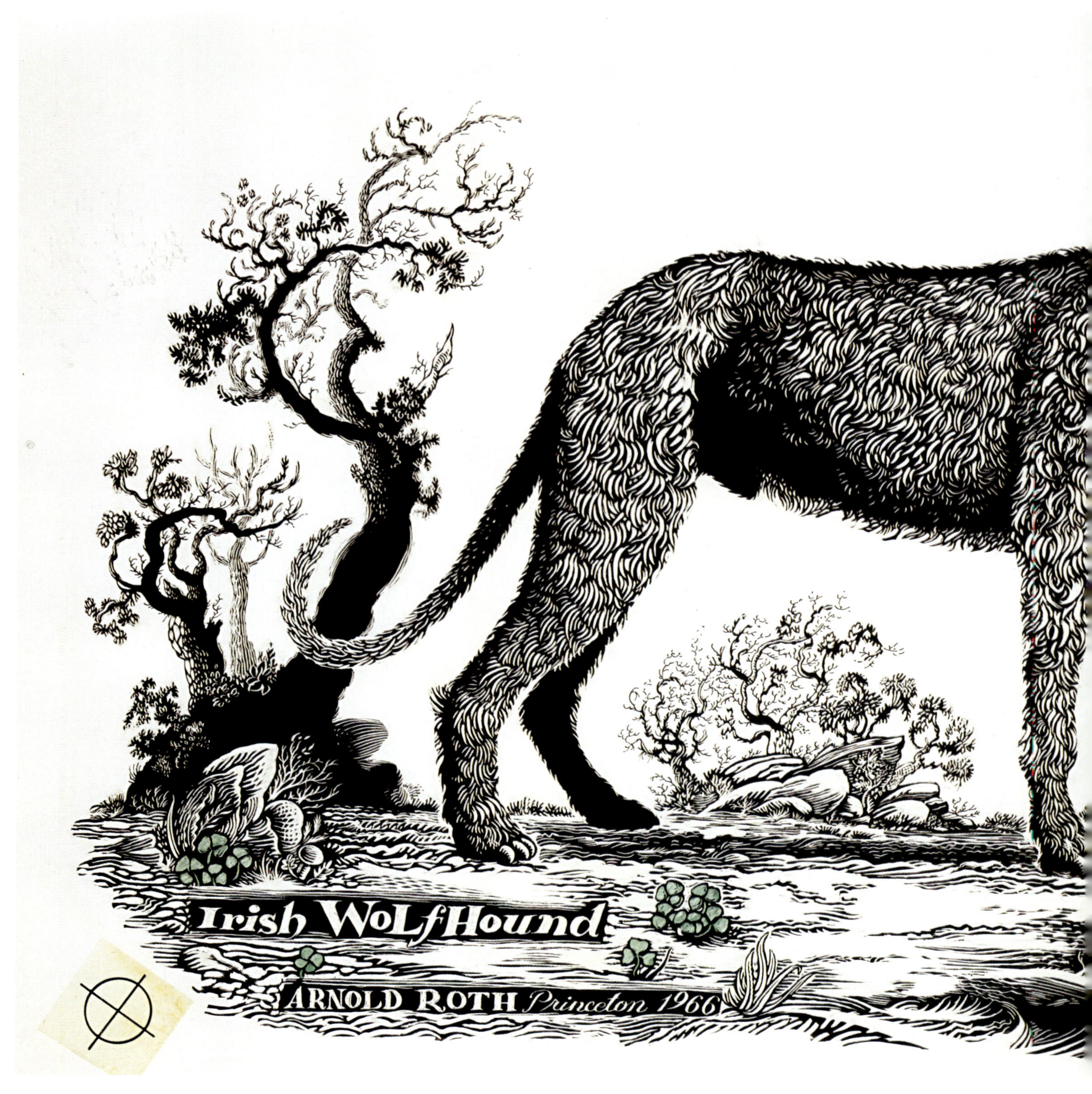

Figure 36
"Irish Wolf Hounds"
Sports Illustrated 1966

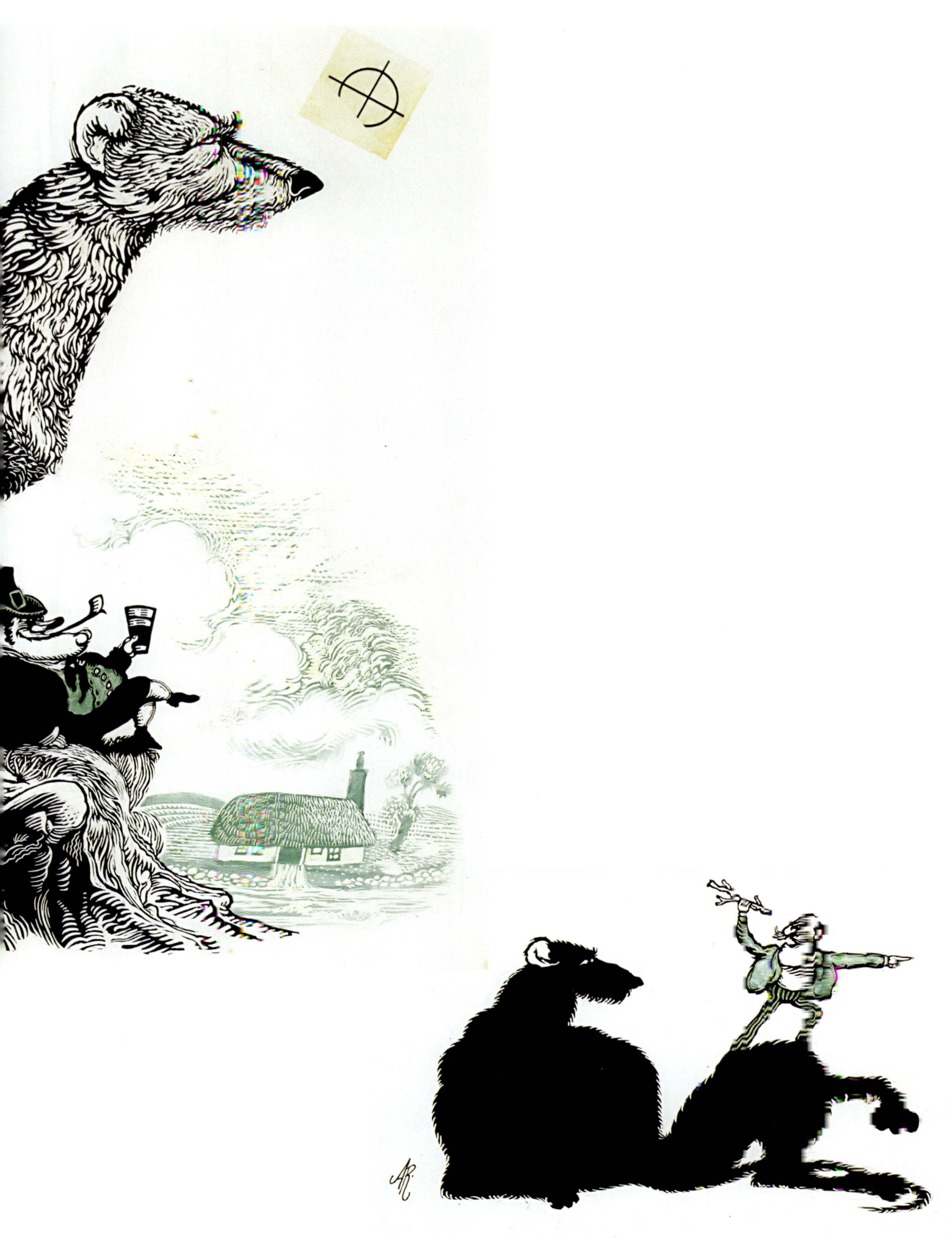

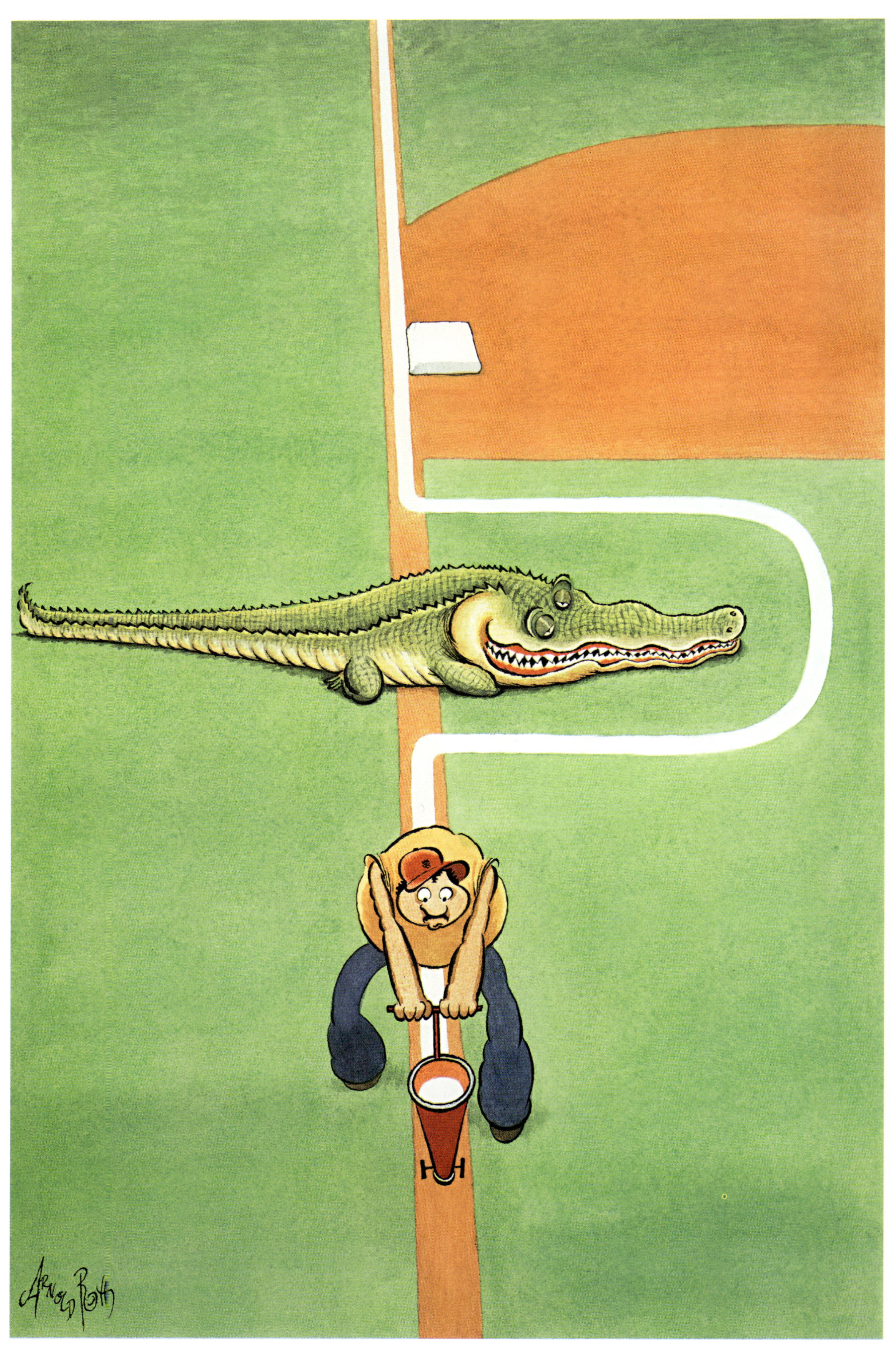

Figure 37
"Spring Training"
Sports Illustrated 1981

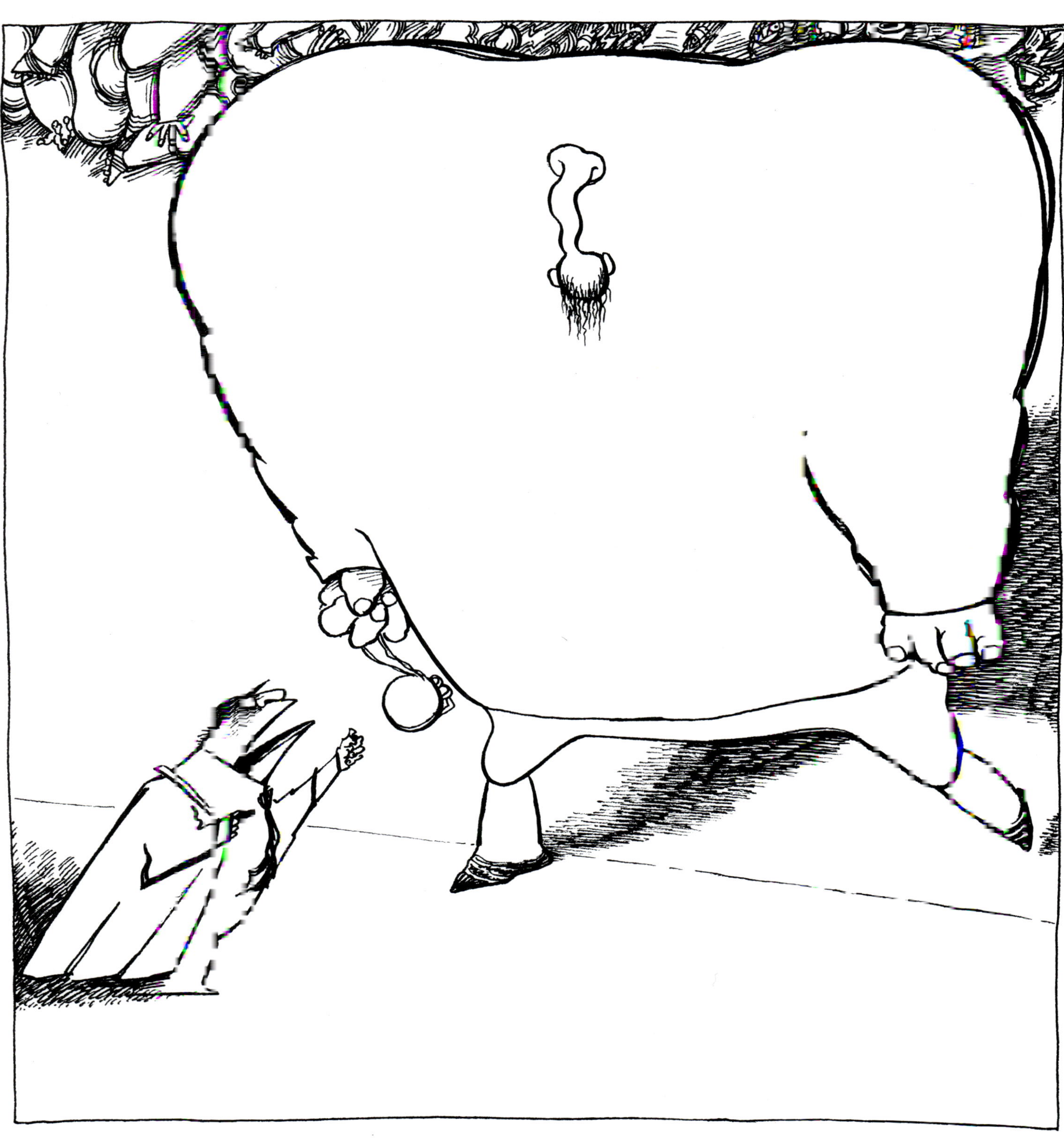

Figure 38
"Coach"
Sports Illustrated

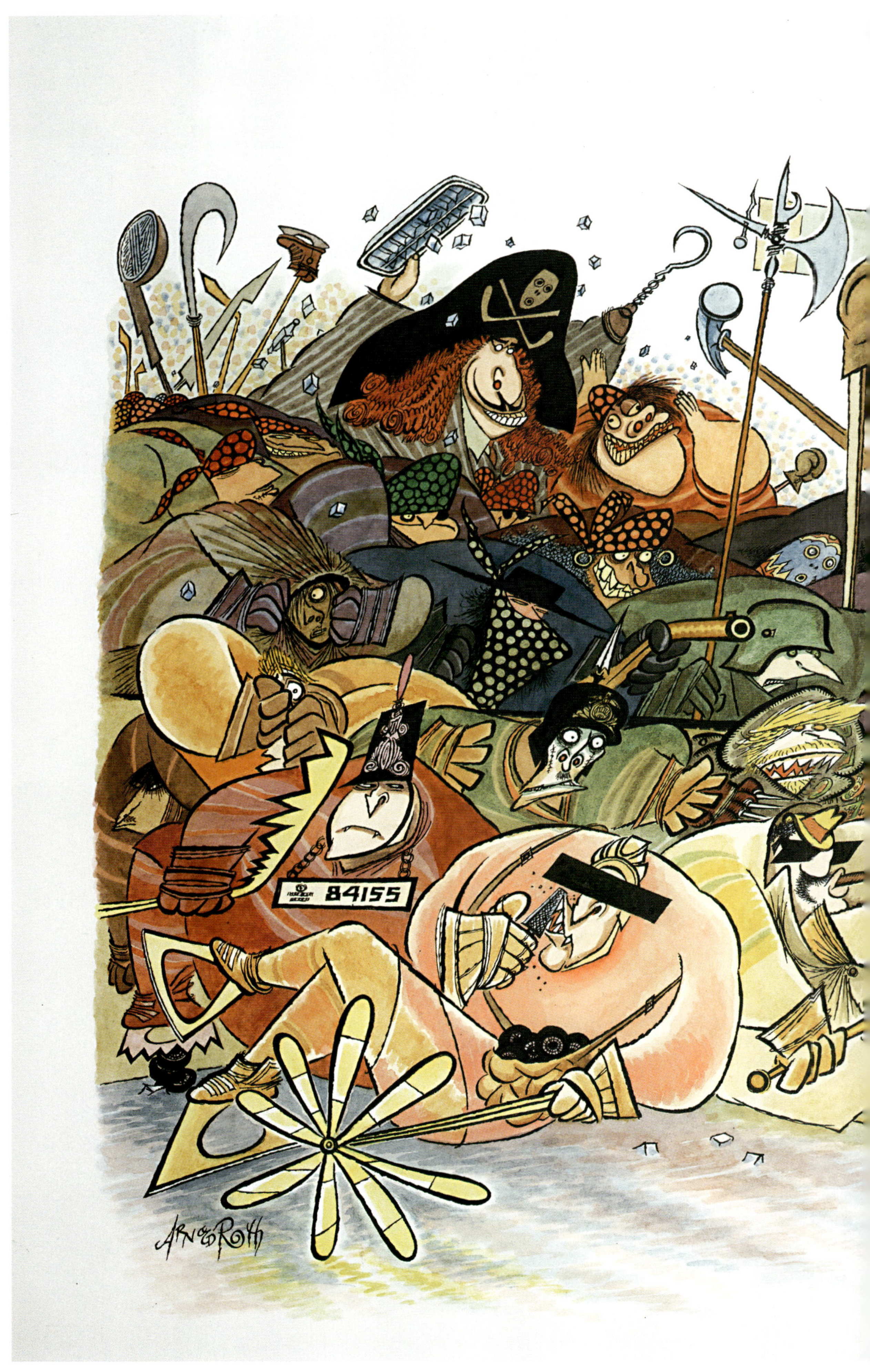

Figure 39
"Hockey Cheats"
Sports Illustrated 2000

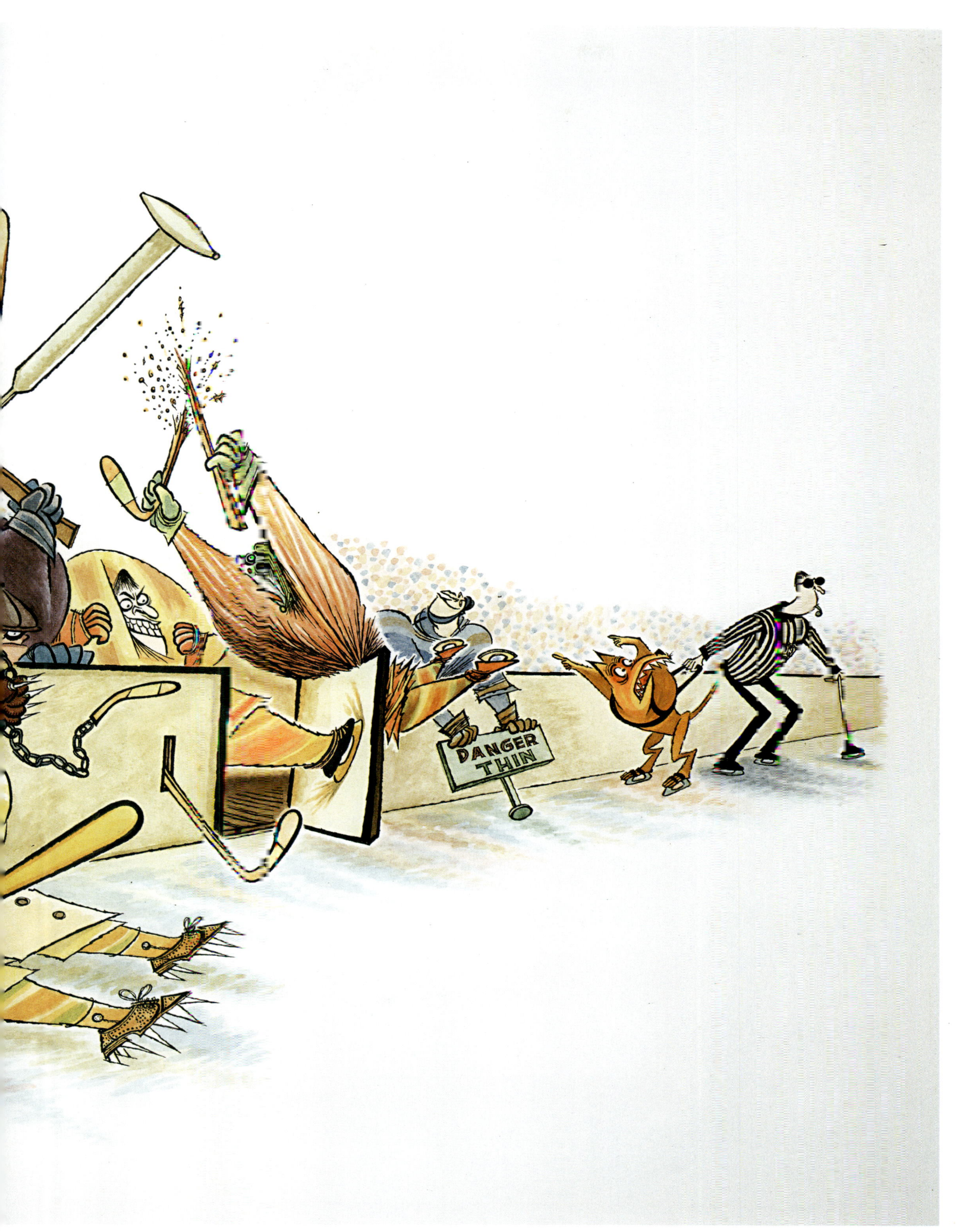

DANGER
THIN

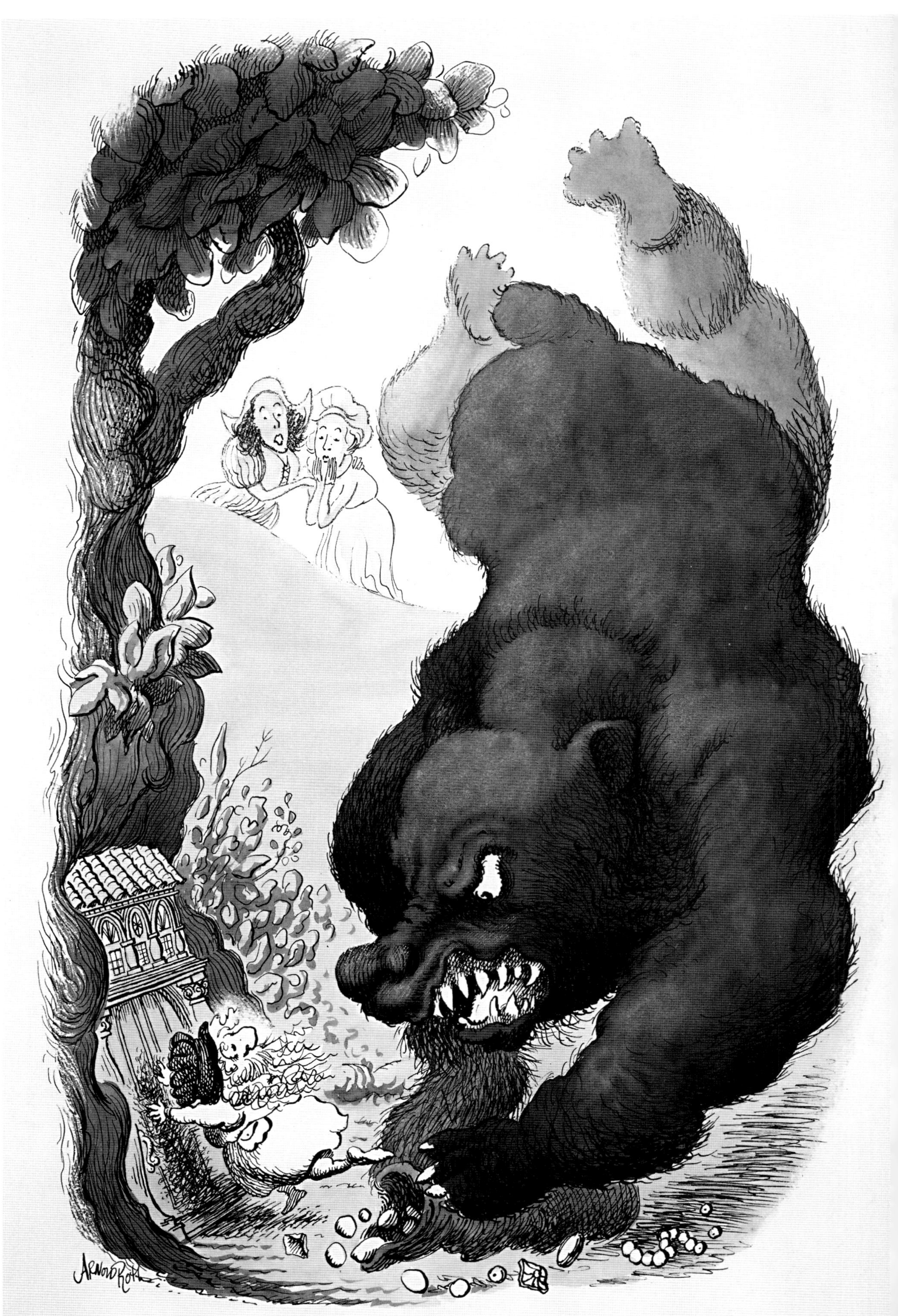

Figure 40
"Snow White & Rose Red"
Grimm's Fairy Tales
1963

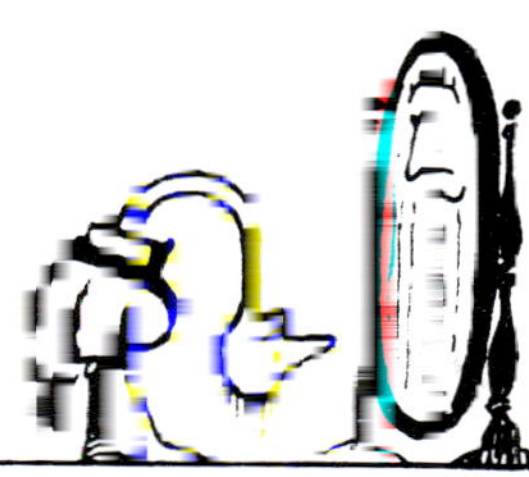

TOPSIDEDOWNSIDEUP PICTURES

Does it really matter whether these pictures are right side up or

upside down?

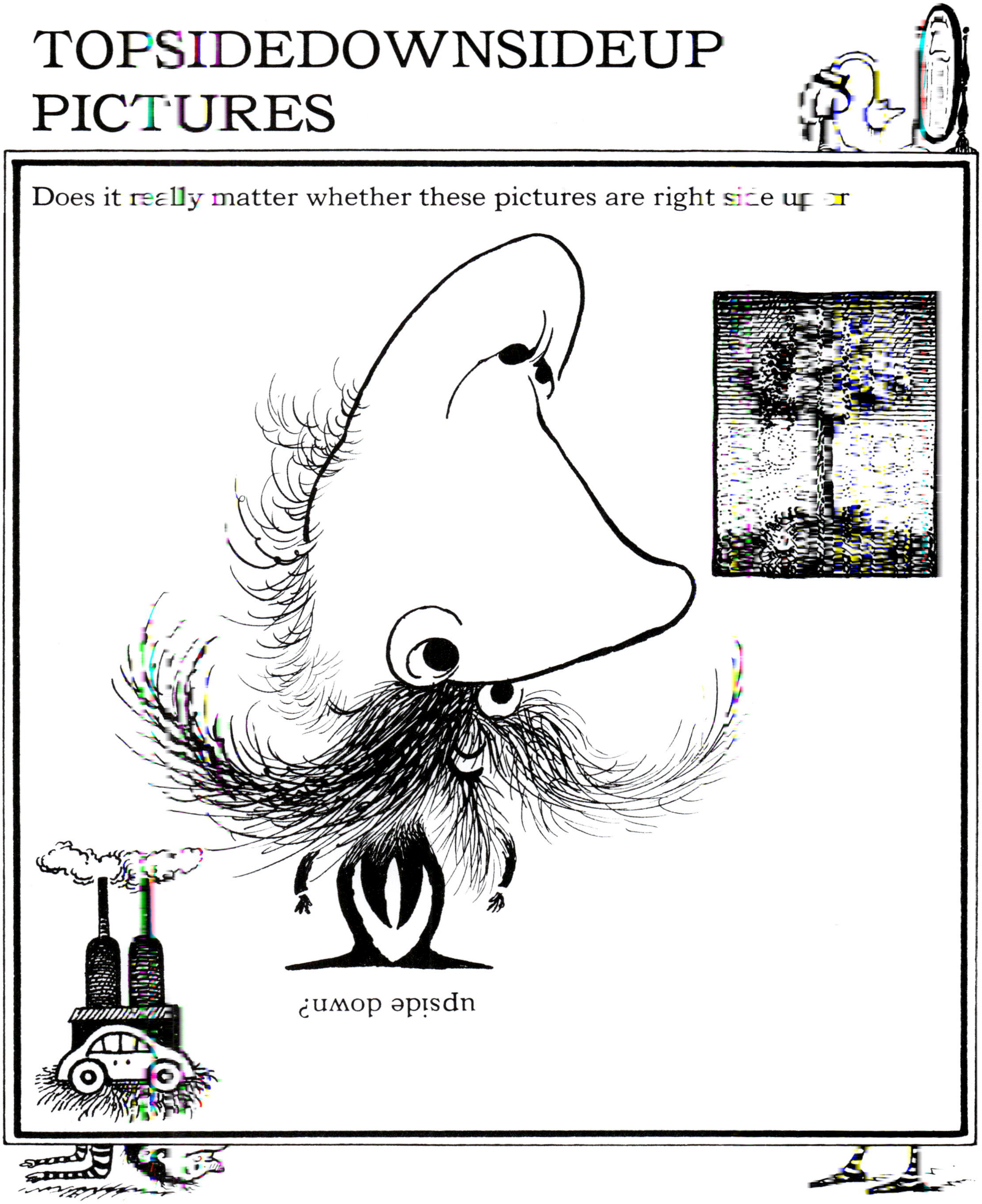

Figure 41
"Topsidedownside Up Pictures"
Pick a Peck of Puzzles 1966

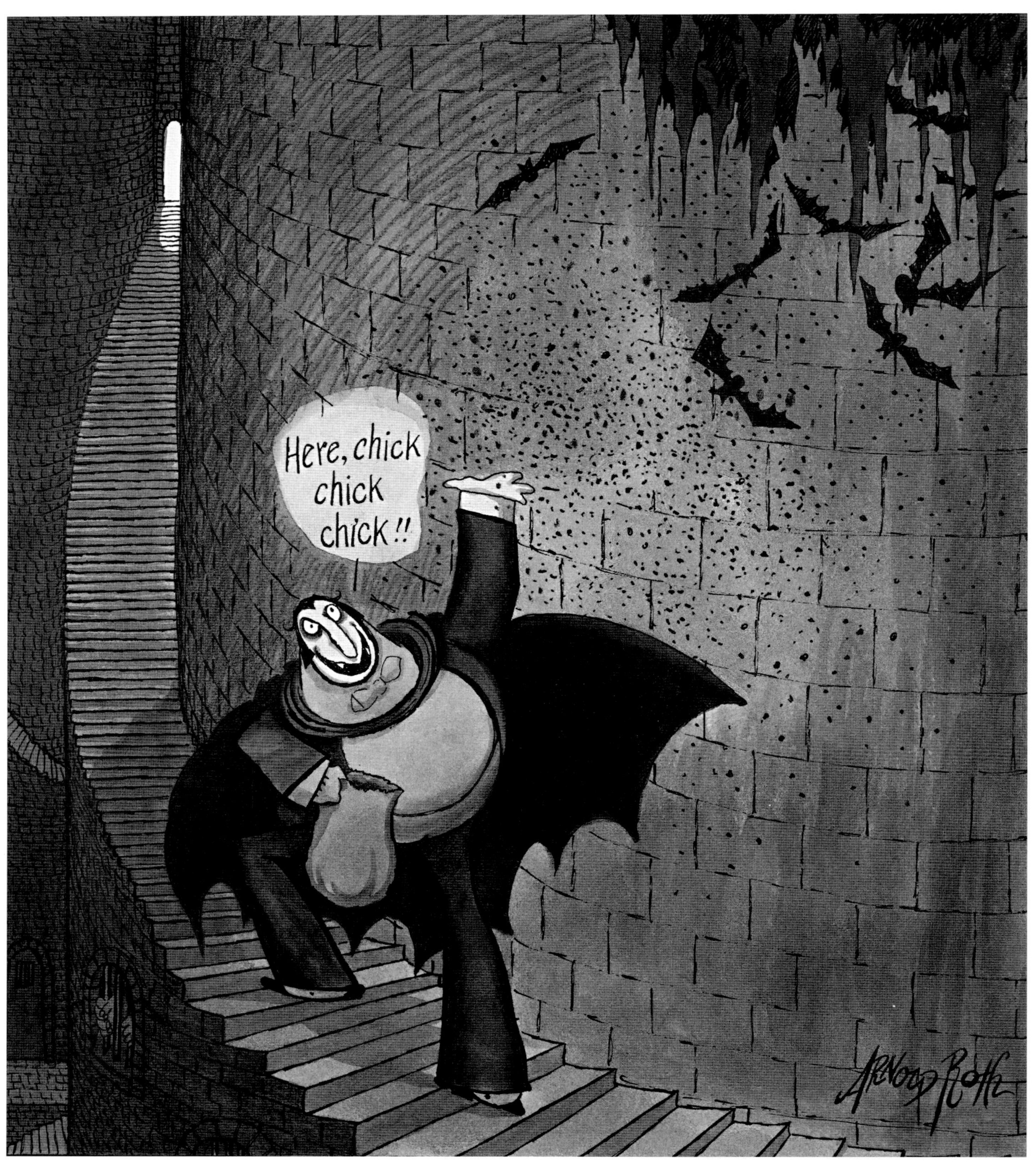

Figure 42
"There Will Always Be Individual Preferences"
Comick Book of Pets 1976

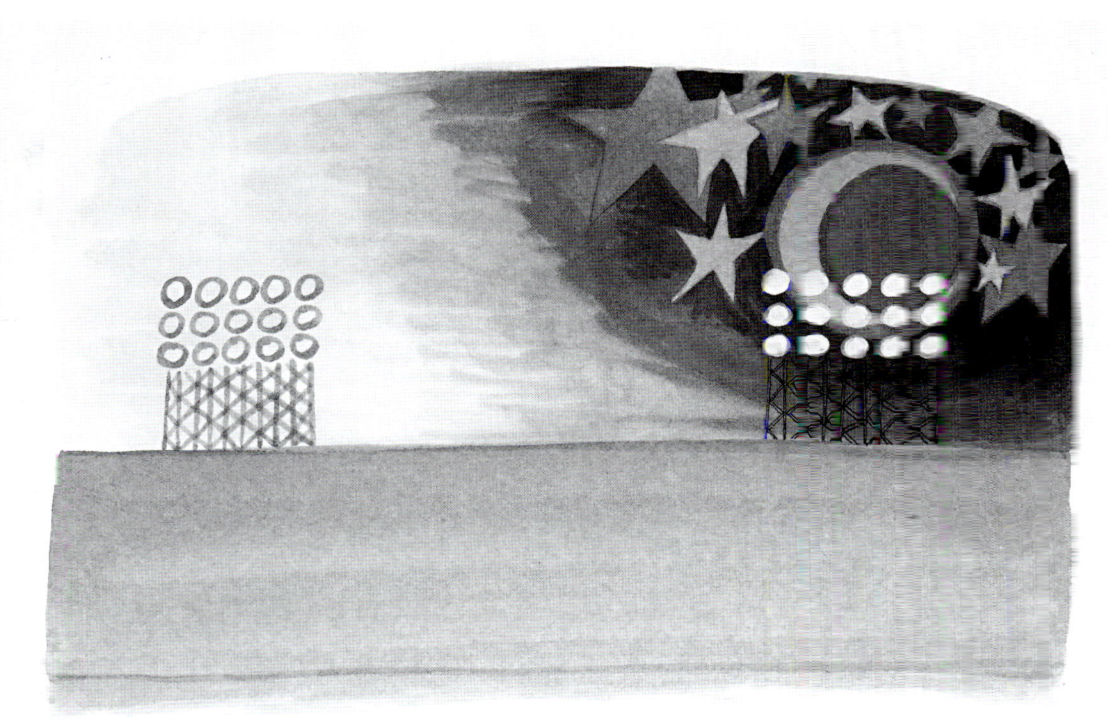

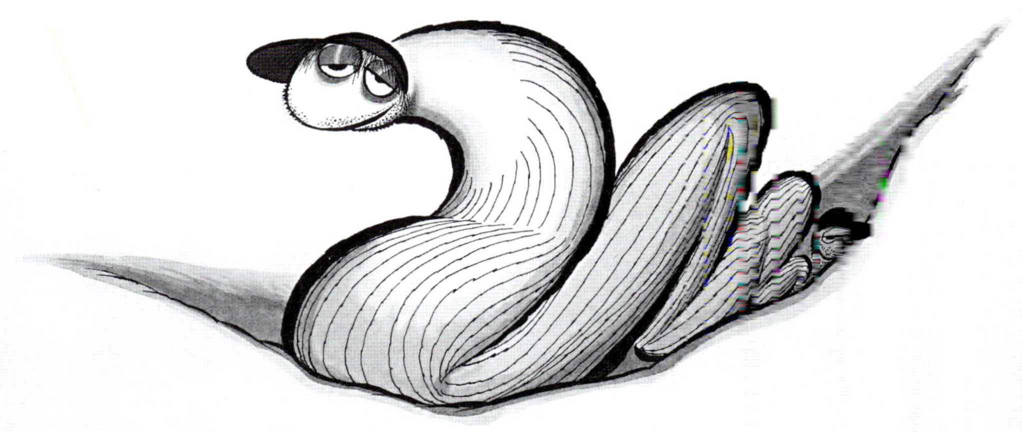

Figure 43
"Twi-Night Double Header"
A Sports Bestiary
1982

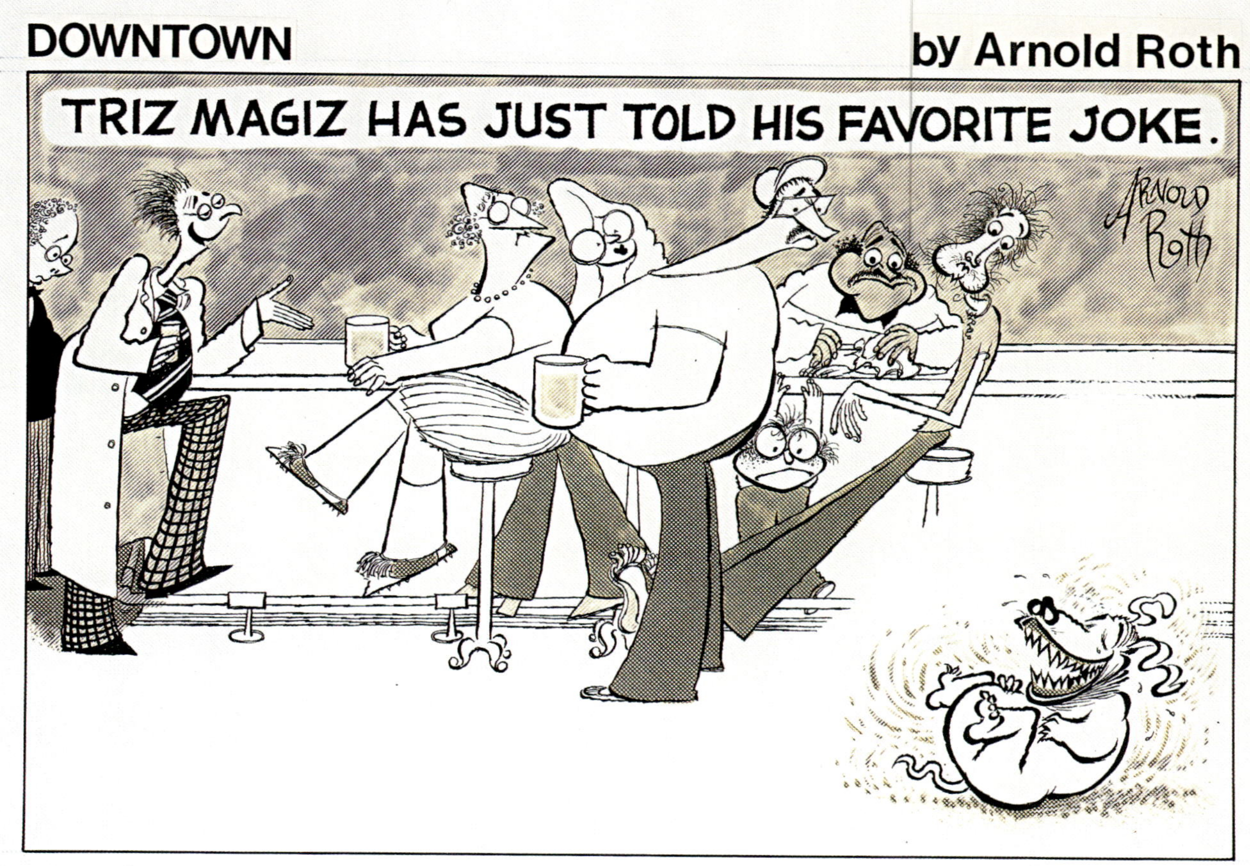

DOWNTOWN

by Arnold Roth

READY! GET SET! **GO!** ...AND THIS IS THE **LAST** GARGLE CONTEST I'M JUDGING!

ARNOLD Roth

Figure 44
"Downtown"
Murdoch News Features
unpublished
1978

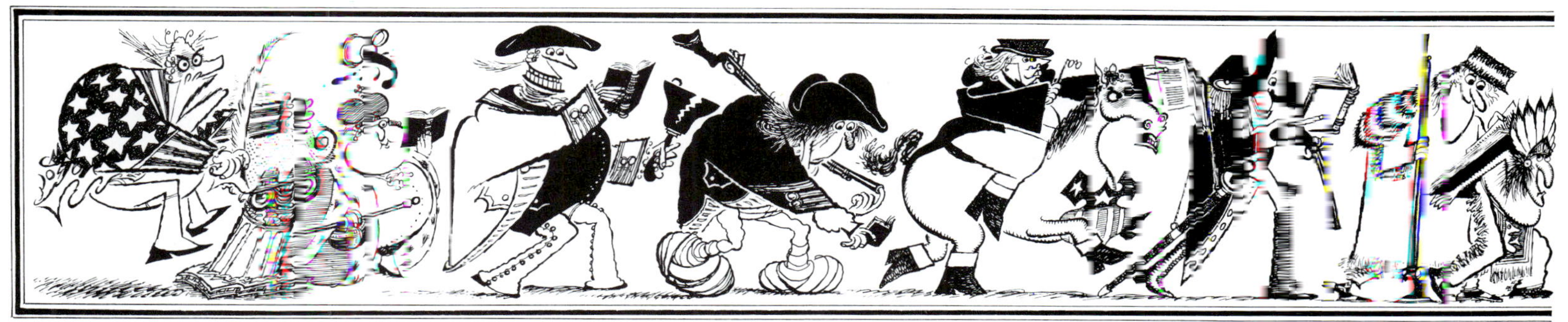

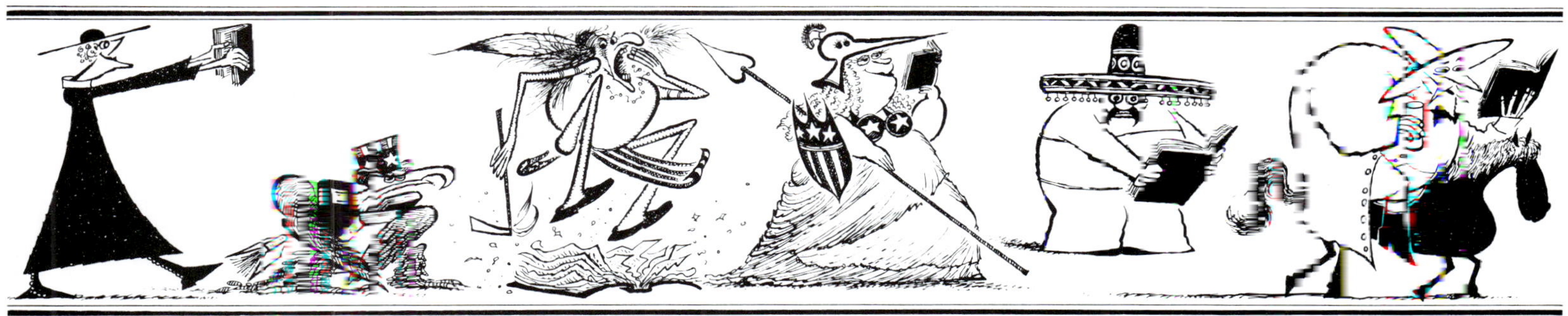

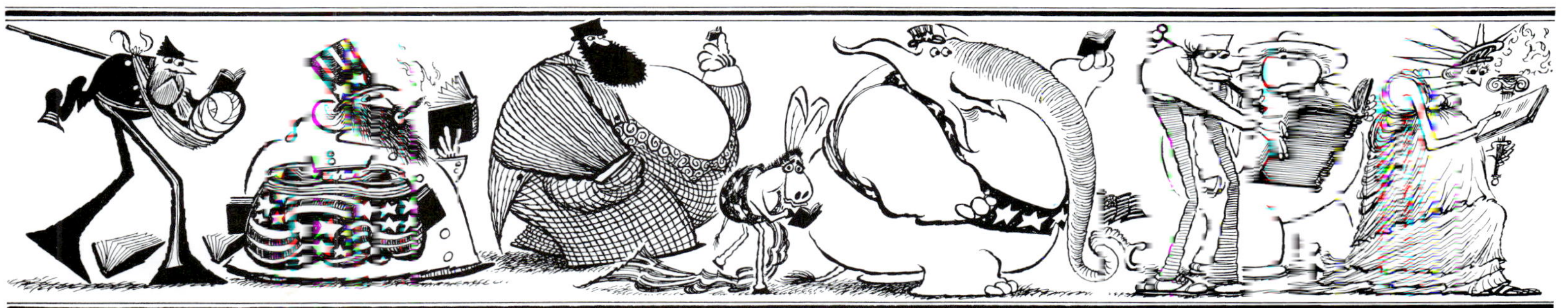

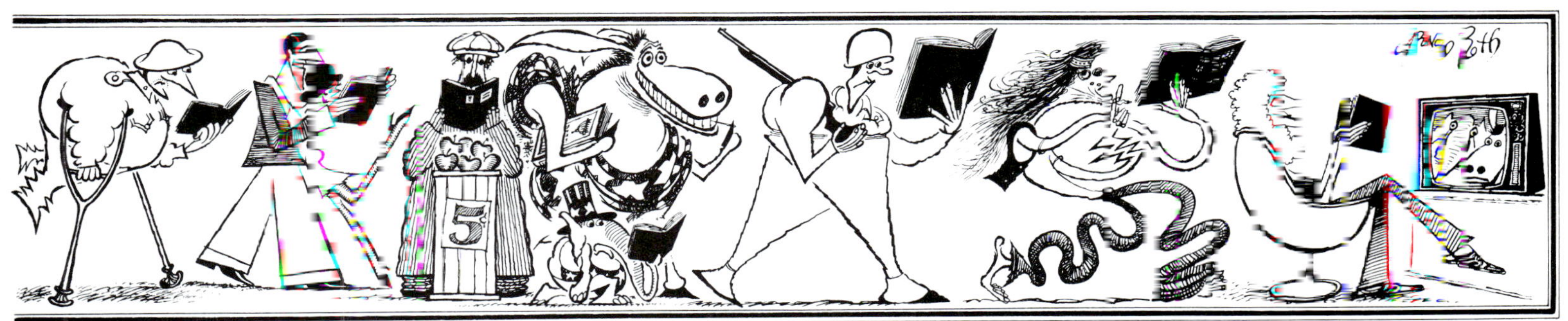

Figure 45
"History of Reading"
The New York Times Book Review 1980

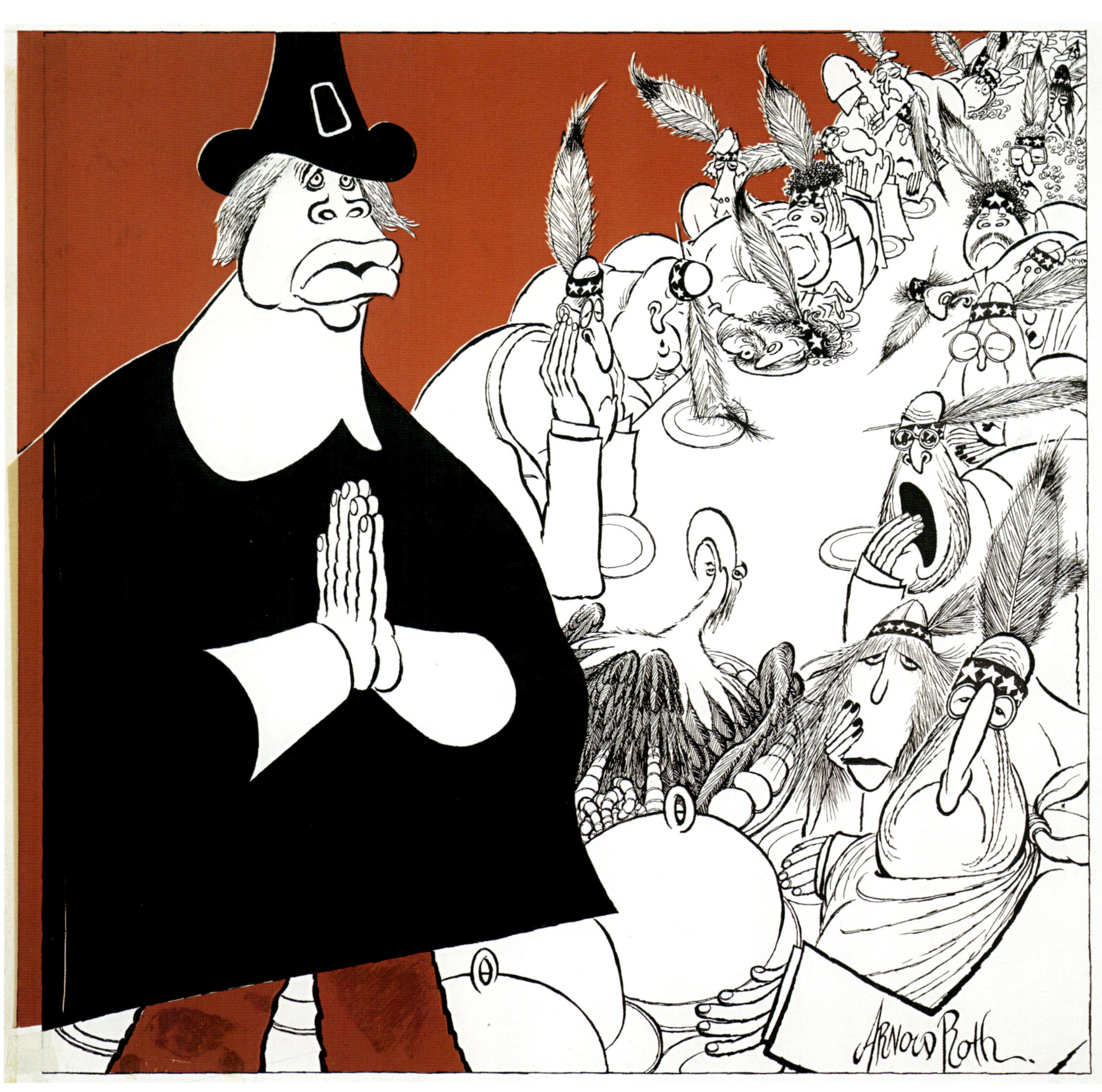

Figure 46
"Jimmy Carter's First Thanksgiving"
Politicks 1977

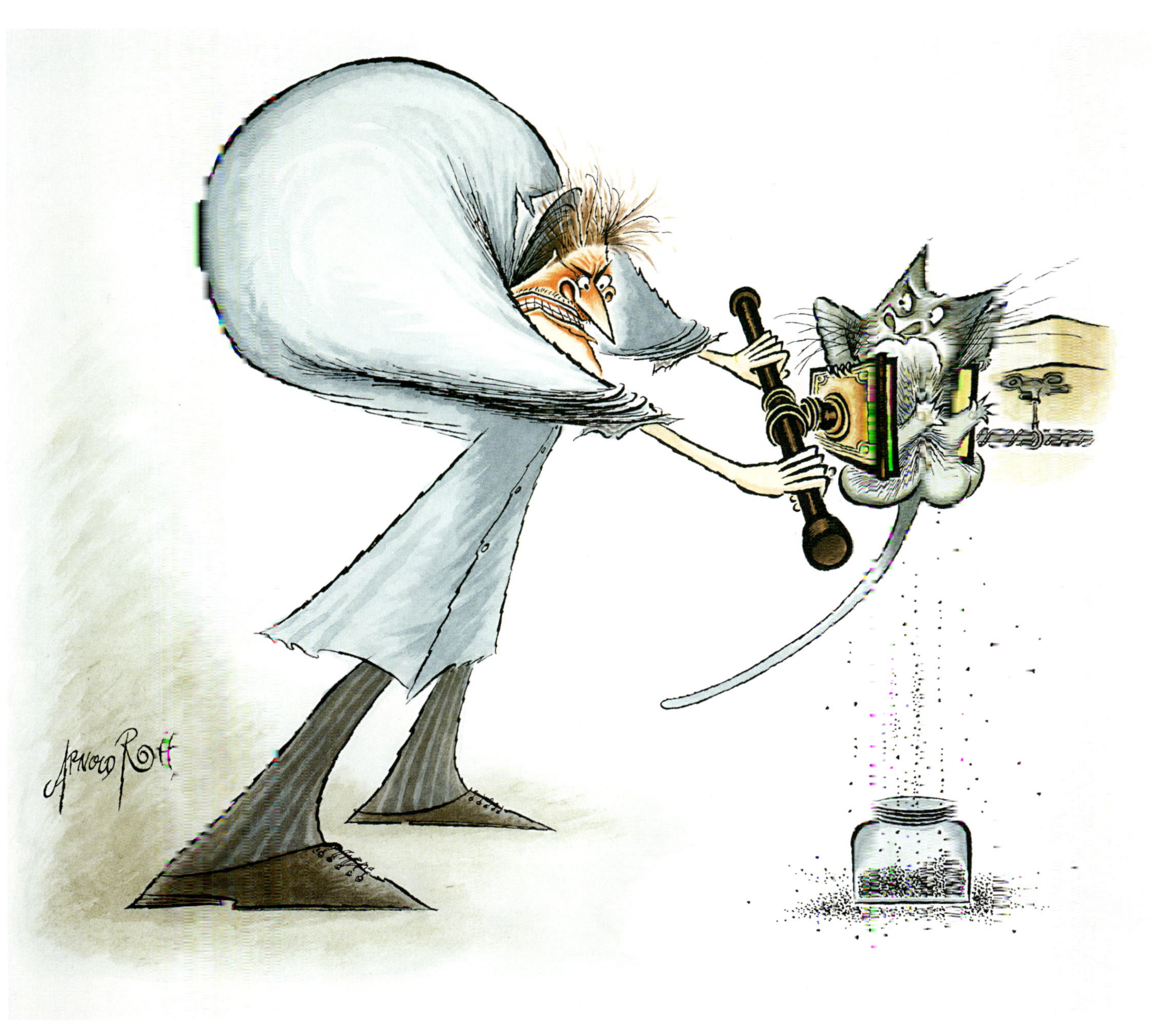

Figure 47
"Fleas"
Discover 1986

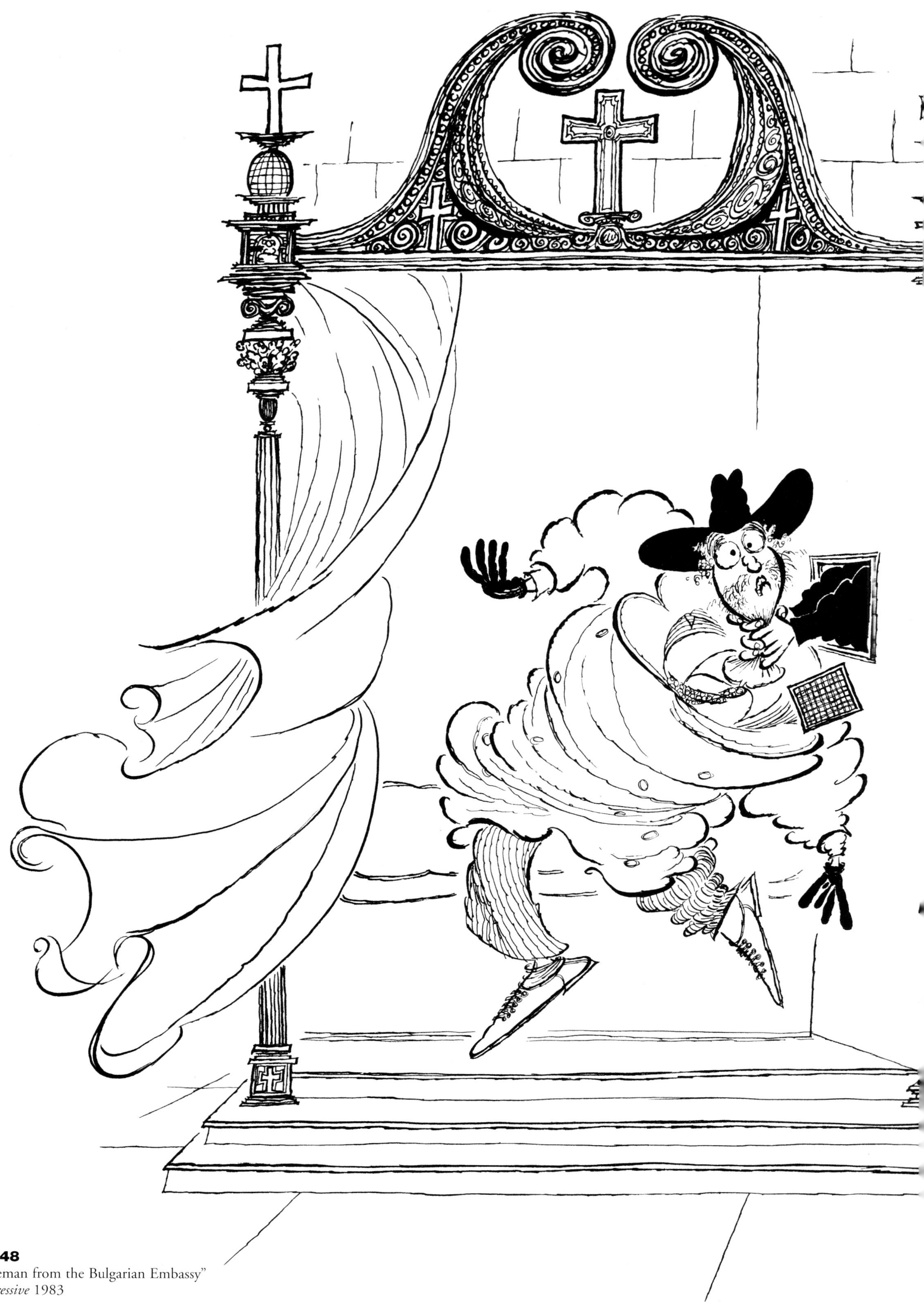

Figure 48
"A Gentleman from the Bulgarian Embassy"
The Progressive 1983

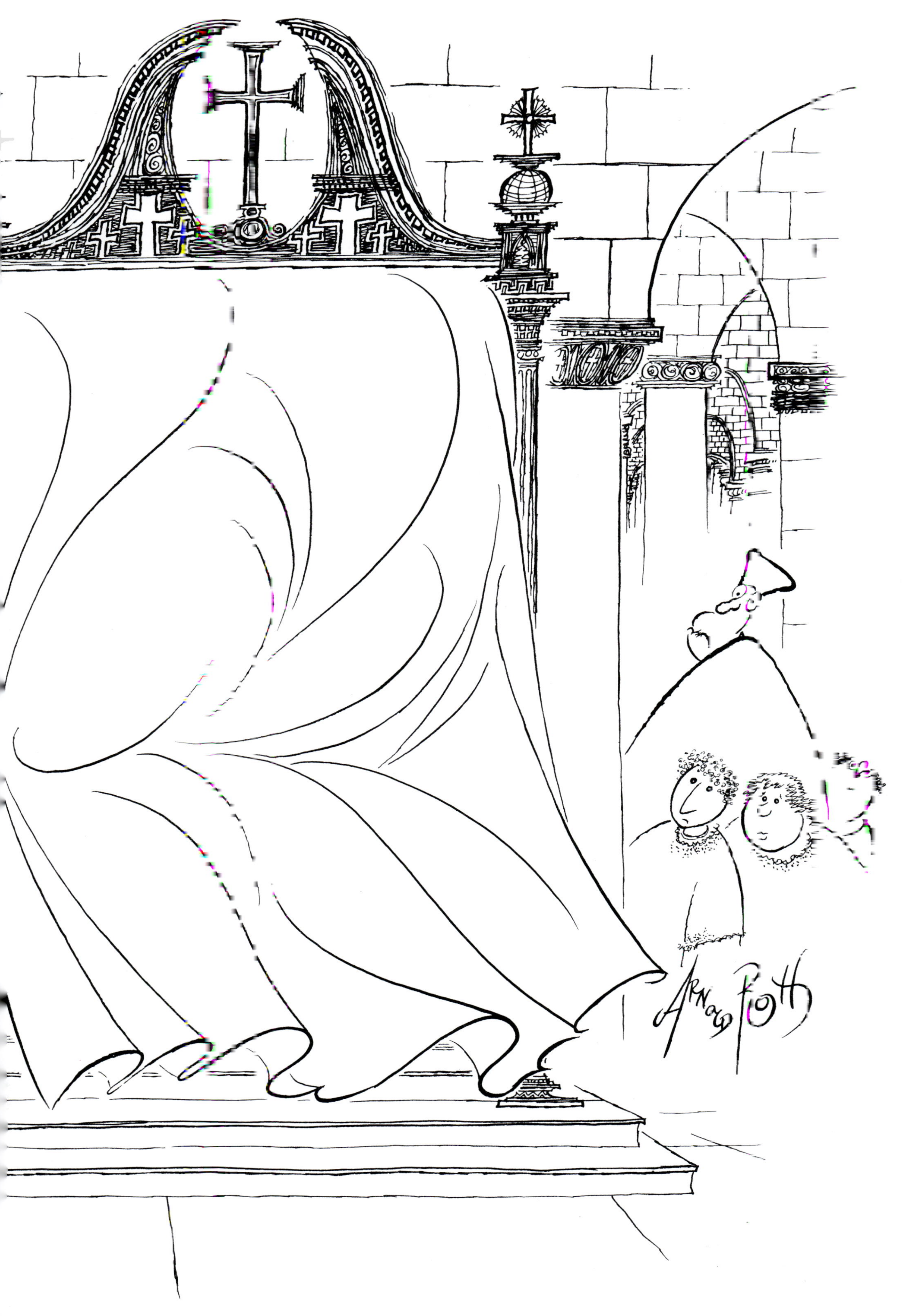
Arnold Roth

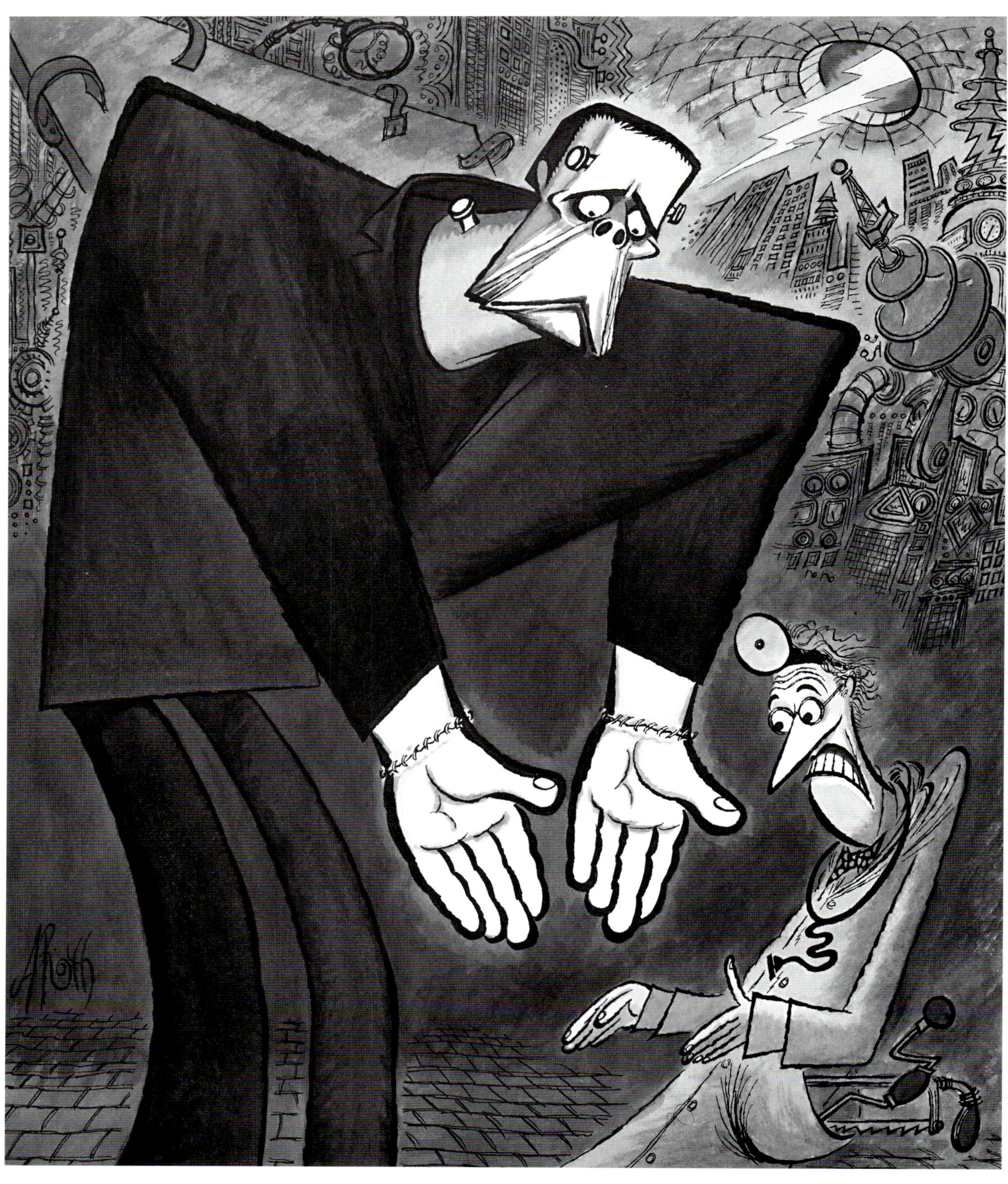

Figure 49
"Sinistrality"
Town and County 1985

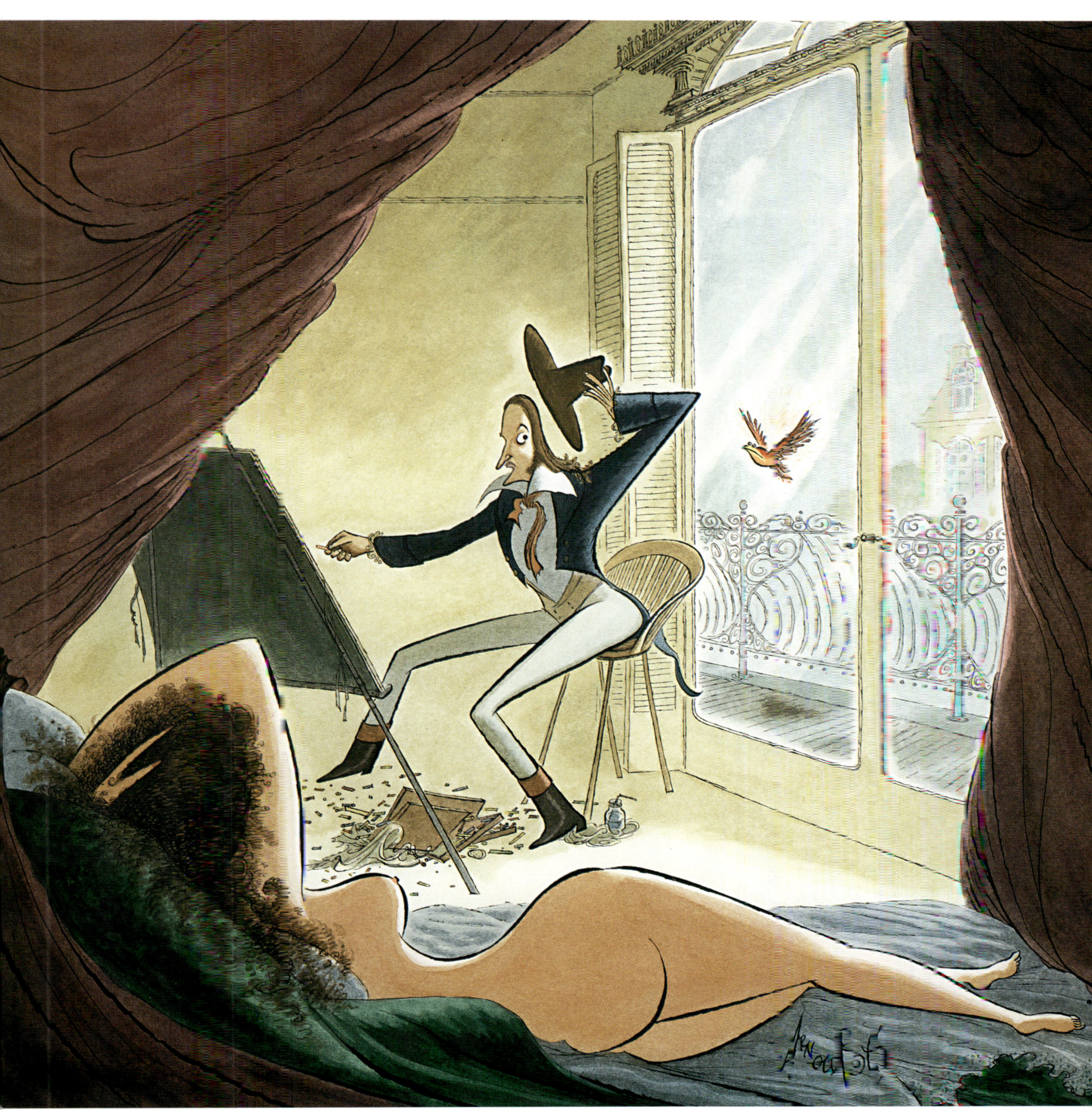

Figure 50
"John James Audubon Draws His One and Only Nude"
Audubon 1985

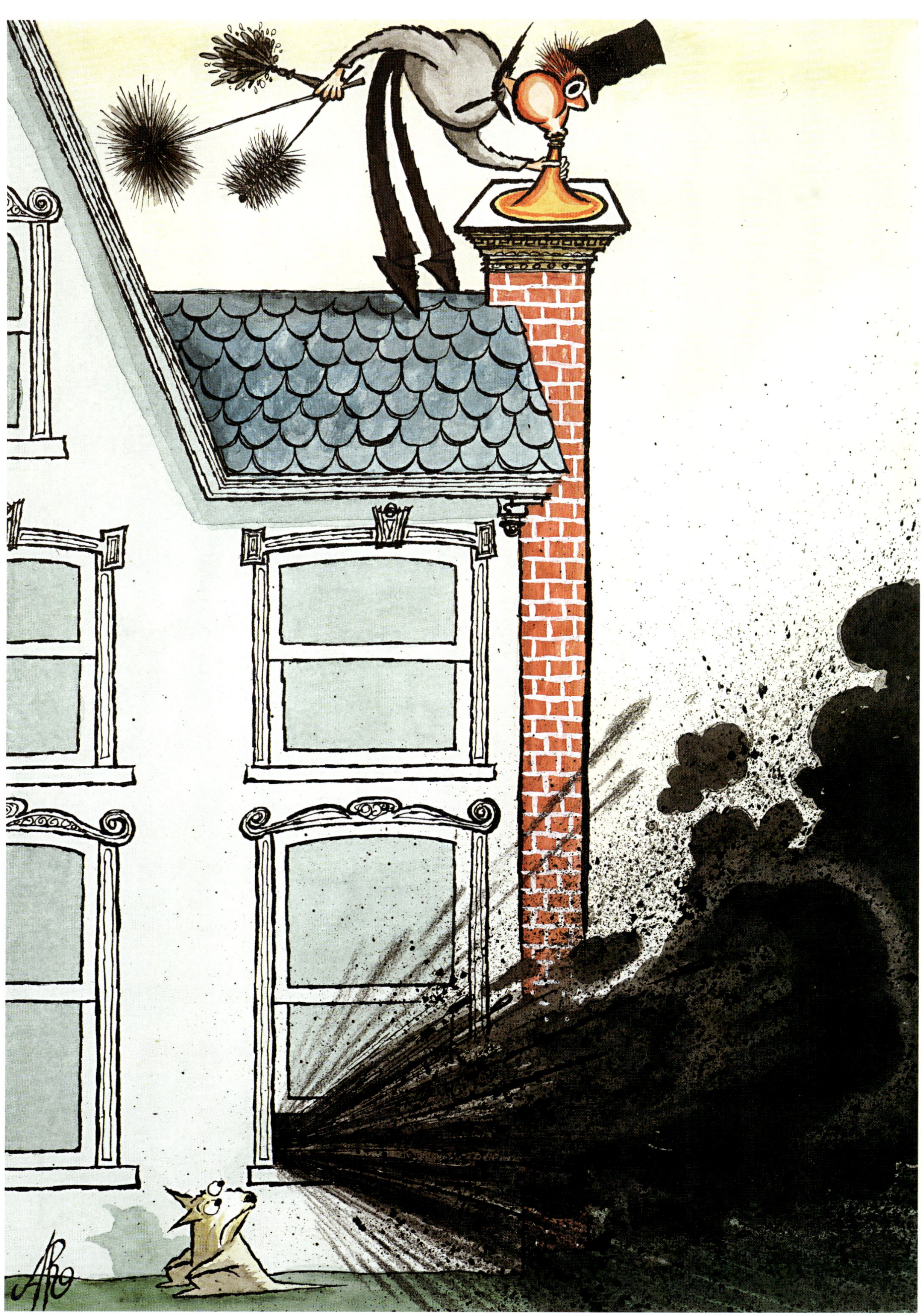

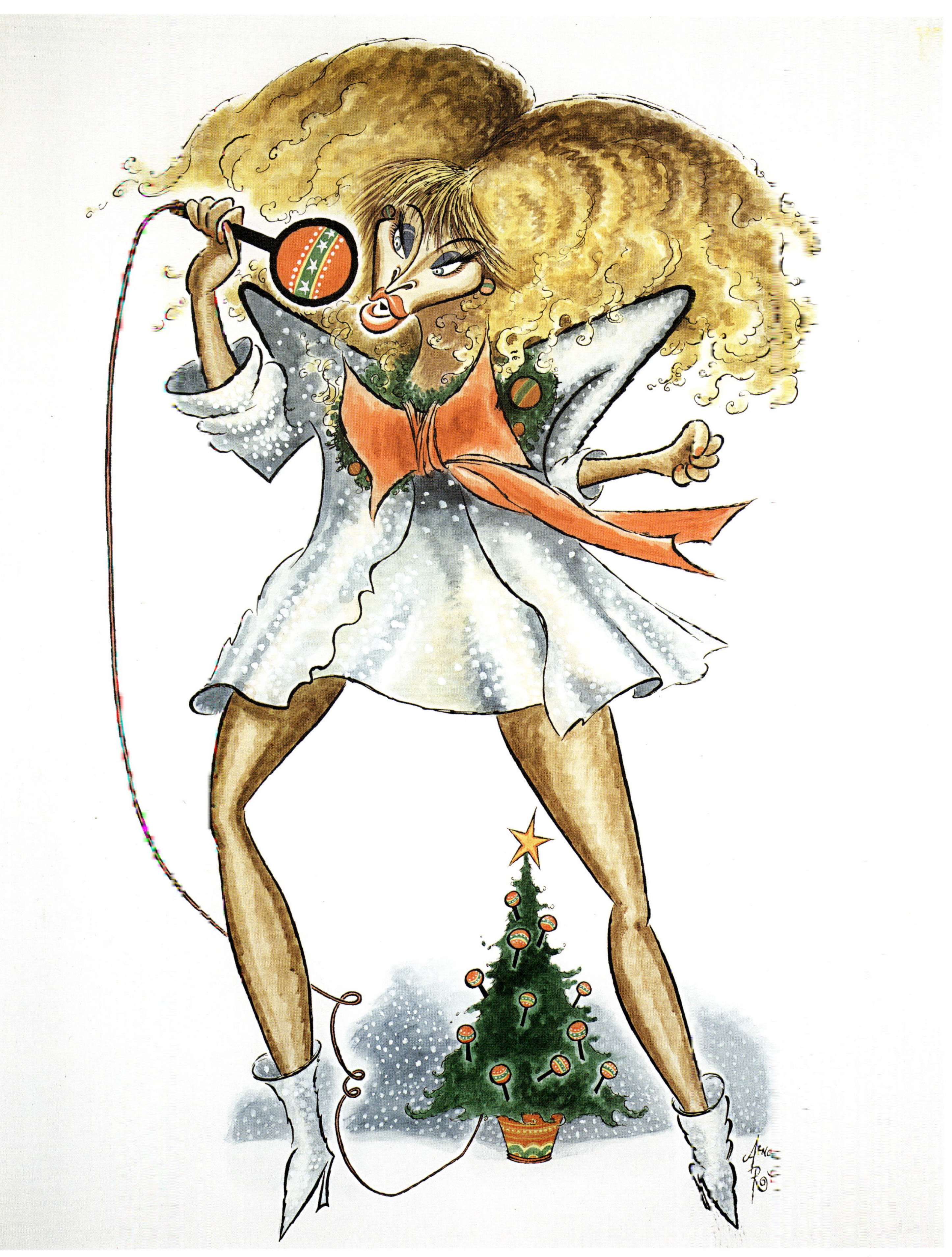

Left:
Figure 51
"I'd Like To Start A Chimney Sweeping Service…"
Money 1983

Above:
Figure 52
"Tina Turner"
Money 1985

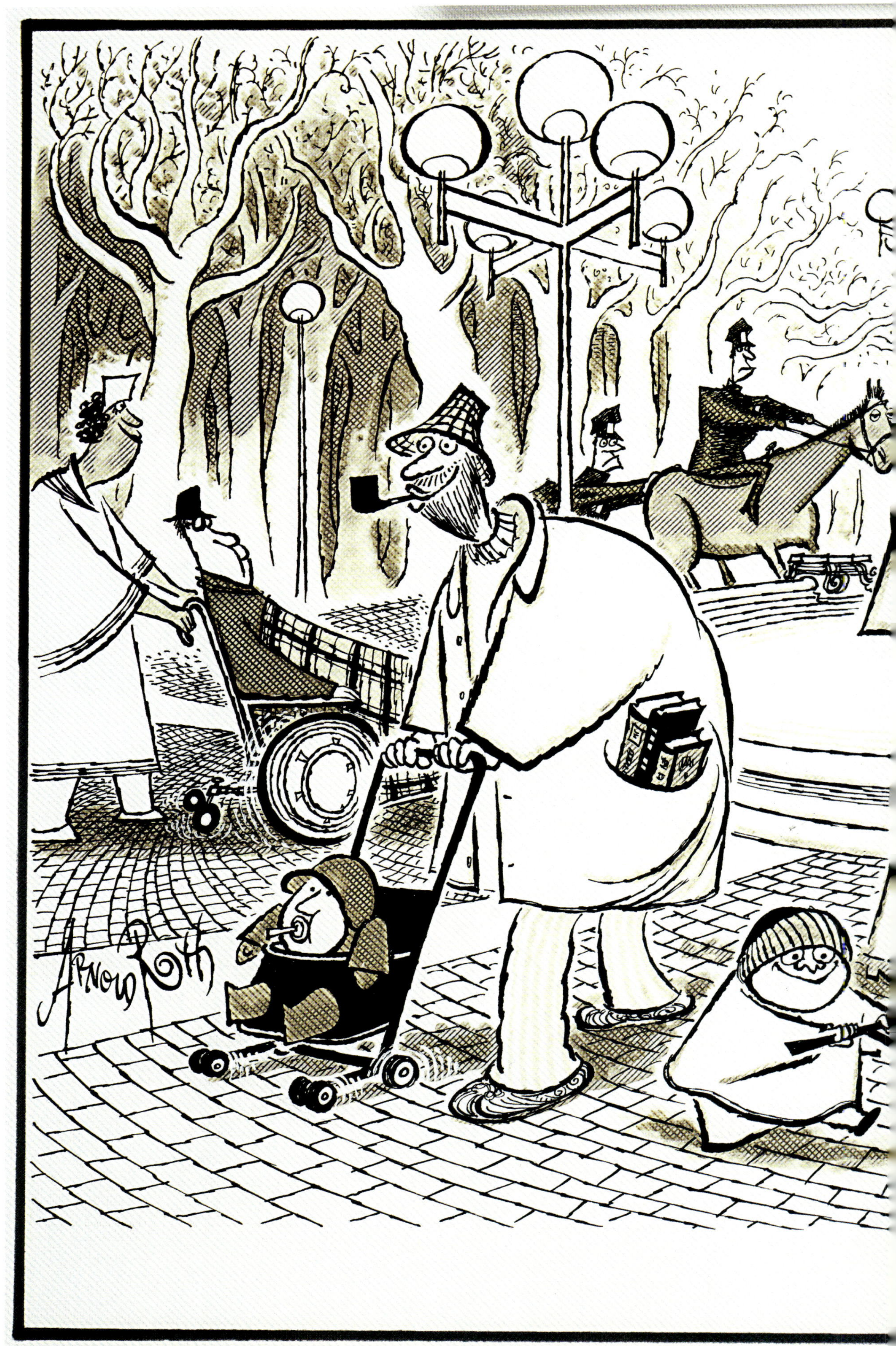

Figure 53
"Original Pushers Return to Washington Square"
New York Post 1987

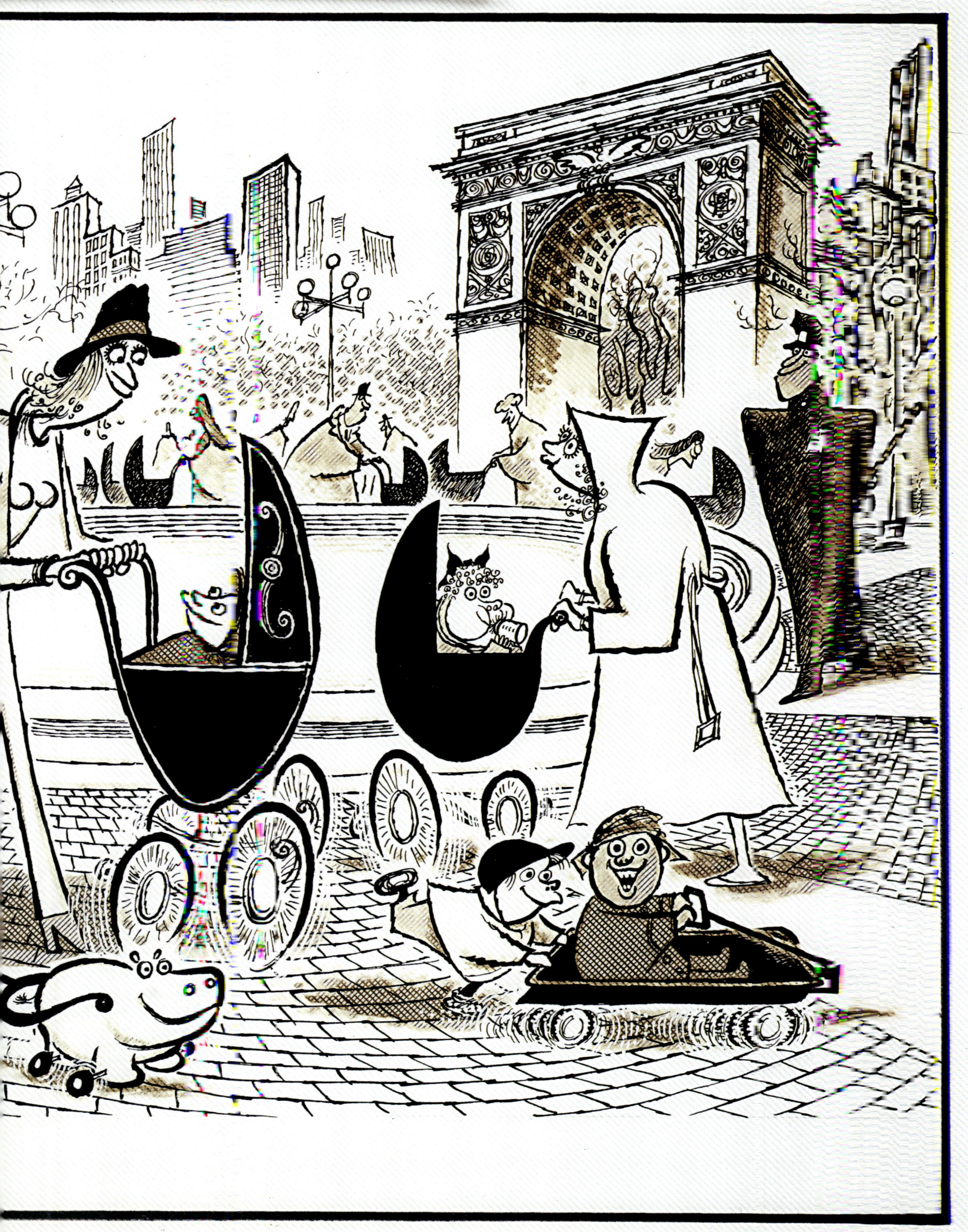

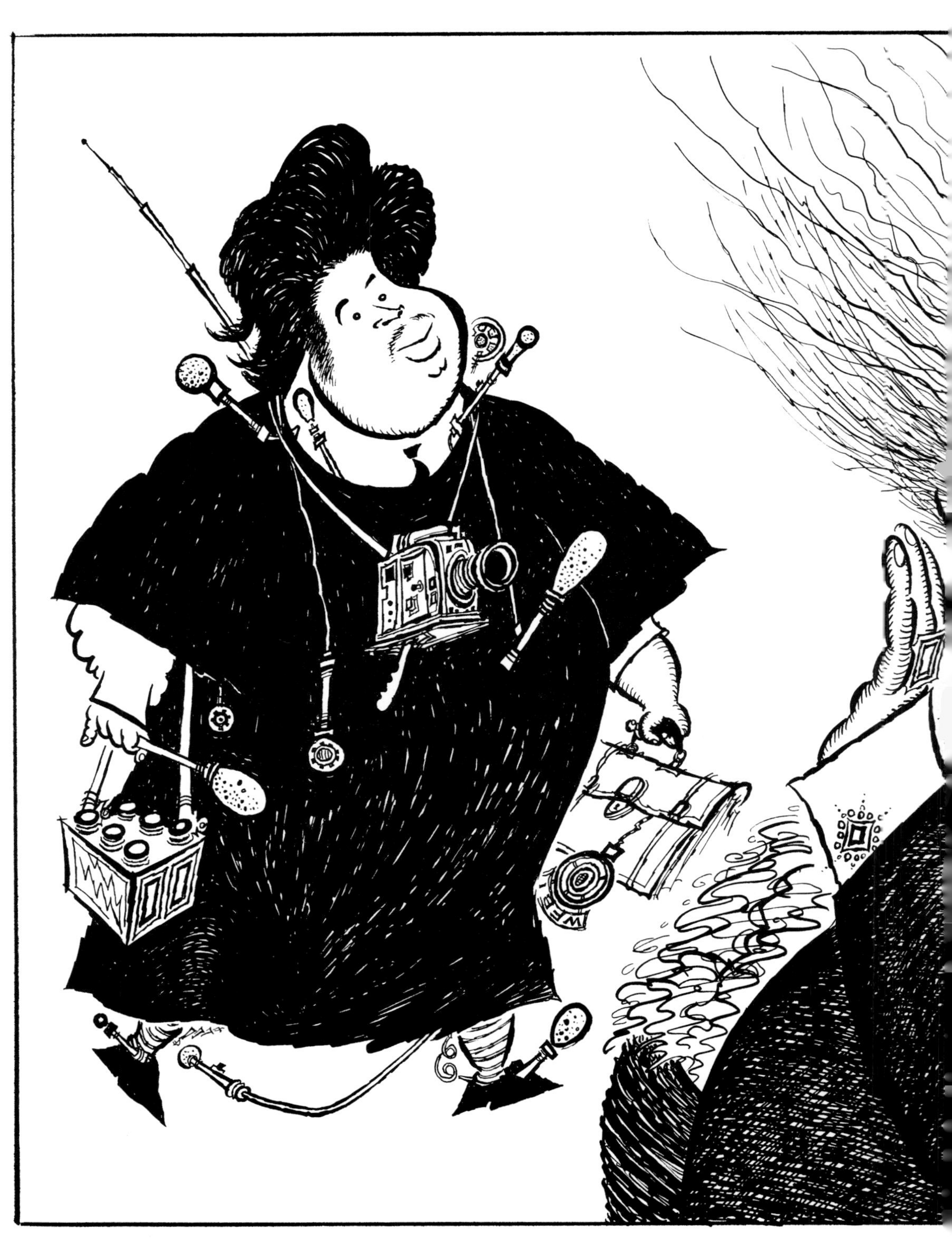

Figure 54
"Here Comes the Reverend Al Sharpton..."
New York Daily News 1988

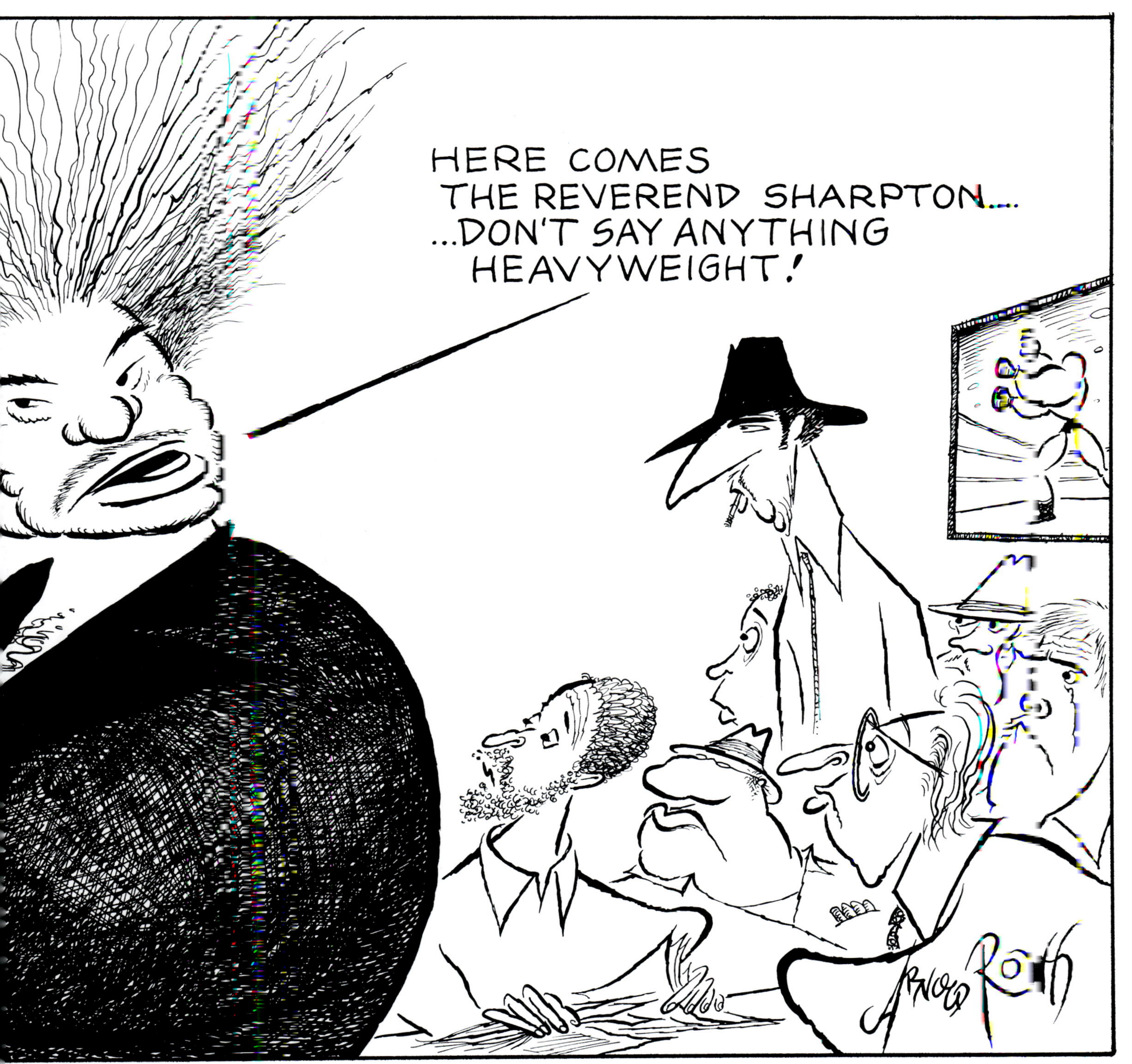
HERE COMES THE REVEREND SHARPTON.... ...DON'T SAY ANYTHING HEAVYWEIGHT!
ARNOLD ROTH

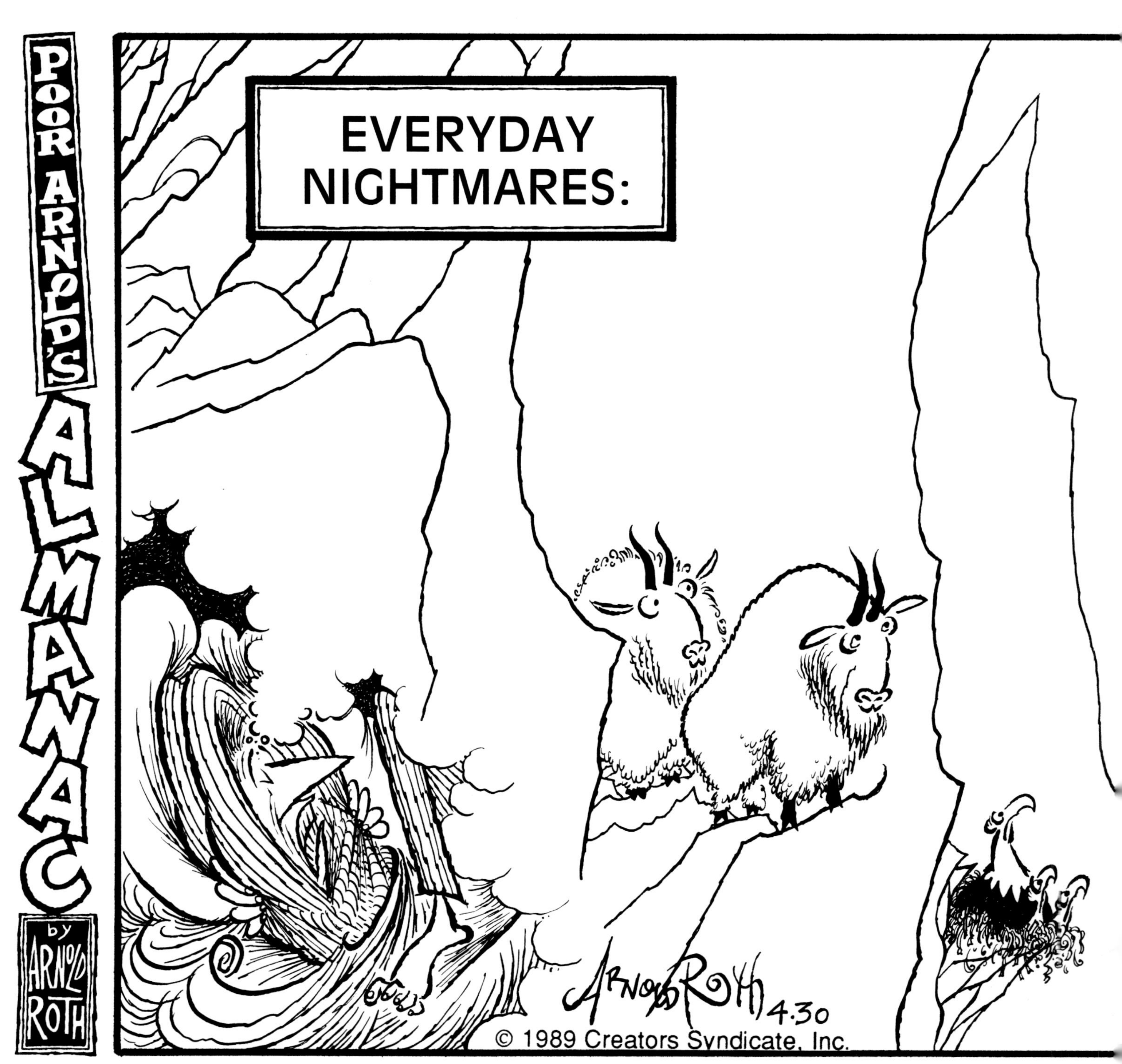

Figure 55
"Poor Arnold's Almanac"
1989

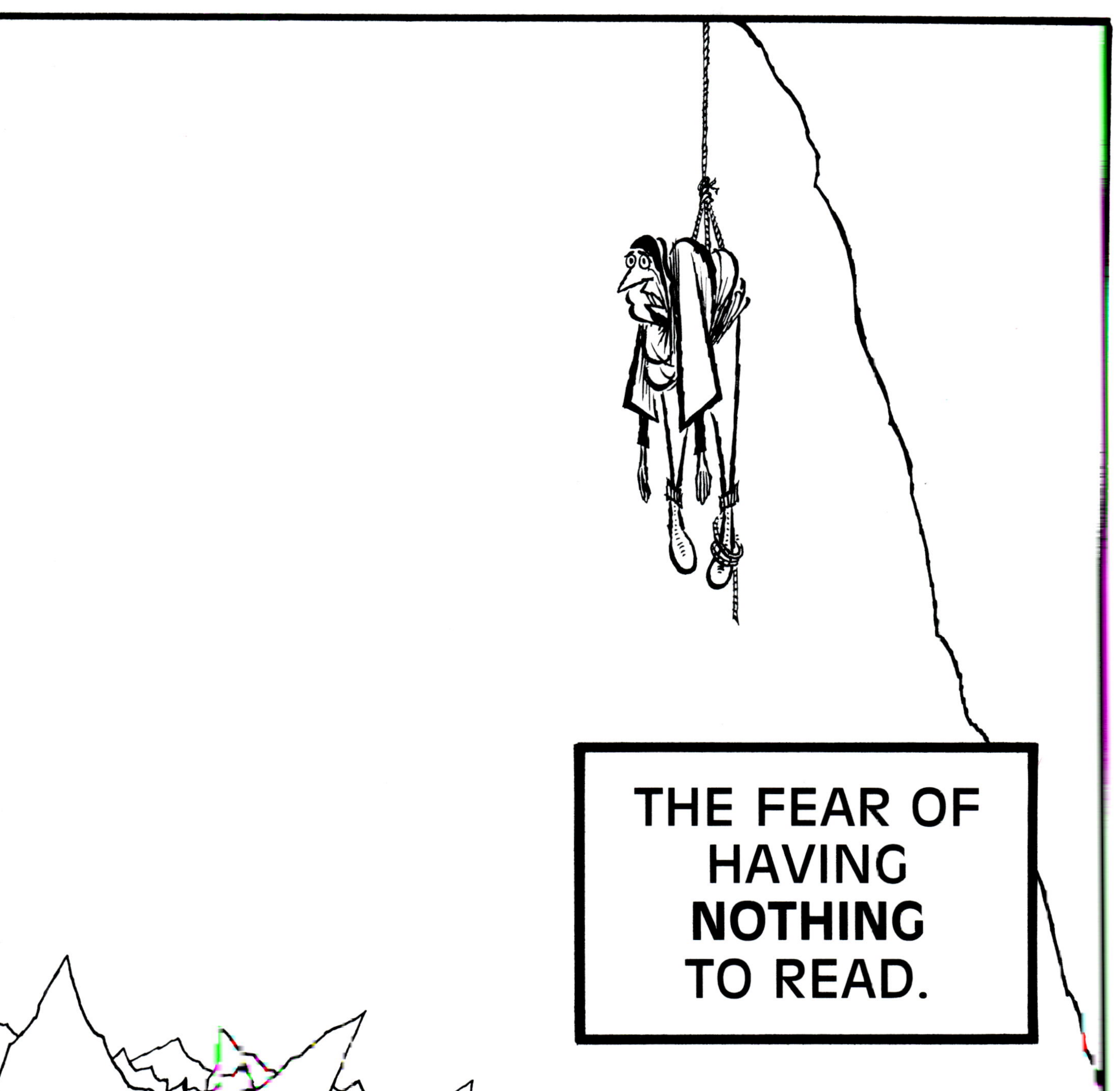
THE FEAR OF
HAVING
NOTHING
TO READ.

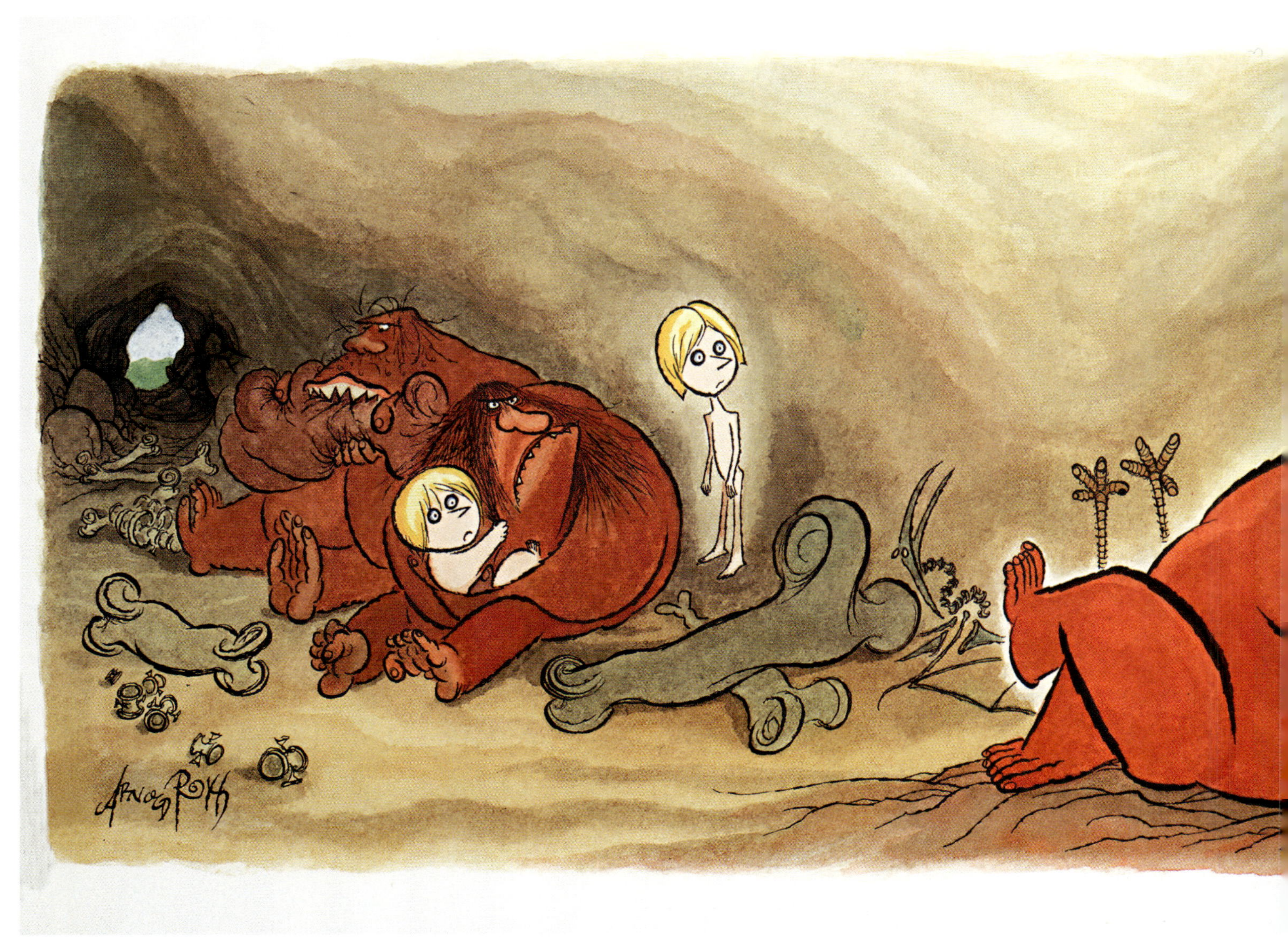

Figure 56
"Gossip"
Smithsonian 1993

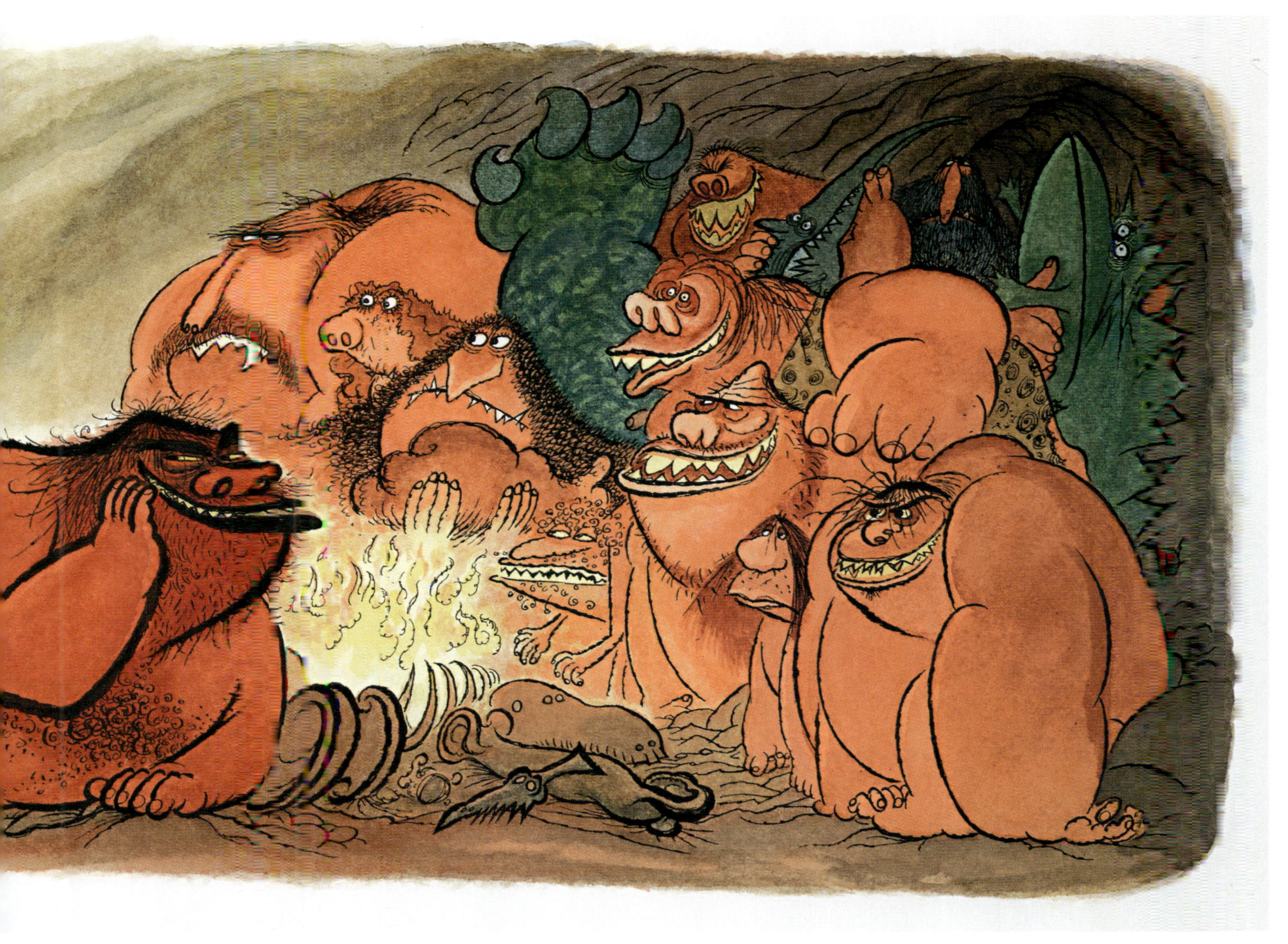

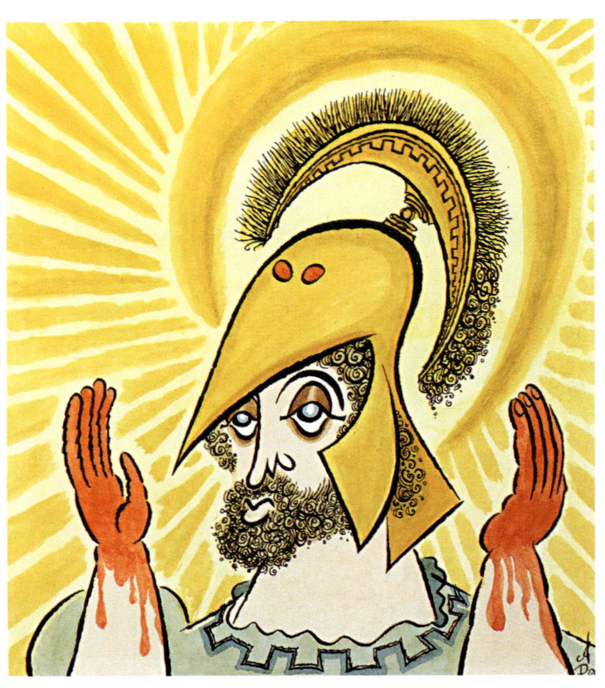

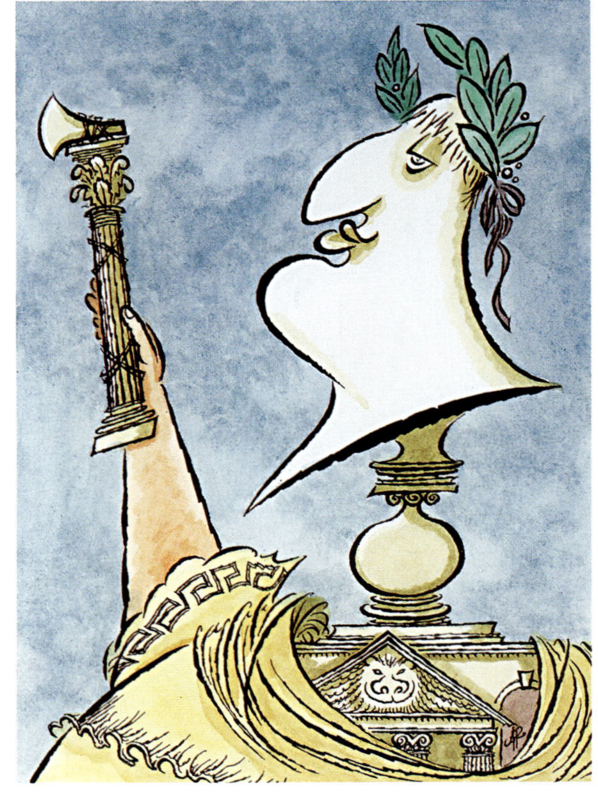

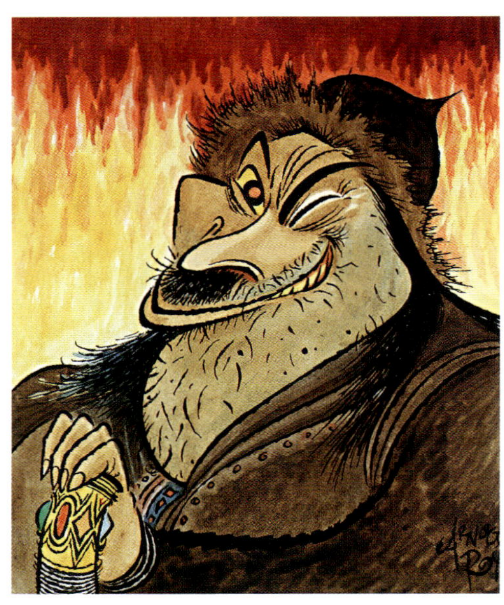

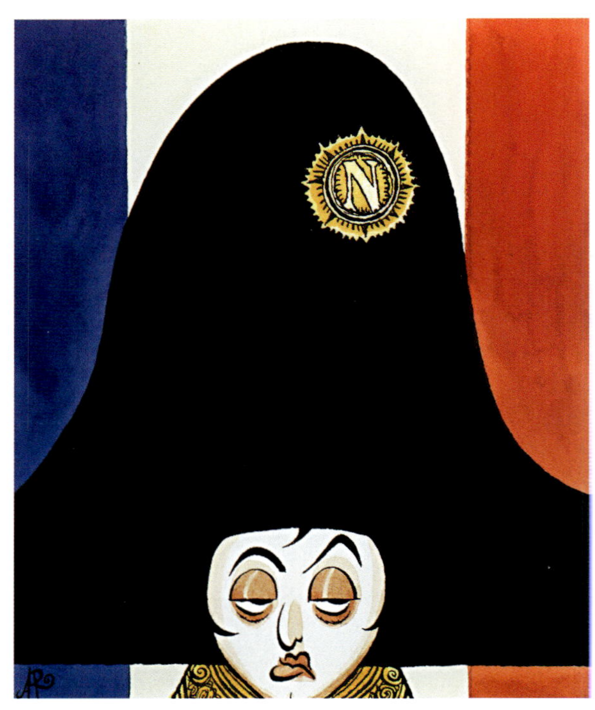

Figure 57
"Alexander," "Diocletian," "Attila," "Napoleon"
Harper's 1998

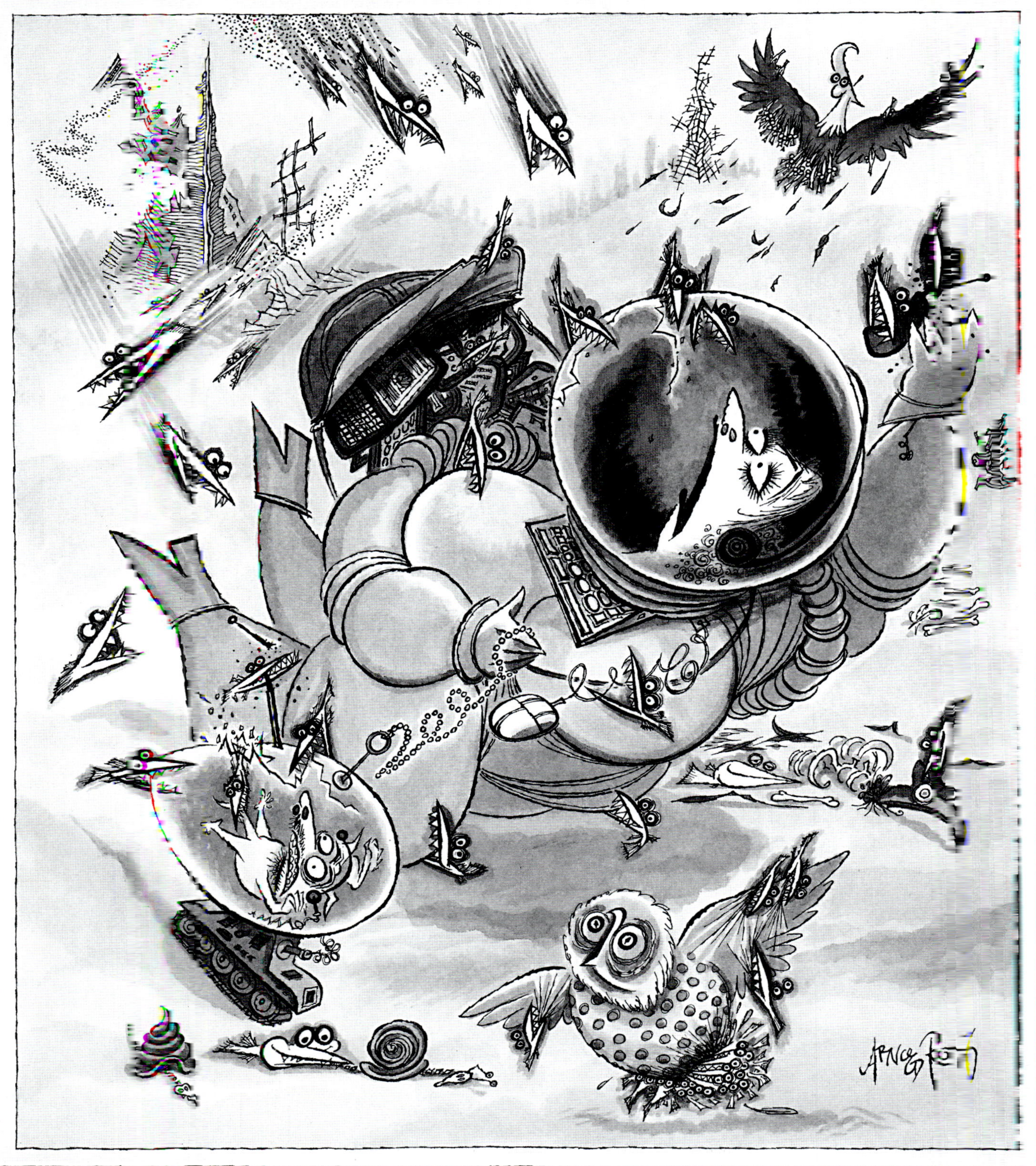

Figure 58
"Ecology Triumphant"
Harper's 2000

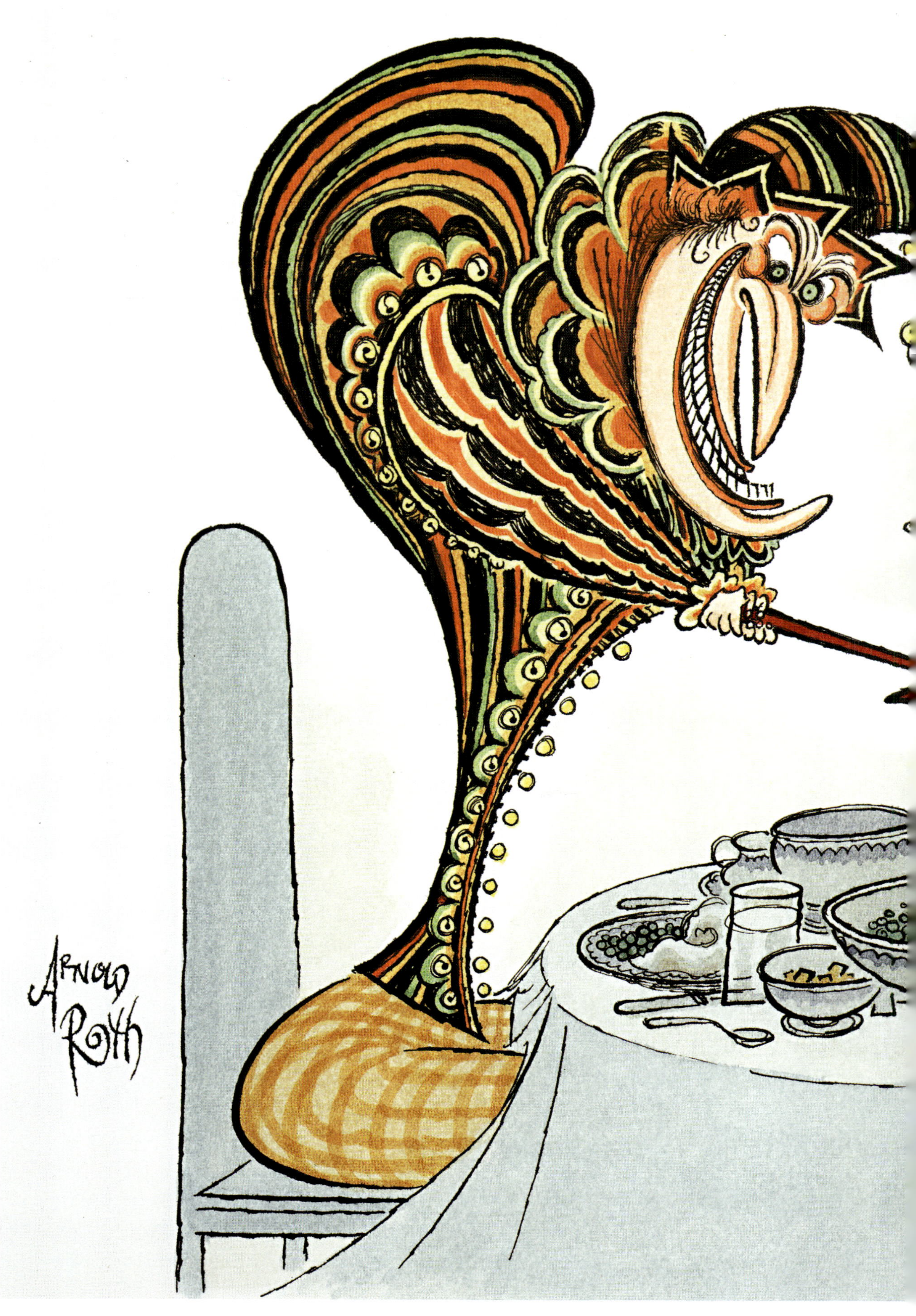

Figure 59
"Teasing"
Parenting 1990

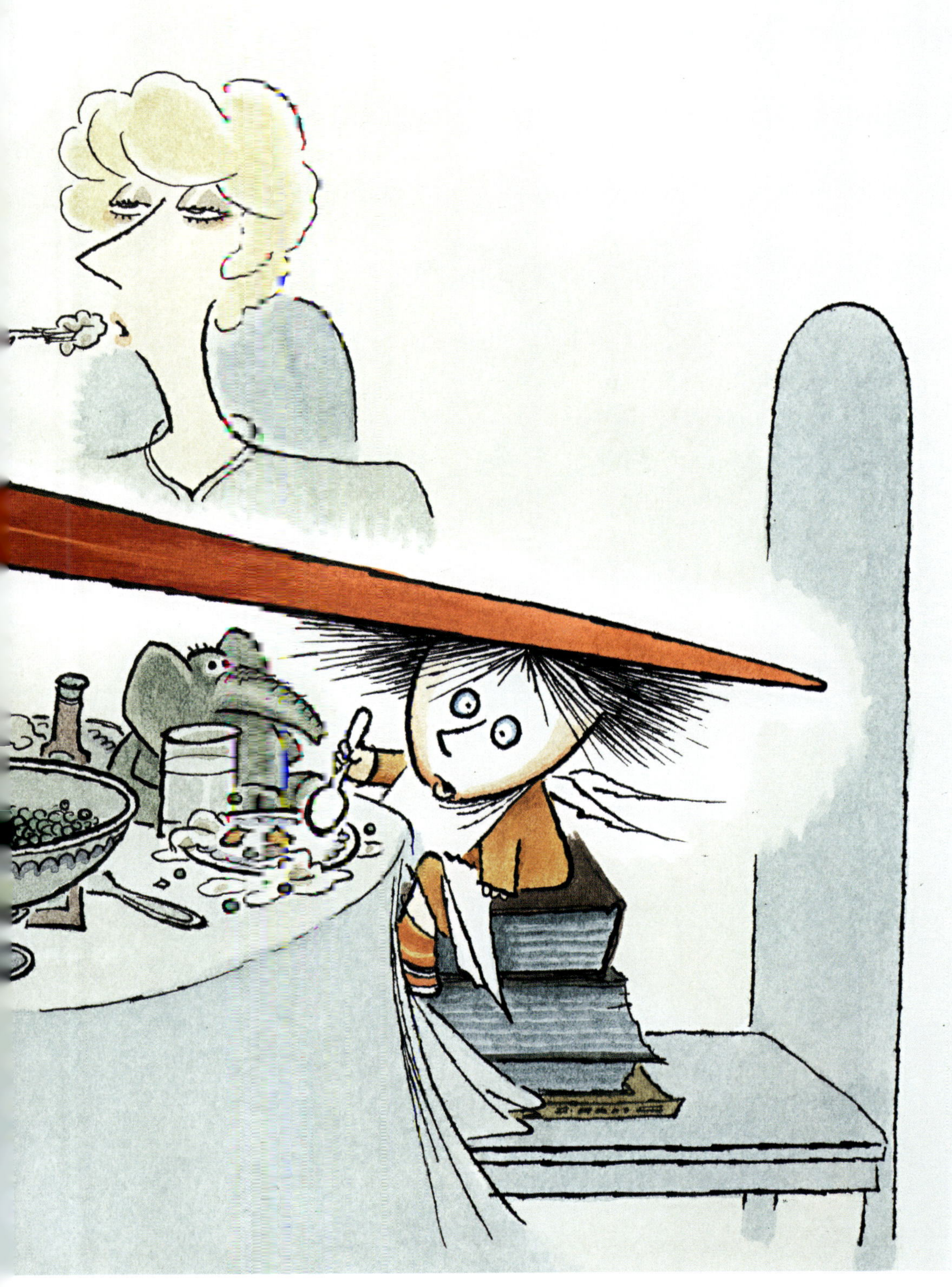

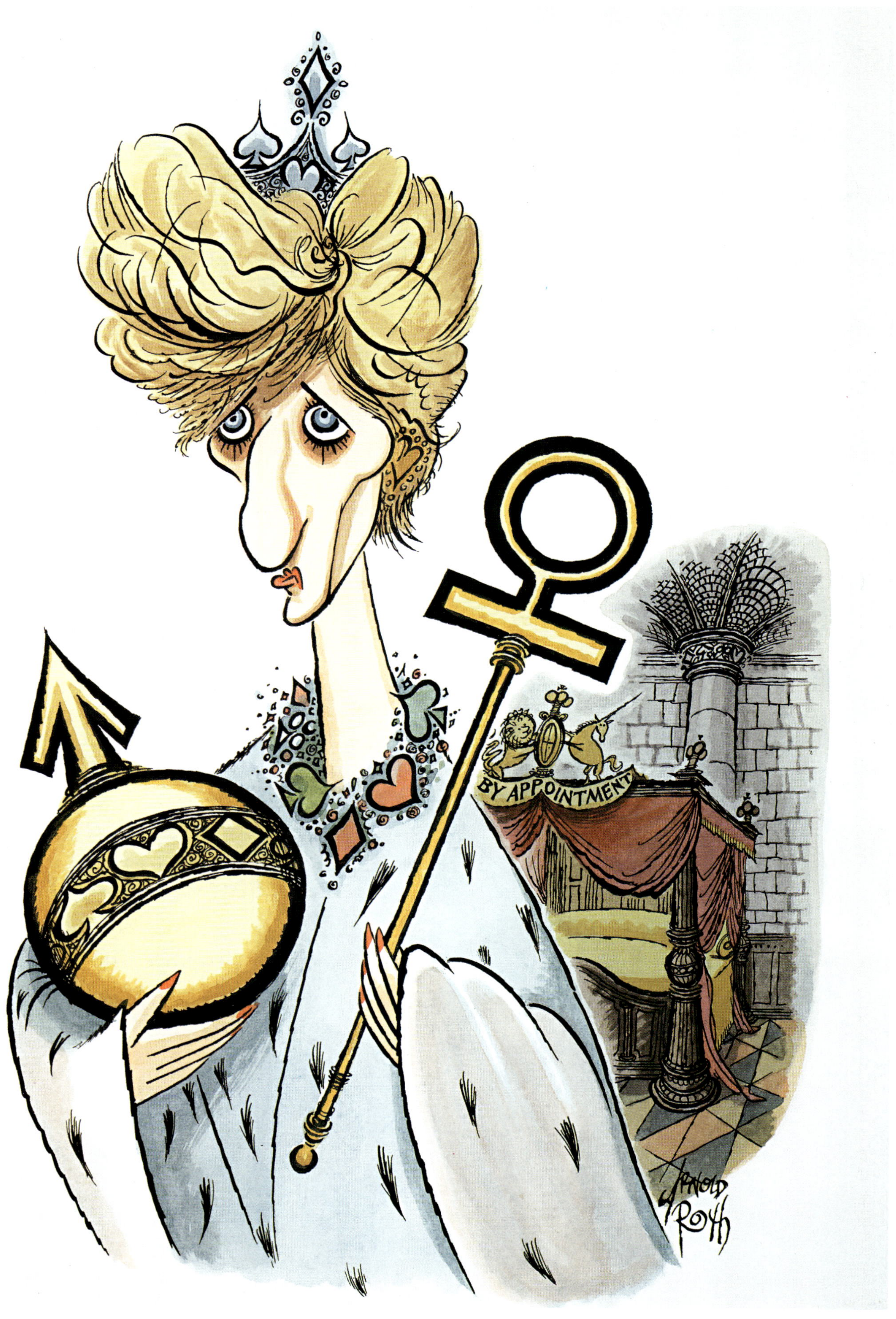

Figure 60
"Princess Di"
Time 1995

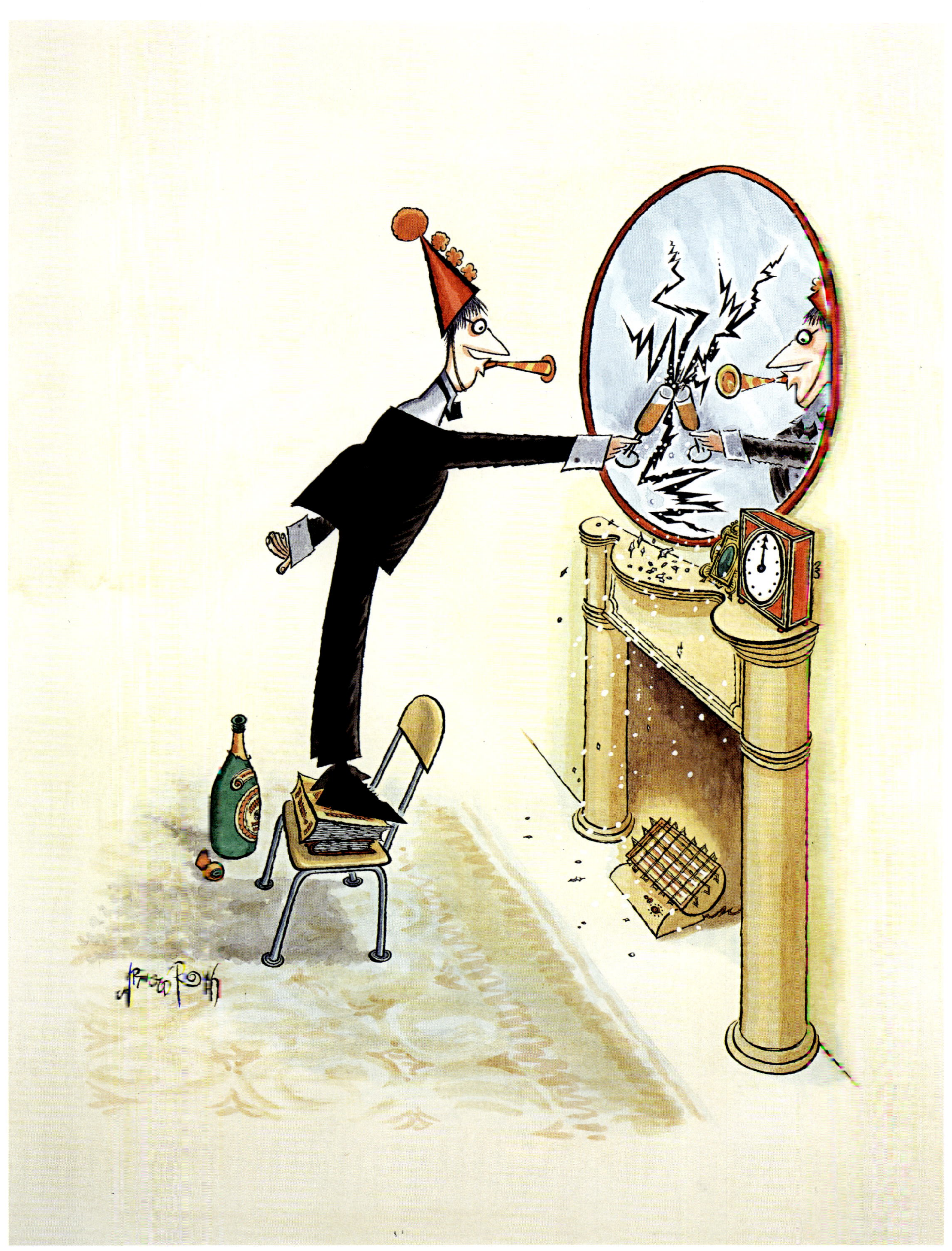

Figure 61
"Millennial New Year's Eve"
Time 1999

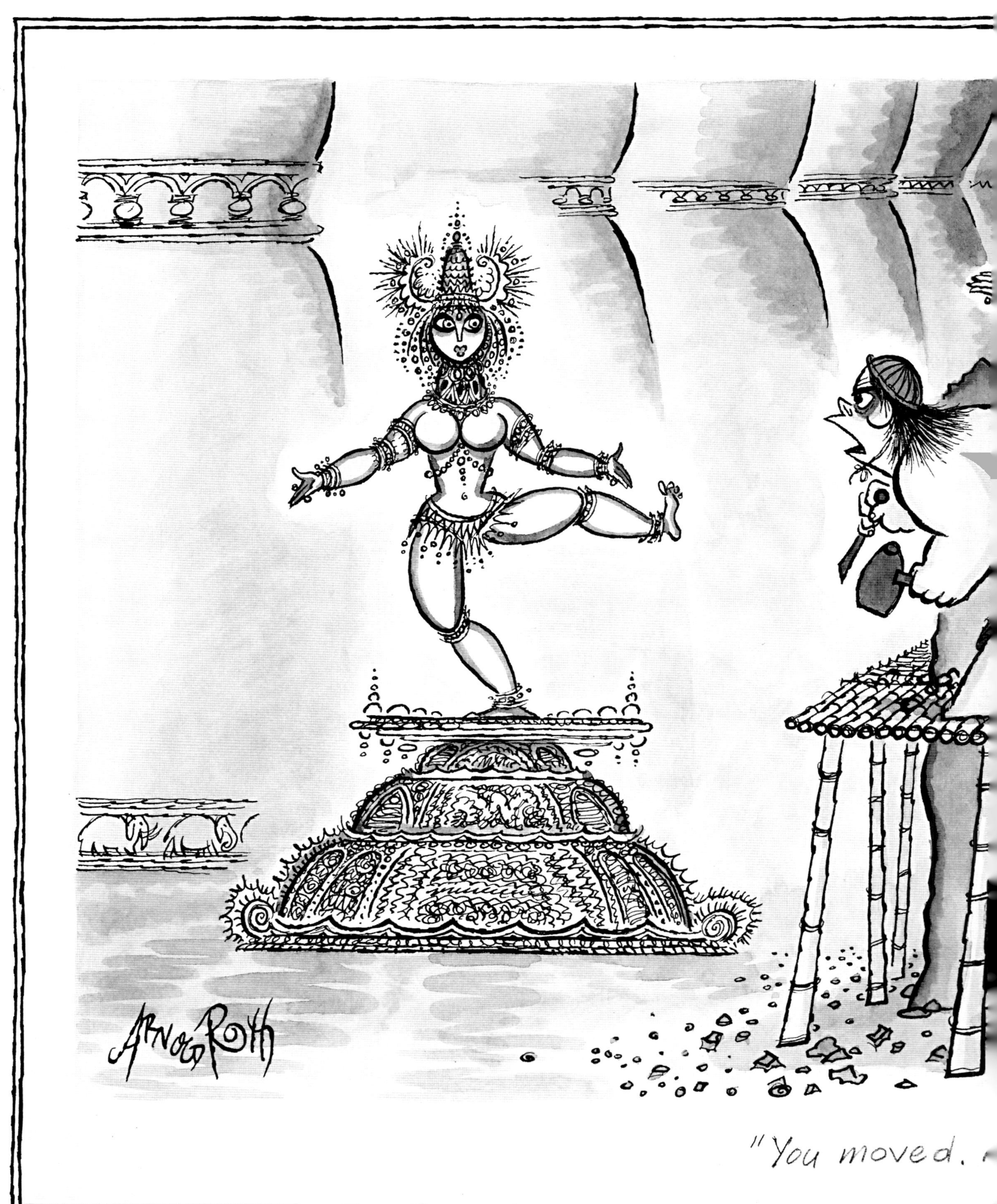

Figure 62
"You Moved Again"
Archaeology 1999

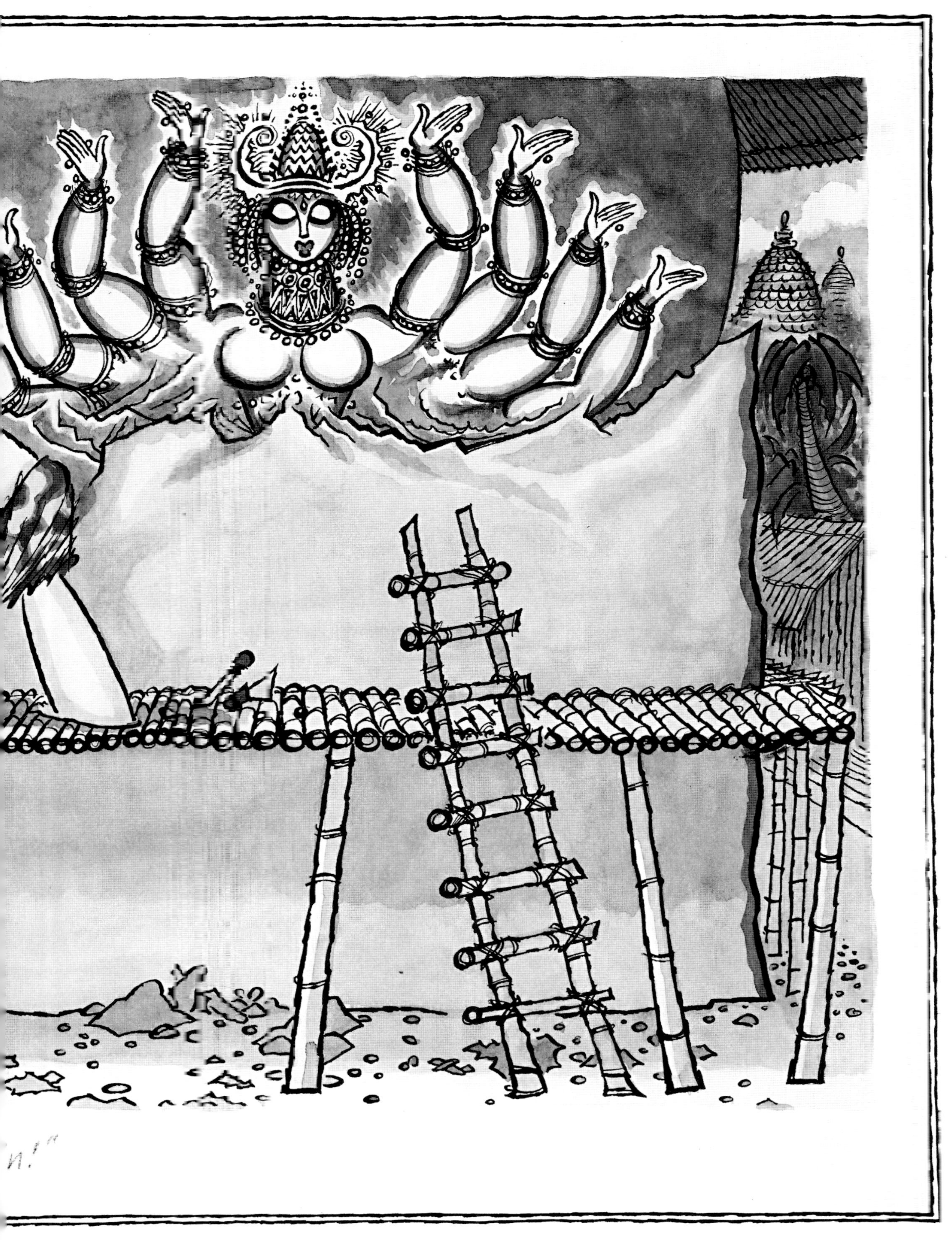

n!"

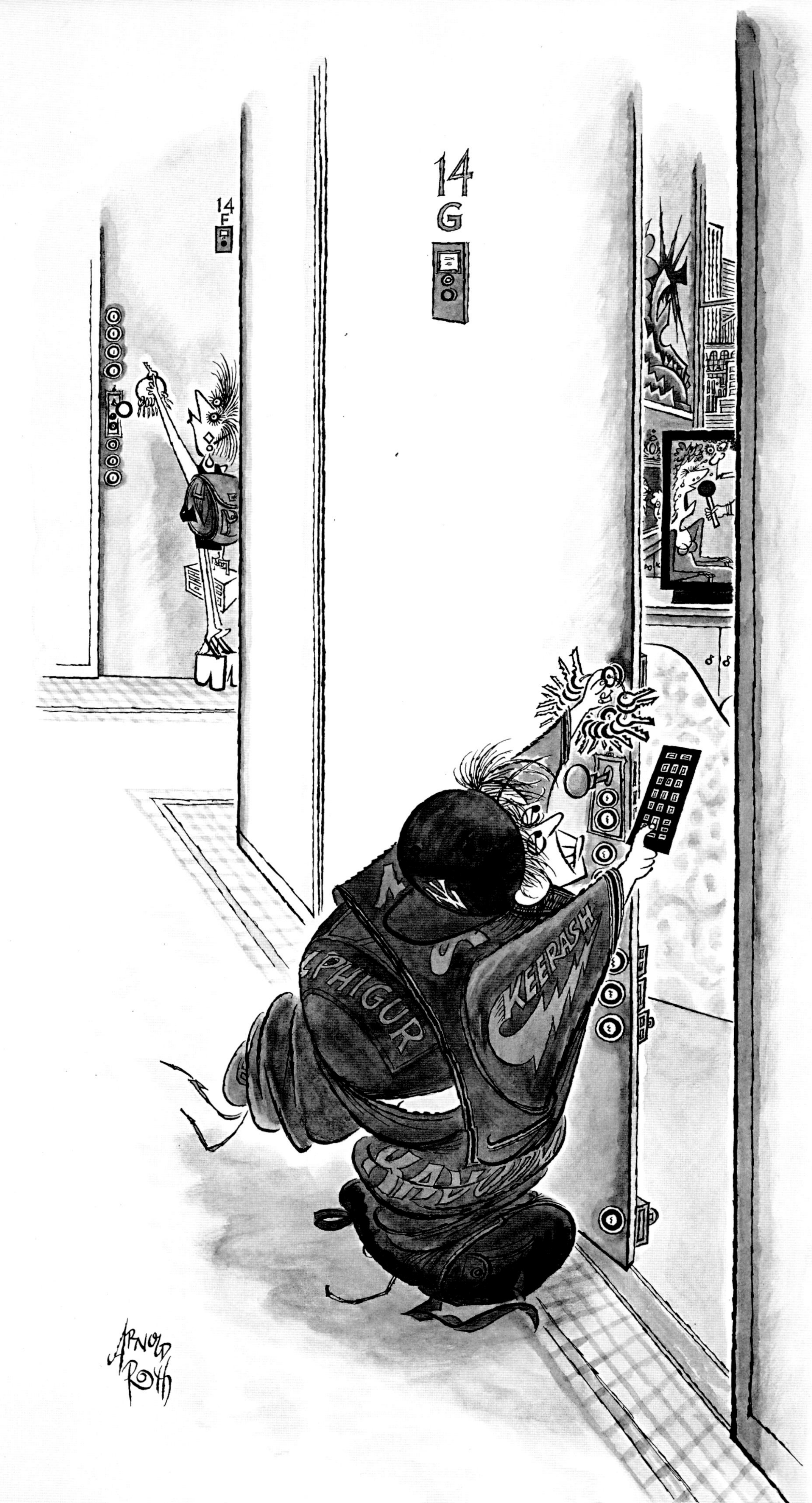

Figure 63
"Ten Going On Sixteen"
City Journal 1998

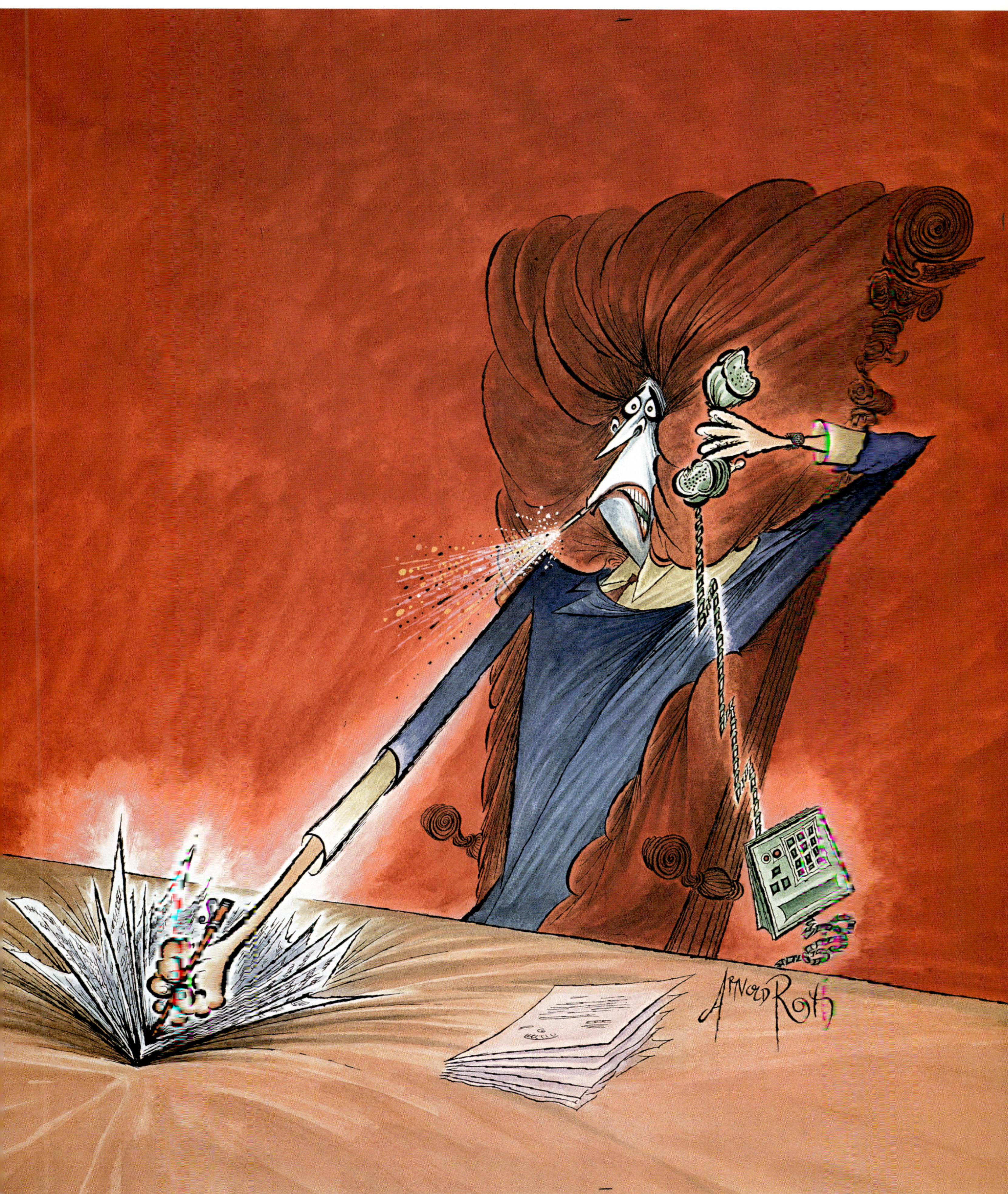
ARNOLD ROTH

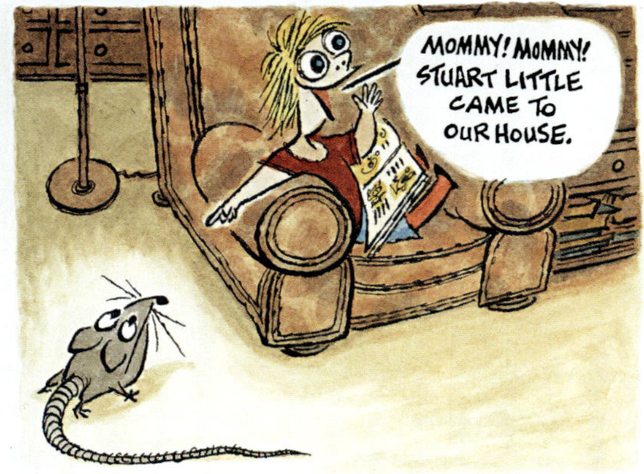

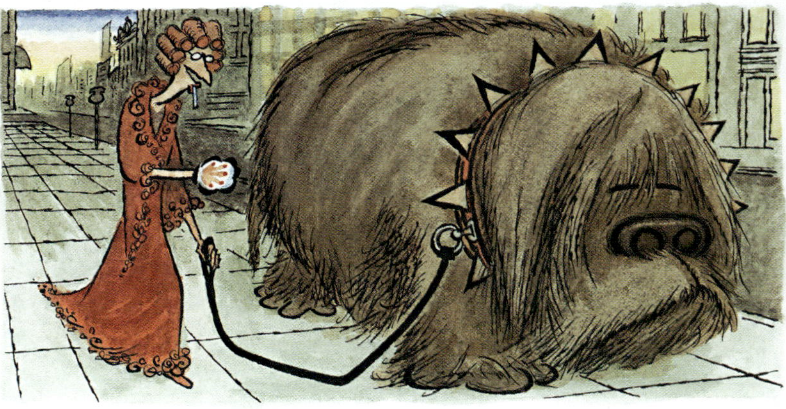

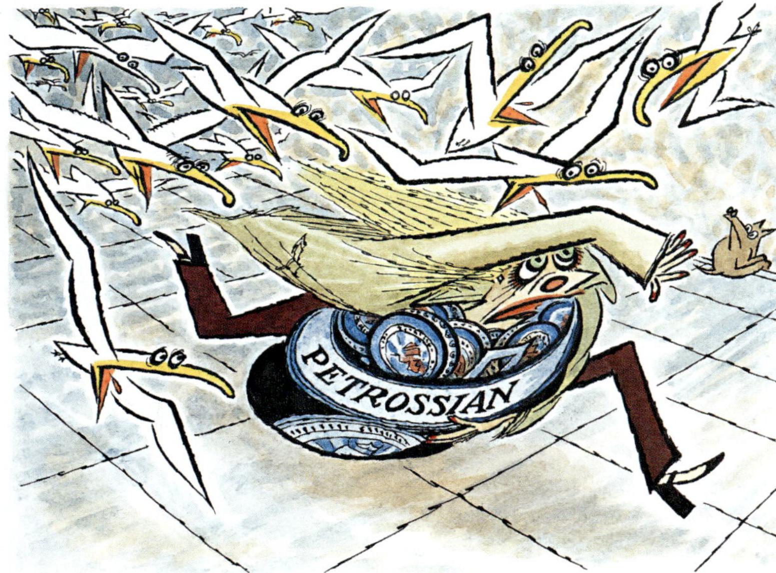

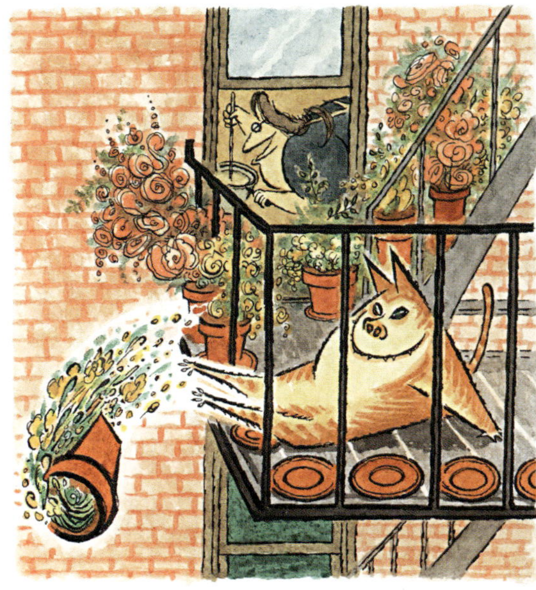

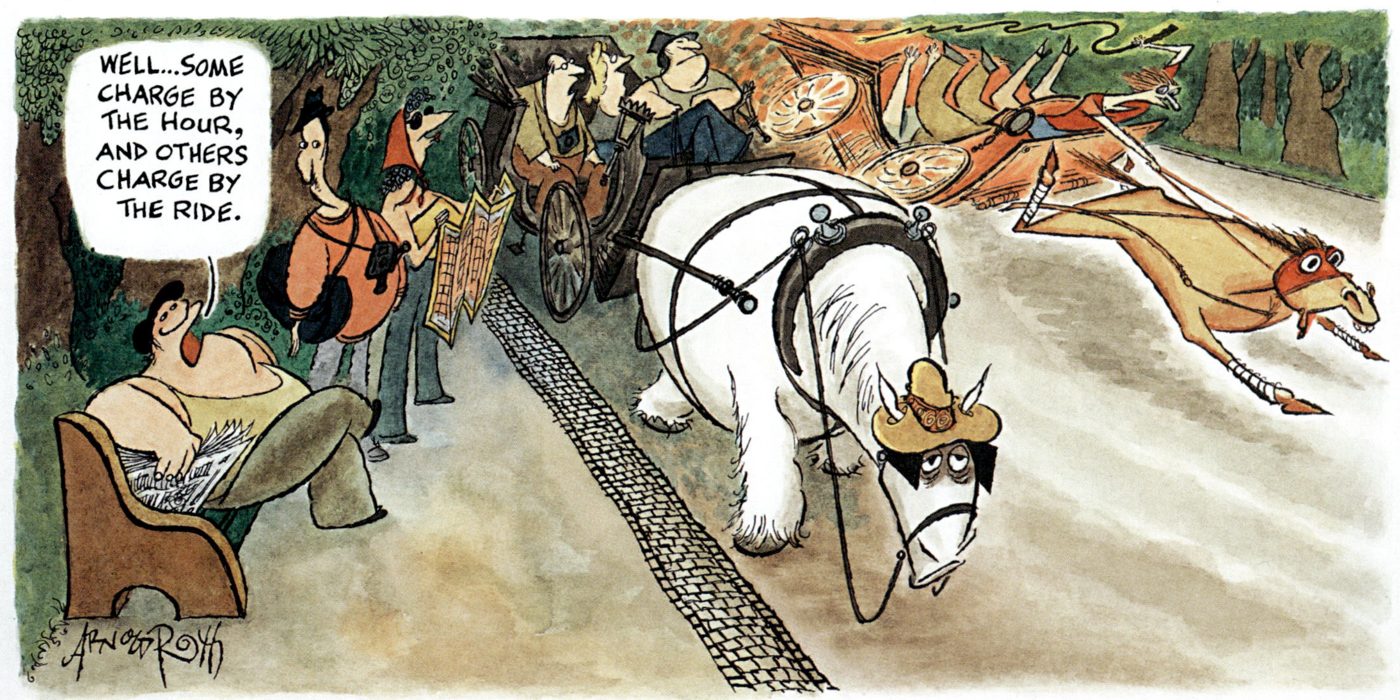

Previous page:
Figure 64
"Stress"
Chicago 1986

Figure 65
"Animal City"
The New Yorker 2000

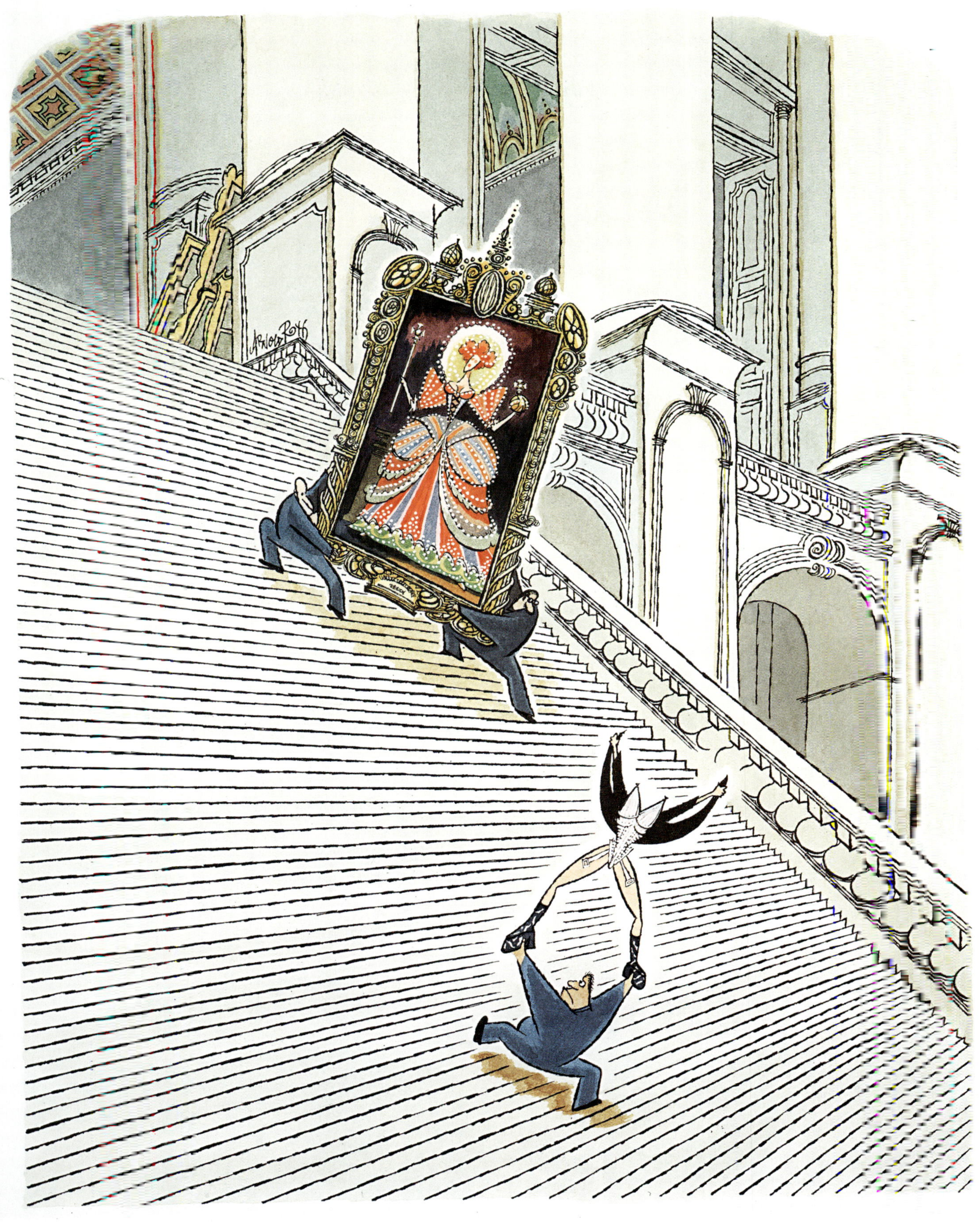

Figure 66
"Rock Star Exhibition."
The New Yorker 1999

CHECKLIST OF THE EXHIBITION

All works are from the personal collection of the artist.

Figure 1
Philadelphia College of Art Poster
Philadelphia College of Art Gallery (1980)
Ink and watercolor on paper. 40.7 x 46 cm.

Figure 2
"The First Pitch"
The New Yorker (April 3, 2000), cover
Ink and watercolor on paper. 48.5 x 37 cm.

Figure 3
"New Talent of 195[illegible]"
Glamour (January 195[illegible]), pages 78-79
Ink on board. [illegible].6 x 50.4 cm.

Figure 4
"The Secret Integration"
Saturday Evening Post (December 1964), pages 19-26
Watercolor on paper. 57.6 x 70.3 cm.

Figure 5
"The Reader"
Holiday (circa 19[illegible])
Ink on paper. 36.[illegible] x [illegible]4 cm.

Figure 6
"Red Wine"
Choosing and Enjoying Wine (New York: Holiday Magazine), 1965, page 70
Ink and watercolor on paper. 32.1 x 29 cm.

Figure 7
"R & R"
TV Guide (September [illegible]7, 1977), page 22
Ink and watercolor on paper. 36.6 x 40.8 cm.

Figure 8
"Charlton Moses Heston"
TV Guide (May 1[illegible], 1987), page 4
Ink and watercolor on paper. 41.3 x 48 cm.

Figure 9
"Poor Arnold's Almanac"
New York Herald Tribune Syndicate (June 7, 1959)
Ink on paper pasted on board. 40.2 x 57 cm.

Figure 10
"Carl Zigrosser"
Philadelphia Print Club (19[illegible]9)
Linoleum cut. 50.3 x 30.[illegible] cm.

Figure 11
"Street Musicians"
Punch (November [illegible], 19[illegible]1), cover
Ink and watercolor on paper. 31.6 x 23.9 cm.

Figure 12
"War Kings"
Punch (November 7, 1960), page 39
Ink on paper. 43.7 x 32.9 cm.

Figure 13
"Roth's Roots and Ruts"
Punch (April 20, 1977), page 666
Ink on paper. 29.7 x 39.1 cm.

Figure 14
"The War Between the Non-Smokers & the Smokers"
Punch (February 22, 1978), pages 328-329
Ink on paper. Both 44.2 x 68.5 cm.

Figure 15
"Assertive Woman"
Punch (August 3, 1977), pages 196-197
Ink and watercolor on paper. Both 45 x 65.6 cm.

Figure 16
"All Jogging Aside"
Punch (March 8, 1978), pages 416-417
Ink on paper. Both 45.1 x 34.8 cm.

Figure 17
"Papal Bull"
Punch (November 7, 1979), pages 842-843
Ink and wash on paper. Both 43 x 64.6 cm.

Figure 18
"Summary Summer"
Punch (June 17, 1987), pages 62-63
Ink and watercolor on paper. Both 46.4 x 35.3 cm.

Figure 19
"The Open Dour Policy"
Punch (October 1, 1986), pages 26-27
Ink and watercolor on paper. Both 46.6 x 34.3 cm.

Figure 20
"Ars Shorta"
Punch (May 5, 1982), pages 732-733
Ink on paper. 36.7 x 29 cm.

Figure 21
"Merry Christmas"
ca. 1963
Ink on board. 51.1 x 39.1 cm.

Figure 22
"A History of Sex Part Four: Olympic Games"
Playboy (April 1975), pages 155-157
Ink and watercolor on paper. 49.3 x 38.9 cm.

Figure 23
"Intermission"
Playboy, (February 1987), pages 74-75
Ink and watercolor on paper. 52.6 x 54.3 cm.

Figure 24
"500 Channels"
Playboy, (November 1993), pages 120-121
Ink and watercolor on paper. 51.3 x 41.9 cm.

Figure 25
"Euphemisms"
Playboy (March 1997), page 129
Ink and watercolor on paper. 52.6 x 65.3 cm.

Figure 26
"Blind Date"
Playboy, (January 1997), page 85
Ink and watercolor on paper. 42.3 x 43.2 cm.

Figure 27
"Camilla Parker Bowles"
Playboy (January 1997), page 87
Ink and watercolor on paper. 49.4 x 46.3 cm.

Figure 28
"For Your Two Legs Only"
Esquire (October 1981), page 146
Black ink, white ink, charcoal, and wash on paper.
37.5 x 41.7 cm.

Figure 29
"First Rate Telescopes"
Esquire (July 1987), page 15
Ink and watercolor on paper. 42.3 x 40.7 cm.

Figure 30
"Seasoned Cook: Tuscan Bread"
Esquire (October 1987), page 52
Ink and watercolor on paper. 37.1 x 47.5 cm.

Figure 31
"Seasoned Cook: New Orleans"
Esquire (July 1985), page 24
Ink and watercolor on paper. 36.5 x 44.3 cm.

Figure 32
"What Every Man Should Know About Opening Oysters"
Esquire (September 1983), page 42
Ink and watercolor on paper. 36.5 x 44 cm.

Figure 33
"Seasoned Cook: Lemon Pie"
Esquire (January 1984), page 34
Ink and watercolor on paper. 36.6 x 44.2 cm.

Figure 34
"Seasoned Cook: Conch"
Esquire (July 1985), page 24
Ink and watercolor on paper. 38.4 x 50.4 cm.

Figure 35
"In Drag Racing, the Machine Is the Man and Vice-Versa"
Sports Illustrated (September 23, 1968), page 63
Ink and watercolor on paper. 31.3 x 39 cm.

Figure 36
"Irish Wolf Hounds"
Sports Illustrated (February 14, 1966), pages 42-43
Ink and colored ink on scratchboard. 18.4 x 26.3 and 29 x 39.2 cm.

Figure 37
"Spring Training"
Sports Illustrated (March 9, 1981), page 44
Ink and watercolor on paper. 48.9 x 35.4 cm.

Figure 38
"Coach"
Sports Illustrated (Unpublished)
Ink on paper. 42.2 x 37 cm.

Figure 39
"Hockey Cheats"
Sports Illustrated (Unpublished)
Ink and watercolor on paper. 43.8 x 60.8 cm.

Figure 40
"Snow White & Rose Red"
Grimm's Fairy Tales (New York: Macmillan, 1963), page 209
Ink and wash on paper. 57 x 39.2 cm.

Figure 41
"Topsidedownside Up Pictures"
Pick a Peck of Puzzles (New York: Grosset and Dunlap, 1966), page 13
Ink on paper, ink on paper pasted on acetate, and color photocopy, mat with color photocopy of printed page showing red ink/position upside down to show reverse drawings. 29.2 x 26.4 cm.

Figure 42
"There Will Always Be Individual Preferences"
Comick Book of Pets (New York: Charles Scribner's Sons, 1976), page 65
Ink, charcoal and wash on paper mounted on board. 44.2 x 39.2 cm.

Figure 43
"Twi-Night Double Header"
A Sports Bestiary (New York: McGraw-Hill, 1982), page 53
Ink and wash on paper. 56.6 x 39 cm.

Figure 44
"Downtown"
Murdoch News Features, unpublished (1978)
Ink and white paint on duo-tone board. 29 x 39.2 cm.

Figure 45
"History of Reading"
The New York Times Book Review (Aug. 10, 1980), pages 3, 7, 9, 11
Ink on paper. [illegible] x 48.2 cm.

Figure 46
"Jimmy Carter's First Thanksgiving"
Politicks (November 22, 1977), cover
Ink on board with acetate overlay. 51.6 x 39 cm.

Figure 47
"Fleas"
Discover (July 198[illegible]), page 22
Ink and watercolor on paper. 36.5 x 44.3 cm.

Figure 48
"A Gentleman from the Bulgarian Embassy"
The Progressive (February 1983), page 17
Ink on paper. [illegible] x [illegible]3.9 cm.

Figure 49
"Sinistrality"
Town and Country (May 1985), page 84
Ink and wash on paper. 37.3 x 31.6 cm.

Figure 50
"John James Audubon Draws His One and Only Nude"
Audubon (January 198[illegible]), page 42
Ink and watercolor on paper. 52 x 52 cm.

Figure 51
"I'd Like To Start A Chimney Sweeping Service…"
Money (July 198[illegible]), page 16
Ink and watercolor with white paint on paper.

Figure 52
"Tina Turner"
Money (December 198[illegible]), page 115
Watercolor on paper. [illegible]1.1 x 37 cm.

Figure 53
"Original Pushers Return to Washington Square"
New York Post (February 22, 1987), page 6
Ink on duotone paper. 34.2 x 45.5 cm.

Figure 54
"Here Comes the Reverend Al Sharpton…"
New York Daily News (January 21, 1988), page 6
Ink on board. [illegible] x [illegible].4 cm.

Figure 55
"Poor Arnold's Almanac"
(April 30, 1989)
Ink on paper, color guide, tear sheet. 24 x 43.3 cm; 21.1 x 41 cm; 19 x 3[illegible] cm.

Figure 56
"Gossip"
Smithsonian (February 1993), pages 76-77
Ink and watercolor on paper. 28.9 x 60.6 cm.

Figure 57
"Alexander," "Diocletian," "Attila," "Napoleon"
Harper's (August 1998), pages 55, 57, 59, 61
Ink and watercolor on paper. All 31.5 x 26.5 cm.

Figure 58
"Ecology Triumphant"
Harper's (June 2000), page 146
Ink and wash on paper. 34.1 x 26.3 cm.

Figure 59
"Teasing"
Parenting (February 1990), page 125
Ink and watercolor on paper. 35.5 x 41.9 cm.

Figure 60
"Princess Di"
Time (December 18, 1995), page 88
Ink and watercolor on paper. 39.2 x 31 cm.

Figure 61
"Millennial New Year's Eve"
Time (1999), unpublished cover
Ink and watercolor on paper. 57 x 39.2 cm.

Figure 62
"You Moved Again"
Archaeology (July/August 1999), page 6
Ink and wash on paper. 29.5 x 42.6 cm.

Figure 63
"Ten Going On Sixteen"
City Journal (Autumn 1998), page 35
Ink and wash on paper. 55.5 x 35.6 cm.

Figure 64
"Stress"
Chicago (March 1986), cover
Ink and watercolor on paper. 50.1 x 46.8 cm.

Figure 65
"Animal City"
The New Yorker (June 5, 2000), page 96
Ink and watercolor on paper. 43.8 x 37.2 cm.

Figure 66
"Rock Star Exhibition"
The New Yorker (December 13, 1999), page 75
Ink and watercolor on paper. 46.4 x 38.7 cm.

ACKNOWLEDGEMENTS

Caroline Roth, my wife, thought that there should be an exhibition to celebrate the fifty years of work that I produced as a freelance cartoonist. It was a good idea. All of Caroline's ideas are good. Mostly because they keep my involvement to a minimum. She always has the best ideas in our house, which gives you an idea not so much of our house but of who else is in it.

When Caroline enlisted the cooperation of the learned and fabulous Lucy Caswell, I knew that the project would be in hands far more capable than mine. Cleaner, too.

Caroline has spent tremendous energy and terrifyingly large numbers of hours and days and months to realize her kind idea, always retaining her cheerful, loving disposition. She is the ideal spouse for a freelance. She is to be admired and thanked. Probably pitied, too.

Lucy Shelton Caswell is a professor at Ohio State University and curator of their Cartoon Research Library. Professor Caswell selected the pictures for the exhibition from the mountain of drawings which were available. And she never flinched.

I thank these brilliant women. If I'd known that they would eventually be involved, I would have done a better job on the work.

I thank all of the many delightful people who caused the pictures to be made but are not mentioned here. They have my, so far, undying gratitude. Cipe Pineles (art director at *Charm*), Frank Zachary (art director at *Holiday*), Merrill Panitt and Alec Joseph (editors at *TV Guide*) gave the work its first national exposure. John Hubley (director of *Storyboard, Inc.*) introduced the drawings into animation. Harvey Kurtzman (editor at *Trump; Humbug; Help!*) and Hugh M. Hefner (publisher of *Playboy*) opened the gates to unrestrained expression and Michelle Urry (cartoon editor at *Playboy*) graciously continues that situation. Harold Hayes, then, Lee Eisenberg (editors at *Esquire*) were a pleasure to work with. Ann Diven (at W.W. Norton; Grosset & Dunlap; and Scribners) was editor of the four books that were written and illustrated at her urging. She was perfect. Rudy Hoglund (art director at *Time*) made life a real pleasure and Richard Gangel (art director at *Sports Illustrated*) made life a real pleasure constantly. Harry Welker (comics editor at the New York Herald-Tribune Syndicate) enabled and titled *Poor Arnold's Almanac* and Richard Newcomb (president of Creators Syndicate) caused its revival. John Updike selected me to depict Henry Bech. Henry had no say. Lee Lorenz (art editor) and Tina Brown (editor) inserted the work into *The New Yorker*. Chris Curry (art director) and David Remnick (editor) continue to allow its appearance there.

The great romance of my career was to work for *Punch*, the great British humor weekly. Bernard Hollowood (editor) and Russell Brockbank (cartoon editor) bought all of the first drawings that I submitted to them. That started a continuous thirty-year association. William Hewison (cartoon editor) suffered this fool too gladly, considering what he had to deal with. William Davis (editor) allowed the continuum to continue.

Alan Coren, the editor of *Punch*, who contributed the introduction to this catalogue, is the maestro of written humor. To be considered a peer by him is the greatest possible praise, as impossible as that seems. His kindness, tolerance and consummate professionalism made working with him a privilege. I thank him for putting up with everything and anything—which, in this case, were usually the same thing.

R.C. Harvey did an excellent essay for this volume and Gary Groth, noble and excellent work in publishing it.

Specific thanks are due for the generosity of the University of the Arts, Philadelphia, Pennsylvania, which I attended as often as possible. President Miguel Angel Corzo has been magnanimous which is usual for him. Eugene Bolt has provided invaluable help and has my vote for best in class.

The Cartoon Research Library of The Ohio State University, Columbus, Ohio, has provided vital assistance, saintly forbearance and the saintly Lucy Shelton Caswell.

If I didn't express gratitude to the helpful people who have labored on behalf of and represent so munificently the institutions and galleries which will exhibit these pictures, I would be a typical cartoonist ingrate. Which I am.

But I shed my grumpy, ink-stained cartoonist's mantle to heartily thank all of them.

Very Much!!!

— Arnold Roth
New York City
March 2001

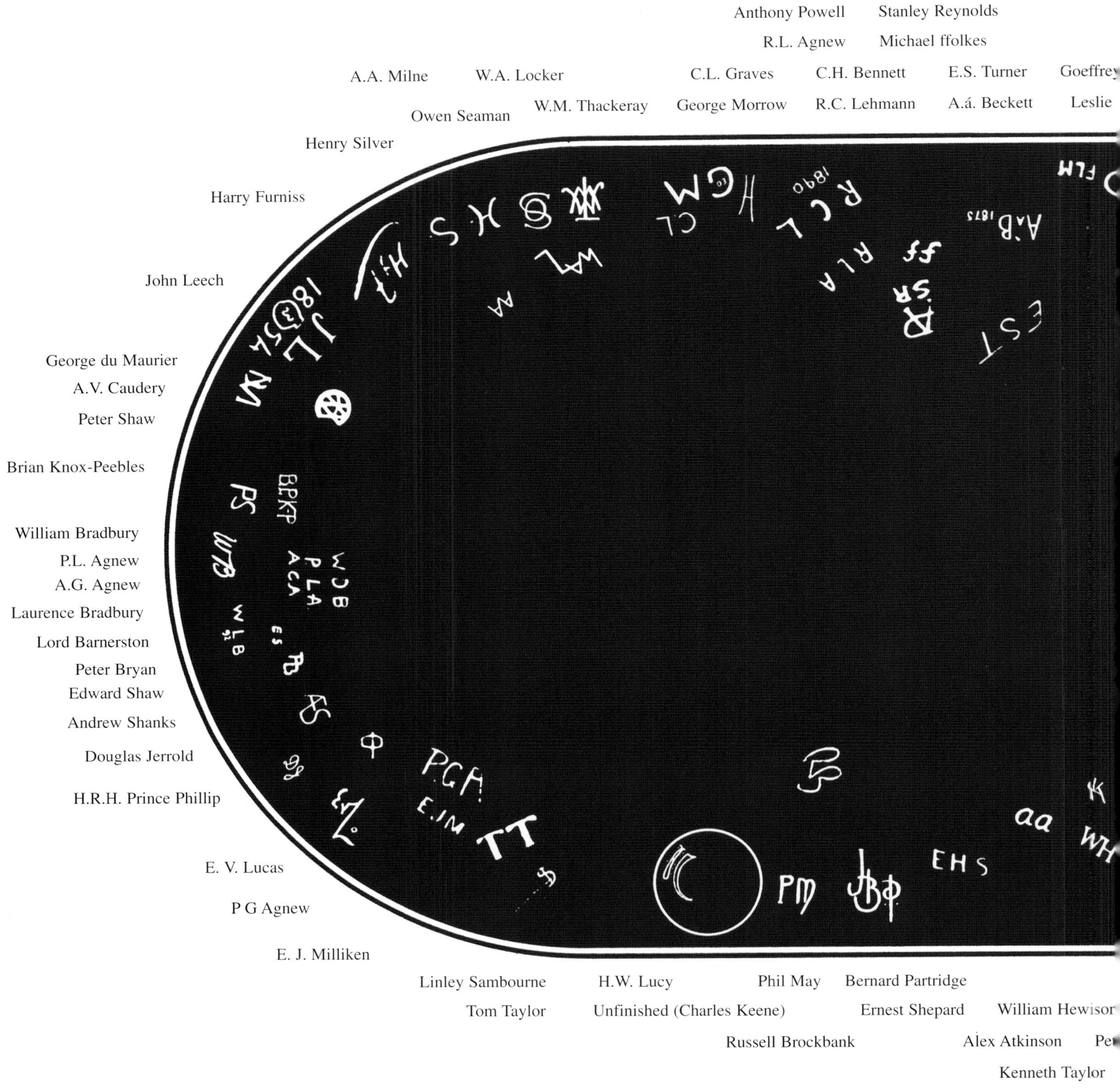

Anthony Powell
Stanley Reynolds
R.L. Agnew
Michael ffolkes
A.A. Milne
W.A. Locker
C.L. Graves
C.H. Bennett
E.S. Turner
Goeffrey
Owen Seaman
W.M. Thackeray
George Morrow
R.C. Lehmann
A.á. Beckett
Leslie
Henry Silver
Harry Furniss
John Leech
George du Maurier
A.V. Caudery
Peter Shaw
Brian Knox-Peebles
William Bradbury
P.L. Agnew
A.G. Agnew
Laurence Bradbury
Lord Barnerston
Peter Bryan
Edward Shaw
Andrew Shanks
Douglas Jerrold
H.R.H. Prince Phillip
E. V. Lucas
P G Agnew
E. J. Milliken
Linley Sambourne
H.W. Lucy
Phil May
Bernard Partridge
Tom Taylor
Unfinished (Charles Keene)
Ernest Shepard
William Hewison
Russell Brockbank
Alex Atkinson
Pe
Kenneth Taylor